TAKE YOUR POSITION

RESTORATION IN THE BODY OF CHRIST

KINGDOM GLOBAL INFLUENCERS PRESENTS

TAKE YOUR POSITION

RESTORATION IN THE BODY OF CHRIST

A 30-Day Devotional

— Volume 2 —

LU ANN TOPOVSKI, M. DIV., MBA
Visionary Author

Dedication

This book is dedicated to all who are seeking restoration within themselves, to the Godhead, and with others. With restoration it is easier for us to see and understand our position within the body of Christ, His church.

Our relationship with Jesus is paramount, and with our daily prayers and communion with Him, He will lead the way.

The chapters within this book point the reader to the Godhead alone. So, this 30-Day Devotional is dedicated to you, the reader. We all wish you well on your journey of discovery as you read each God-inspired chapter.

Thank You

Ann Marie Thrives

Arlana Holland Scola

Kelly Williams Hale

Libby George

Peggy Grimes

There have been countless hours put into this book by our contributing authors. There have been even more hours by the women named above, even before our contributing authors were selected.

Thank you, Ann Marie, Arlana, Kelly, Libby, and Peggy. This inner core team has helped to fine tune with their countless talents, keen observations, and prophetic observations.

Thank you for your teamwork, your love for our Lord, and your love for our readers. Together, we worked on a masterpiece in this 30-Day Devotional—Plus! My sincere thank you ladies!

Contents

— BONUS —

PROPHETIC DECLARATIONS
— AND PROPHETIC WORDS —

Introduction

We live in a natural world, but our fight is in the spiritual realm. When we understand this fact, it is easier to proclaim who we have been created to be and accept our position within the body of Christ. It all becomes clearer as we walk hand-in-hand with the Spirit of God. When we walk in this power and confidence, with our Lord and Savior, Jesus Christ, we remain in Him, and in our active role within His Kingdom.

Studies show that it takes 21-30 days to change a habit. By reading this devotional each day, your confidence in who you were created to be will become more evident; and your relationship with God will become more real. You will have a peace which passes all understanding even when you walk through the valley of the shadow of death. You will fear no evil, but rather you will have the confidence Christ gives you as He rises within you. In that very moment, you will know exactly what you must say or do.

We are in the beginning stages of the Kingdom era and have already transitioned from the Church era. People from all nations are sensing the shift and are about to see one of the biggest moves by the Holy Spirit the church has ever seen.

Part of this movement points its finger back to the individual. As we walk with Christ, we are restored to God, our families, and communities. We then more fully take our position within the church, the ecclesia, which is the governmental ruling Kingdom of Jesus Christ. This is the shaking going on within us and what we are sensing, and seeing, in the world around us.

In order to take our position within the church/ecclesia, we first must know our identity in Christ. Then we must take the next step and speak it out loud to claim it within the atmosphere and thereby into the spiritual realm. This begins a stirring in our heart and soul bringing restoration back to God, relationships, and in our world.

As mentioned, we have moved from the Church era into the Kingdom era. The Church era was more about religious traditions. The era of the Kingdom of God is the time in which we have outgrown the Pharisees and Sadducees of our time, and we walk into the modern-day Book of Acts with knowledge of what Jesus did for us, and in the power of Christ within us.

As sold-out, Holy Spirit (Christ) filled Christians, even when we walk through the *shadow* of the valley of death, we fear NO evil because we know Christ in us is greater than the enemy in this world. This might sound cliché, but it is the truth for millions of 'born-again' believers in Jesus Christ, our Messiah.

God bless you on your adventurous journey.

Opening Prayer

Dear Heavenly Father,

We thank You and honor You for this opportunity once again to share and edify Your people. We will speak for all that read these words in saying that we come before You with hearts open to Your presence and Your guidance. We thank You for the gift of this time to explore Your Word and to seek a deeper understanding of Your restoration in our lives. We invite You, Holy Spirit, to be with us and to light up Your Word and speak to our hearts as we journey together in this exciting exploration.

May Your truth resonate within us and lead us to a deeper relationship with You. Please grant us wisdom, discernment, and a spirit of humility as we dive into the theme of taking our position and restoration renewal in Your plan for our lives. May this time of reflection draw us closer to You and equip us to be agents of Your restoration and renewal in this world. We commit this 30-day devotional into Your hands, knowing that You are the source of all wisdom and truth. May Your name be always glorified in our midst.

In Jesus' Mighty Name... Amen!

Prayer by: Misty Dawn Allen

Sharon Baker

Sharon Baker, founder of *Embracing Abundance Life Coaching*, has profoundly impacted the personal and professional growth sectors throughout her 25-year career. A certified business professional, life coach, speaker, and best-selling Author. Sharon began her professional journey in the corporate world, emphasizing forward-thinking leadership, development, and employee engagement. Her coaching platform combines her deep business knowledge with innovative coaching techniques, helping clients unlock their passions and achieve their goals.

Overcoming personal limiting beliefs has equipped Sharon with special insights into defeating scarcity mindsets. Beyond individual coaching, she collaborates with corporations to boost workforce potential and resilience, frequently speaks at major events, and has authored best-selling books. Sharon is also a Presidential Lifetime Achievement Award recipient, honored for her significant contributions to societal advancement.

embracingabundancelifecoaching.com
facebook.com/sharon.baker.50552
linkedin.com/in/sharon-y-baker
instagram.com/embracingabundancellc

Day 1

Sharon Baker

Beyond the Surface

Unveiling Your Identity in Christ

Therefore if any man be in Christ, he is a new creature: old things are passed away; behold, all things are become new.
— 2 Corinthians 5:17 (KJV)

What Defines You?

A few years ago, when I started a business, I had a conversation with God about the individuals in whom I felt called to serve. My question was this: *"God, what do you want me to share with those I have been called to serve?* His reply was this: *"Remind them of who they are. They have lost perspective and need a shift in their thinking. They have forgotten who they are and what they are capable of.*

I went on to name my company, *Embracing Abundance Life Coaching*, where we help individuals focus on shifting belief systems and adjusting their mindset about themselves and their lives. In John 10:10, it states, *"I came that they may have life and may have it abundantly."* He wants us to have life to the full because once we become members of the Household of Faith, we take on God's identity, relinquishing our own.

We will not be able to live in abundance until we embrace our true identity. Identity in the natural sense can be defined as the traits that make

1

up a person in their entirety. Someone's beliefs, personality, and a number of countless qualities all play a role in how they are identified. This isn't limited to physical attributes; it includes some psychological makeup. All these details play a role in how we are viewed and how our being is perceived. It's so easy to find ourselves placing our value in things that will never give us an accurate measurement of the greatness that God intended for us.

Unfortunately, it is so easy to get lost in the things that we believe make us who we are. If we don't understand who we truly are, it could not only be a stumbling block, but it could be what hinders us from walking in the fullness of Christ. If we don't know who we are, we run the risk of missing out on our full potential.

What Does God Say About Me

Believe it or not, our true identity is not derived from what people think about us or even what we think about ourselves. Our true identity is solely based on what God says about us. When we get into alignment with his thoughts towards us, it is then and only then that we can walk in confidence. Once we gain an understanding of what it means to be the handiwork of the Master Creator, *who has prepared us in advance to do good works* (Ephesians 2:10), we will find that our potential is unlimited.

The Bible tells us that once we have accepted Jesus as Savior and Lord, His work on the cross, and have been reconciled to the Father, we become children of God. A new creation is identified as justified, beloved, and the righteousness of God. Romans 8:17 speaks of *being a child of God and informs us that we are not only children of the Most High God but also fellow heirs with Christ.* This implies a lineage of royalty. 1 Peter 2:9 confirms that we are a *"chosen people, a royal priesthood, a holy nation, God's special possession."*

One of my favorite movies is *Overcomer,* which was released in 2019 and addresses the topic of identity head-on. It was a faith-based movie and one of the many movie projects of Christian filmmakers and brothers, Alex and Stephen Kendrick. There is a scene in the movie when Hannah, the main character, shares with her principal, Ms. Brooks, her emotions regarding her biological father who abandoned her as an infant.

She explained that this left her feeling unloved, unwanted, and even like she was a mistake. Principal Brooks comforts Hannah by introducing her to the concept of a different father; a flawless father, the only wise God who has always desired her, loved her, and cared for her. Together, they pray, and during this moment, Hannah invites Jesus Christ into her life.

Principal Brooks then encourages Hannah to explore the first two chapters of Ephesians in the Bible and to jot down everything that God says about her. This was an eye-opening process as she reads and writes on her notepad, "blessed, chosen, adopted, sealed, forgiven, redeemed, loved, and God's child." Every time I see this part, it makes me want to shout, "Hallelujah!" The key here is to discover who we are, then take hold of it, believe it, and then receive it. Scripture is filled with so many reminders of who we are in Christ.

Discovering Your Identity in Hard Times

In the story of the prodigal son as depicted in Luke 15:11–32, we read how a father seems to lose his son after he leaves home. Many people think that this story is solely about redemption, reconciliation, mercy, and grace, but it is also about identity. This instance shows us how we can lose our rationality because of sin and the struggles in our lives. Although the son is from a wealthy family, he found himself in unfamiliar territory. Even though he was far away from home, had sinned against his father, and wasn't in an ideal situation, he was still his father's son. The son returns with a heart of repentance and is readily received by his father. Sound familiar?

In the song *"Prodigal Son"* by gospel singer and songwriter Fred Hammond, there is a line that expresses the words, *"Whatever you've done, I cannot even remember."* This is an amazing illustration as it pertains to Father God and His heart towards us. Despite our sin, God is ready to receive us. His grace is sufficient.

So, why are you in the pigpen? Don't you know who you are? Loss, failure, and heartbreak all cloud our judgment. Truth be told, all of us have had a pig-pin experience at some point in our lives. When we were down and out and lost hope. Let's focus on the bigger picture. Yes, we may fall short, but this does not change who we are in Christ.

> *For I am convinced that neither death nor life, neither angels nor demons, neither the present nor the future, nor any powers, neither height nor depth, nor anything else in all creation, will be able to separate us from the love of God that is in Christ Jesus our Lord.*
> — *Romans 8:38-39 (NIV)*

If we look at another prominent figure in the Old Testament named Moses, we can clearly see that his journey began with an identity crisis. He was a Hebrew born to be enslaved but was chosen to live as an Egyptian and would ultimately lead his people to freedom. It has been stated by some historians that although Moses lived his early life as a royal, he knew that he was Hebrew. But instead of accepting one or both titles, he chose to define himself by his negative actions.

The murder of the Egyptian brought fear, regret, and shame and changed the trajectory of his life. It was then that he found himself running from everything he had grown accustomed to as he came to the end of himself. It wasn't until his supernatural encounter with the God of

Abraham, Isaac, and Jacob that he was made aware of who he truly was. Although everything leading up to that moment prepared him to be the one who delivered the Israelites from the hand of Pharaoh, an entire nation was impacted by one man's revelation of identity through fellowship with Elohim.

Standing Your Ground: The Power Within

You have power if you understand who you are. Despite all the odds, Daniel accepted who he was, and this won him favor with both God and people. The account goes as follows: following his conquest of Jerusalem, King Nebuchadnezzar ordered the brightest and best Israelites from the royal families and aristocracy to undergo a three-year training program before joining his service. The ones chosen were Azariah, who became Abednego; Mishael, who became Meshach; Hananiah, who became Shadrach; and Daniel, who became Belteshazzar.

The irony of this situation is that, despite having their names changed and being taken from their home and everything they knew to Babylon, they refused to change who they were on the inside and maintained their identity while being schooled by the Babylonians. Daniel declined to eat from the king's table and to sip wine to avoid defiling himself. He chose water and vegetables as a sign of respect for God. Daniel and the other three young men benefited from divine provisions because of this conduct.

To these four young men, God gave knowledge and
understanding of all kinds of literature and learning. And
Daniel could understand visions and dreams of all kinds.
— Daniel 1:17 (NIV)

These young men exceeded their peers and were superior in every way. This is a prime example of what happens when you preserve your identity even when everything around you shifts.

The Impact of You

When we are uncertain where our value lies, it is easy to fall into the snare of the fear of man. When we seek the praise and affirmation of others to find worth, our certainty and security will be short-lived, which often leads to rejection. Human beings can be fickle, loving you one minute and abandoning you the next. This, in turn, leaves us broken, hurt, and dejected. As a believer in our Christ identity, there will be times that you will face rejection. No matter how good, nice, or kind you are, even as a Christian, there will be people who will not receive you.

Rejection in one place means adoption somewhere else. There is a profound statement that reinforces this truth: "You weren't rejected; I hid your value from them because they were not assigned to your destiny." Jesus himself faced rejection. This is something that we will endure as well. Even though He was the Son of God, He never insisted on anyone validating who He was. There was a moment in Jesus' life where, after He was baptized, God identified Him as *"my beloved Son, with whom I am well pleased."*

Even before Jesus began doing miracles, healing the sick, and delivering the captives, God identified and affirmed Him. This shows us that who we are to God isn't based on the things we have, or even the things that we do well, but on who God is. In Isaiah 43:1, he even tells us,

Fear not, for I have redeemed you;
I have called you by name; you are mine.

Cultivating Clarity

We begin to gain full awareness of our identity when we choose to seek God through fellowship, communion, and reading His word. Awareness is paramount. Once we are in pursuit of the truth of God and His word, we will also begin gravitating towards our true identity.

As we step into this place of certainty about who God is and what He says about us, we become more assured as we move along in our journey. So much so that, no matter what obstacles we may face, we are certain that we are walking in the authority which comes with belonging to the Almighty.

When it comes to your walk, it needs to be so strong and so personal that if you wake up one day and no one believes in God but you, you will be able to go on.

The fulfillment of our purpose and reaching our destiny are also tied to our recognition of our true identity and what or who it is based upon. We are all born with a particular purpose, and until we can come to terms with what that is, we may move through life searching for something that cannot be found outside of the One who created us. Without a grip on our identity, we can be left feeling as if something is missing and we are unfulfilled.

The ultimate goal on this journey to having a full awareness of our identity in Christ will be found in eternity. As children of God and beneficiaries of Christ, we must have hope in what God has spoken over us. Even before the foundations of the earth, it was His intention to make us citizens of Heaven. Simply stated, your true identity is found in Jesus Christ, and the sooner we accept this truth, the sooner we can live an abundant life, because nothing will be unattainable.

Exhortation

As you embark on each new day, rest assured of who you are in Christ. In order to keep it at the forefront of your mind, you must be deliberate in your approach, as this will not always come naturally. Start your day with prayer, reading His Word, and listening to affirmations.

Prayer of Affirmation

Lord Jesus, thank You that I am fully aware of who I am. I receive everything that You say about me because I know it to be true. I rebuke anything that is in opposition to what You have said in Your Word. I affirm daily who I am and whose I am by meditating and speaking Your words. I will do this until I become everything You intended me to be. In Jesus name, I pray. Amen.

THINGS TO PONDER...

1. What Does Your Identity in Christ Mean to You?

_____

_____

_____

_____

_____

_____

2. How Do External Factors Affect Your Sense of Identity?

_____

_____

_____

_____

_____

3. Based on the scripture Ephesians 2:10, how can you actively align your thoughts about yourself with God's thoughts? What practical steps can you take to embrace your identity as God's handiwork?

_____

_____

_____

_____

_____

4. In What Ways Have You Experienced an 'Identity Crisis' Like the Prodigal Son or Moses?

_____

_____

_____

----

5. Share a time when you felt lost or uncertain about your identity. How did your faith help you rediscover your true self?

----

6. How Do You Stand Firm in Your Spiritual Identity Amidst Life's Challenges?

----

7. Drawing inspiration from Daniel's story, how can you maintain your spiritual integrity and identity even when faced with external pressures or adversities?

_____

_____

_____

_____

_____

_____

8. Reflect on the importance of starting your day with prayer, reading the Word, and listening to affirmations. How do these practices strengthen your understanding and acceptance of your identity in Christ?

_____

_____

_____

_____

_____

_____

Peggy A. Grimes

Peggy A. Grimes is a best-selling author, public speaker, spiritual coach, and mentor. Her greatest passion is helping women succeed on their emotional healing journey, empowering them to become Kingdom Women who can take back their marriage, children, families, and communities for the Kingdom of God. She served as CEO of the Montana Food Bank Network prior to moving to her current home in Jacksonville, North Carolina.

Peggy has been featured on various episodes of *The Kingdom View* TV Show, *1Kingdom TV,* and *The Renegade Women* and *Women Rise Up!* Podcasts. She is prophetic and a woman's leader in her church, the current board chair of *White Raiment Ministries, Inc.,* and a course leader for *Kingdom Women Rising,* a nonprofit ministry for women suffering from deep traumatic wounds.

KingdomWomenRising.org
facebook.com/TheKingdomLifeCoach
instagram.com/KingdomWomenRising
KingdomWomenRising@gmail.com

Day 2

Peggy A. Grimes

Spiritual Renewal

The Vital Role of Restoration in Our Faith Journey

All this is from God, who reconciled us to himself through Christ and gave us the ministry of reconciliation: that God was reconciling the world to himself in Christ, not counting people's sins against them. And he has committed to us the message of reconciliation.
— 2 Corinthians 5:18-19 (NIV)

The Reason for and Nature of Restoration in the Body of Christ

Restoration in the body of Christ is a profound and essential concept that addresses the healing, renewal, and revitalization of individuals and communities within the church. This process is not merely a return to a previous state but a transformation into a more vibrant, faithful, and fruitful existence in Christ.

Understanding the reasons for and the nature of restoration helps believers grasp its significance and pursue it actively in their spiritual journeys. There are biblical foundations, theological significance, and practical implications for restoration in the body of Christ.

The Biblical Foundation of Restoration

The concept of restoration is deeply rooted in the Scriptures, from the Old Testament narratives to the teachings of Jesus and the Apostles in the New Testament. God's desire to restore His people is a recurring theme, demonstrating His love, mercy, and commitment to His covenant people:

1. **The Restoration of Israel:** Throughout the Old Testament, God repeatedly promises to restore Israel after periods of rebellion, exile, and suffering. For instance, in Joel 2:25 (NIV), God says, *"I will repay you for the years the locusts have eaten."* This promise signifies not only the physical restoration of crops but also the spiritual renewal of the nation.

2. **The Psalms:** Many Psalms reflect a longing for restoration and renewal. Psalm 51:10 (NIV) says, *"Create in me a clean heart, O God, and renew a right spirit within me."* Here, David seeks personal restoration, acknowledging the need for a purified heart and a steadfast spirit.

3. **The Prophets:** Prophets like Isaiah and Jeremiah frequently speak of God's restorative plans. Isaiah 61:1-3 (NIV) describes the coming of the Messiah who will *"bind up the brokenhearted"* and *"comfort all who mourn,"* highlighting the spiritual and emotional aspects of restoration.

New Testament Foundations for Restoration

1. **The Ministry of Jesus:** Jesus' ministry on earth was marked by acts of restoration. He healed the sick, raised the dead, and forgave sins, demonstrating the holistic nature of His restorative work. Luke 19:10 (NIV) encapsulates His mission: *"For the Son of Man came to seek and to save the lost."*

2. **Paul's Epistles:** The apostle Paul frequently addresses the theme of restoration. In 2 Corinthians 5:17 (NIV), he writes, *"Therefore, if anyone is in Christ, the new creation has come: The old has gone, the new is here!"* This verse emphasizes the transformative restoration that occurs through faith in Jesus Christ. Jesus and His Apostles performed many miracles demonstrating the restorative power of the Word of God to heal and deliver us from sin and its grip on us.

3. **Revelation:** The book of Revelation concludes with a vision of ultimate restoration. Revelation 21:5 (NIV) declares, *"He who was seated on the throne said, 'I am making everything new!'"* This promise assures believers of the complete restoration that awaits at the end of times. In the meantime, Father God wants us to walk in abundance in every area of our lives! This includes the restoration of our spirit and our soul.

Biblical Significance of Restoration

Restoration is not merely a return to a previous state, but a transformative process that aligns believers with God's original design and purpose. This transformation is multi-faceted, encompassing spiritual, emotional, relational, and communal dimensions.

1. **Spiritual Restoration:** At its core, restoration involves the reconciliation of the believer with God. Sin disrupts this relationship, but through Christ's redemptive work, believers are restored to a right standing with God. 1 John 1:9 (NIV) states it this way: *"If we confess our sins, he is faithful and just and will forgive us our sins and purify us from all unrighteousness."* This spiritual restoration is foundational to all other forms of restoration. Luke 19:10 (NIV) *"For the Son of Man came to seek and to save the lost."*

2. **Emotional Restoration:** Trauma, sin, and the fallen nature of the world can leave deep emotional and psychological scars. Biblical restoration addresses these wounds, offering healing and peace. Philippians 4:6-7 (NIV) encourages believers to present their anxieties to God, promising the peace of God which transcends all understanding. 3 John 1:2 (NKJV) states *"Beloved, I pray that you prosper and be in health, even as your soul prospers."*

3. **Relational Restoration:** Sin not only separates individuals from God but also disrupts human relationships. The process of restoration seeks to mend these broken relationships, fostering forgiveness, reconciliation, and unity within the body of Christ. Ephesians 4:31-32 (NIV) urges believers to forgive one another as God in Christ Jesus forgave them.

4. **Church Restoration:** The church, as the body of Christ, experiences restoration on a communal level. This involves building a healthy, vibrant community that reflects Christ's love and unity. Acts 2:42-47(NIV) provides a model of a restored church, characterized by fellowship, breaking of bread, and prayer.

The Nature of Restoration in the Body of Christ

Restoration in the body of Christ is a dynamic, ongoing process that requires intentionality and cooperation with the Holy Spirit. It involves several key elements:

Repentance and Confession: Restoration begins with repentance and confession. Acknowledging sin and turning away from it is essential for personal and relational healing. 1 John 1:9 (NIV) promises *"If we confess our sins, he is faithful and just and will forgive us our sins and purify us from all unrighteousness."*

Forgiveness: Forgiveness is central to the process of restoration. It involves releasing resentment and extending grace to others. Jesus emphasized the importance of forgiveness in the Lord's Prayer (Matthew 6:12) and in His teaching on reconciliation (Matthew 18:21-22).

Healing: Restoration includes physical, emotional, and spiritual healing. James 5:16 (NIV) encourages believers to *"pray for each other so that you may be healed."* The healing process often involves prayer, counseling, and the support of the Christian community.

Reconciliation: Reconciliation is the restoration of relationships that have been broken by sin. It involves efforts to restore trust and rebuild fellowship. 2 Corinthians 5:18-19 (NIV) describes believers as ministers of reconciliation, tasked with restoring relationships both with God and with others. *"All this is from God, who reconciled us to himself through Christ and gave us the ministry of reconciliation: that God was reconciling the world to himself in Christ, not counting people's sins against them. And he has committed to us the message of reconciliation."*

Renewal: Restoration leads to renewal, a fresh start that aligns individuals and communities with God's purposes. Romans 12:2 (NIV) speaks of the renewal of the mind, which transforms believers, and enables them to discern God's will. *"Do not conform to the pattern of this world, but be transformed by the renewing of your mind. Then you will be able to test and approve what God's will is—his good, pleasing and perfect will."*

Transformation: The ultimate goal of restoration is transformation into the likeness of Christ. 2 Corinthians 3:18 (NIV) describes this process *"And we all, who with unveiled faces contemplate the Lord's glory, are being transformed into his image with ever-increasing glory."* As we are transformed from sinners saved by Grace to Sons and Daughters of God the Father, we then begin the process of "sanctification," the renewing of our minds, which encompasses our thoughts and attitudes. Romans 12:2

(NIV) states it this way *"Do not conform to the pattern of this world, but be transformed by the renewing of your mind. Then you will be able to test and approve what God's will is—his good, pleasing and perfect will."*

Practical Implementation of Restoration

Understanding the reasons for and nature of restoration in the body of Christ has practical implementation for individuals and communities.

1. **Personal Application:**

   • *Daily Repentance:* Believers should practice daily repentance, seeking God's forgiveness and guidance. 1 John 1:9 (NIV) *"If we confess our sins, he is faithful and just and will forgive us our sins and purify us from all unrighteousness."*

   • *Embracing Forgiveness:* Practicing forgiveness, both receiving it from God and extending it to others, is crucial for personal healing. Matthew 6:12 (NIV) *"And forgive us our debts, as we also have forgiven our debtors."*

   • *Pursuing Healing:* Seeking emotional and psychological healing through prayer, counseling, and community support is important for holistic restoration. James 5:16 (NIV) *"Therefore confess your sins to each other and pray for each other so that you may be healed. The prayer of a righteous person is powerful and effective."*

   • *Renewing the Mind:* Engaging in spiritual disciplines such as Bible study, prayer, and meditation helps renew the mind and align it with God's truth. Romans 12:2 (NIV) *"Do not conform to the pattern of this world, but be transformed by the renewing of your mind. Then you will be able to test and approve what God's will is—his good, pleasing and perfect will."*

2. **Community Application:**

• *Fostering Unity:* Churches must strive for unity, addressing conflicts with grace and seeking reconciliation.

• *Supporting Healing:* Providing support for those who are hurting through counseling ministries, support groups, and prayer is essential.

• *Promoting Renewal:* Encouraging others in their spiritual growth and renewal through discipleship programs, retreats, and regular teaching on restoration.

• *Engaging in Outreach:* Extending the message of restoration to the broader community through evangelism and opportunities to speak to a broader audience about restoration and renewal.

Examples of Restoration

1. **Personal Restoration:**

• *John's Journey:* John, a member of a local church, struggled with addiction for many years. Through the church's recovery program, he found support and guidance. As he confessed his sin, repented, and sought God's help, he experienced not only sobriety, but a deep spiritual and emotional renewal. His relationships were restored, and he now serves in the church's recovery ministry, helping others find restoration.

2. **Relational Restoration:**

• *The Reconciliation of Sarah and Emily:* Sarah and Emily, long-time friends and church members, had a falling out over a misunderstanding. The conflict affected not only their relationship, but also the church body. Through the church's mediation efforts and their willingness to forgive, they reconciled. Their restored relationship strengthened the unity within the church and served as a testimony to the power of forgiveness and reconciliation.

3. Church Restoration:

• *The Renewal of First Church:* First Church had been declining for years, struggling with internal conflicts and a loss of vision. A new pastor led the congregation through a process of repentance, healing, and renewal. The church embraced a new vision focused on community outreach and discipleship. As they sought God's guidance, they experienced growth, unity, and a renewed sense of purpose.

Conclusion

All this is from God, who reconciled us to himself through
Christ and gave us the ministry of reconciliation: that God
was reconciling the world to himself in Christ, not counting
people's sins against them. And he has committed
to us the message of reconciliation.
— 2 Corinthians 5:18-19 (NIV)

Restoration in the body of Christ is a multifaceted process that involves spiritual, emotional, relational, church, and community renewal. It is deeply rooted in biblical teachings and is essential for the health and vitality of individual believers, churches, and communities. Understanding the reasons for and nature of restoration helps believers actively pursue it, leading to transformed lives that reflect Christ's love and grace.

By embracing the principles of repentance, forgiveness, healing, reconciliation, renewal, and transformation, the body of Christ can experience profound restoration. This process not only brings personal and community healing, but also equips the church to fulfill its mission in the world, demonstrating the power of God's restorative work.

We, as believers, must strive on our journey towards restoration. Let us be encouraged by the words of Jesus *"Come to me, all you who are weary and burdened, and I will give you rest. Take my yoke upon you and learn from me, for I am gentle and humble in heart, and you will find rest for your souls"* (Matthew 11:28-29 NIV).

In Christ, restoration is not only possible but promised!

Father God, You sent Your one and only Son, whom You loved, to this earth to restore mankind through reconciliation by Your Holy Word through Your Prophets.

Jesus brought to earth the way of reconciliation and showed us how to walk in it. Adam and Eve lost their direct relationship with You when they were tempted through deception and stepped into disobedience.

Jesus, through His perfect obedience, even to His death on the cross, restored our right to be reconciled to You.

We are now given the "ministry" of reconciliation to bring to our family and friends, our church and community, and all to whom You send us.

Thank you, Father God, for Your sacrifice, and may we all come to understand the power of reconciliation which brings restoration to us as individuals and to our world. We are so grateful to You, Father, the Holy Spirit, and to Jesus, our Savior, in whose name we now pray. Amen.

THINGS TO PONDER...

1. What past hurts or sins do I need to repent of and seek God's forgiveness for?

   _____

   _____

   _____

   _____

   _____

   _____

2. Have I genuinely forgiven those who have wronged me, or am I still holding onto bitterness or resentment?

   _____

   _____

   _____

   _____

   _____

   _____

3. How can I initiate the process of reconciliation with someone I have wronged or who has wronged me?

   _____

   _____

_____

_____

_____

_____

4. What specific steps can I take to restore a broken relationship in my life?

_____

_____

_____

_____

_____

5. In what areas of my life do I need to experience God's restorative power?

_____

_____

_____

_____

_____

_____

6. How has my pride or stubbornness hindered my willingness to seek or offer forgiveness?

_____

_____

_____

_____

_____

_____

7. Am I willing to humble myself and ask for forgiveness from those I have hurt?

_____

_____

_____

_____

_____

_____

Denise C. Herndon Harvey

Denise C. Herndon Harvey is a published author of the children's book called, *Growing up Sassafras—Where is my daddy?* and *Emergence of Me—Discovering My Identity and Courage Within.* She also participated in three best-selling, multi-author books, *Unlock Your Voice, A Kingdom Word Now,* and *Women Rising.*

She is a Liberty University graduate with a Master of Arts in Human Service Counseling—Family Advocacy and Public Policy. She earned a BS degree in Psychology—Christian Counseling and a BS degree in Psychology—Crisis Counseling, with a minor in Biblical Studies, along with a Life/Mental Health Coaching Certification.

Denise and her retired Air Force husband have been married for 40 years; they have two grown children and six grandchildren.

facebook.com/groups/emergeandrestore
instagram.com/deecharvey
deniseharvey.com
deniseharvey.icanvoice.com

Day 3

Denise C. Herndon Harvey

Are You Submitted?

You will keep him in perfect peace, whose mind is stayed on You,
because he trusts in You.
— Isaiah 26:3 (NKJV)

Reflecting back with renewed hope, our only true hope is in our gracious Jesus and His Word. Still, reflection is sometimes burdensome, and it can even be painful. The memories are not all love and peace, there can be a lot of pain and disappointments, coupled with misunderstandings and hurt hearts. Hurt and bleeding hearts want nothing more than for the pain to go away and the trials and tribulations to end. Yet, didn't I pray for it? Do we not all pray for restoration in our homes, lives, and families?

The rebuilding that we desire when we are searching for the peace that appears to be just in the distance, just around another corner. The corner, that perpetual corner, that turns into another and another, as we seek, and as we wait, and as we do our best not to give up, knowing that in His time, it will make sense and it will take place. God's Word says,

And not only that, but we also glory in tribulations, knowing that
tribulation produces perseverance; and perseverance, character;
and character, hope. Now hope does not disappoint, because the
love of God has been poured out in our hearts by the Holy Spirit
who was given to us. — Romans 5:3-5 NKJV

Still, on reflection, no one would want to remain in the pit of despair. I don't desire for the despair to continue; however, in this world, the pain, the hurt, the betrayal, and the disappointments come with the living. At times, it can even be considered a prerequisite for living.

So many remain unhealed in their soul, generation after generation, and continue to yield the same heart wounds, not having the understanding, nor seeking the one and only true lover of our soul. The One that wants us to come to Him with repentant hearts, laying down all the pain, the loss, the unforgiveness, the disappointment, the confusion, the betrayal, and the abuse, and misuse.

Lay it at the feet of Jesus! With Jesus we all find the truth when we truly seek the Way, the Truth, and the Life, with our whole heart, and with everything within us.

My brethren, count it all joy when you fall into various trials,
knowing that the testing of your faith produces patience.
But let patience have its perfect work, that you may
be perfect and complete, lacking nothing.
—James 1:2-4 (NKJV)

Just like years past, we lift our hands, close our eyes, bow our heads, and seek the favor of God. Our faith leads us down the right path, but have we truly submitted? Have you and I come under submission to the Word of God for our life? Have we yielded or surrendered the life we are experiencing? Have you laid down your ways and how you desire your life or situations to be, turning it over to Holy Spirit, or do you believe that you still know better? True restoration can only occur when we have laid down our way, and allow for His way to operate in our life and that of our family.

For so many years now, I prayed for restoration in my family. I prayed for restoration for different loved ones and situations, and what I began to see, and what started to happen, was a shaking. It was as if everything began to come unglued, to fall apart. It became a significant disruption in my life and that of my family.

Past years, which may have been filled with hurt, pain, betrayal, great sorrow, and never-ending tears, are topped with prayers of "Please, Lord, hear my cries." How do you stand when all around you is crumbling into pieces. How do you hold your head up and be strong for others when you only want to crawl in a ball and cry your eyes out? How often has the pain and heartache hit so hard it feels like it was never-ending.

Disruption, on the way to restoration, causes life eruptions, the prelude to restoration. The tearing down, the revealing, the unearthing of what has been hidden away must be revealed for true restoration to take place. The new beginning of the prayed restoration had begun; but wait, Lord, where is the "real" restoration? Where is the peace that we believe we are in need of? Where are the beautiful days and lavishing love we desire to be shown down over us, covering us with everlasting joy? That great peace, great joy, and undying love are so necessary in our lives. How are we to go on without it, Lord?

Let me share what I learned from Holy Spirit. Yes, we serve a God of restoration; however, on the road to restoration, we will be met with a breaking, a shaking, and a disruption. The disruptions will cause eruptions to occur in life. These eruptions are the prelude to restoration.

We all desire that restoration when we see the brokenness, the hurt, the pain, and the heartache. We know the despair and the loneliness, and we want it all to stop so badly. Seeking restoration will require work, and it will also require exposure. The breaking, revealing the lies, the secret hidden sins to be exposed.

Yet, I've only come to understand what it means to desire restoration and be totally submitted. Submission implies that something is to be presented, or considered, or a decision that awaits approval. Meanwhile, the word yield is the act of submitting or surrendering.

Finally, surrender goes right back to the word yield or agree. It means entrusting our plans and our lives to Jesus and now aligning with the will that He has for our lives. Our surrender will bring about peace, and we will discover freedom. After all, remember it is not about us; it is all about Him.

The surrendering, the laying down of human ambition, and seeking only after the one and only Redeemer, the One who laid down His life, who loved me, and loved me more than I can ever love myself. The One who saw all the shaking before we were ever born. The one who knew us, who still knows us, and loves us.

He loves us in our brokenness and inadequacies, buried in fault, and ever-repentant sin. Instead of getting better, we wonder, "How could this be?" How could life as we know it suddenly look as if it is someone else's life, not ours/mine?

Lesson in Lanes

Learning to seek His perfect way will keep us in our lane. What is this lane? The lane of seeking after God.

Then Jesus said to his disciples, "If anyone desires to come after Me, let him deny himself, take up his cross, and follow Me. For whoever desires to save his life will lose it, but whoever loses his life for My sake will find it. For what profit is it to a man if he gains the whole world and loses his own soul? Or what will a man give in exchange for his soul?" — Matthew 16:24-26 (NKJV)

1. The lane of a daughter or son blessed and striving to stay in the necessary position of humility, knowing that it is and will never be about them.

   a. *"Therefore humble yourselves under the mighty hand of God, that He may exalt you in due time"* (1 Peter 5:6, NKJV).

2. The lane of obedience to what God has declared in His Word for our life is:

   a. *"If you love Me, keep My commandments"* (John 14:15, NKJV).

3. The lane of repentance is necessary for us all to take up, as it helps to not only heal us individually, but God's land as well.

   a. *"If My people who are called by my name will humble themselves, and pray and seek My face, and turn from their wicked ways, then I will hear from heaven, and will forgive their sin and heal their land"* (2 Chronicles 7:14, NKJV).

4. The necessary lane of sacrifice, of laying down our own desires and seeking first after the Kingdom of God also helps us to stay in our lane.

   a. *"But seek first the kingdom of God and His righteousness, and all these things shall be added to you"* (Matthew 6:33, NKJV).

5. The lane of forgiveness.

   a. *"If we confess our sins, He is faithful and just to forgive us our sins and to cleanse us from all unrighteousness"* (1 John 1:9 NKJV).

Reflecting the image of Jesus, by sowing the fruit of the spirit: love, joy, peace, patience, kindness, goodness, gentleness, faithfulness, and self-control, in all things, even in these hard places, is restoration is taking place.

We must understand that the hurt, the pains, and all our life experiences will be used. It will all be used! In the end, the good, the bad, and the ugly will be used for our desired restoration.

And we know that all things work together for good to those who love God, to those who are the called according to His purpose.
— Romans 8:28 NKJV

That restoration is not only necessary, but already in progress, even when it is not yet visible to the naked eye or experienced in our life. Eventually, we will continue to count it all joy.

Others may have lavished in years passed. They may not have felt the sting of the loss of a loved one, or the loss of a relationship. They may not have had to worry about the loss of income they needed for everyday life expenses, or family members who broke away and never wanted to reunite. Nevertheless, we wake up and tackle the day passionately, longing for the restored hope we believe in. Great hope that in all we have done, prayed, and believed for others, the hope we desperately need will peek around the corner and announce its presence to us.

This is the power of submission and surrender as we enter into a new process and find restoration and transformation. We discover a new way of living, a new way of being, and a new way of relating to God and others, with a renewed mind in the process according to the Word of God.

And do not be conformed to this world, but be transformed by the renewing of your mind, that you may prove what is that good and acceptable and perfect will of God. — Romans 12:2 (NKJV)

That transformation takes place on the inside of mankind and reflects the character of Jesus on the outside as well as within our spirit and heart. This new understanding is that we must all be image bearers of the one true image of Jesus. We must all lay down our life and pick up the submitted life. This is the grace of the Father, already revealed to us when our Savior laid down His life for us while we were still in our sinful state, allowing us to have the mind of Christ as we ought, in holiness and righteousness when we submit.

That you put off, concerning your former conduct, the old man which grows corrupt according to the deceitful lusts, and be renewed in the spirit of your mind, and that you put on the new man which was created according to God, in true righteousness and holiness. — Ephesians 4:22-24 (NKJV)

Finally, the yearning to have the restoration, has deposited the necessary peace. It brought all the important attributes of Jesus, keeping us seeking, repenting, and submitting to the Father as we wait for what we sense in our spirit to manifest in the natural. With it all, we count it all joy. The joy we have received from God is smothered in His love, mercy, and grace.

Love suffers long and is kind; love does not envy; love does not parade itself, is not puffed up; does not behave rudely, does not seek its own, is not provoked, thinks no evil; does not rejoice in iniquity, but rejoices in the truth; bears all things, believes all things, hopes all things, endures all things. — 1 Corinthians 13:4-7 (NKJV)

THINGS TO PONDER...

1. Are you submitted? When you look back on your life, can you see areas that are not surrendered to the Father.

_____

_____

_____

_____

_____

_____

2. When difficult times occur, do you keep standing, knowing that as God's Word declares:

For our light affliction, which is but for a moment, is working for us a far more exceeding and eternal weight of glory, while we do not look at the things which are seen, but at the things which are not seen. For the things which are seen are temporary, but the things which are not seen are eternal.
— 2 Corinthians 4:17-18, (NKJV)

Or, are you like a lot of people, throw in the towel, believing that it's all over. What is your stance? Have you submitted?

_____

_____

_____

_____

_____

3. Healing cannot take place if it's hiding, not being dealt with, and out of sight. Are you ready to unveil to heal and restore, giving it all to Jesus because He is more than aware of your situation? He is waiting and He loves you dearly! ARE YOU SUBMITTED?

_____

_____

_____

_____

_____

_____

Lindsey Parson

Lindsey Parson is a former corporate healthcare leader, nurse practitioner, author, and speaker. She has been married to the love of her life for 17 years, and God has blessed them with 2 beautiful children. Lindsey, her marriage, and her family have been restored by the Grace of God. Lindsey is committed to expanding the Kingdom for HIS glory and restoring families back to HIM. Lindsey serves as secretary on the Board of Officers for *Forged in His Fire Ministries,* a nonprofit organization dedicated to bringing submitted vessels to allow restoration of families back to HIM.

lindseyparson.com
forgedinhisfireministries.org
msha.ke/lindseyparson
lindsey@lindseyparson.com

Day 4

Lindsey Parson

Restoration Back to Self
With the Priceless Love of Jesus

Truly I tell you, unless you change and become like little children,
you will never enter the kingdom of heaven.
— *Matthew 18:3 (NIV)*

I was standing there so proud as I heard over the loudspeaker "would the parent or guardian of Lindsey Mitchell please come to the service desk to retrieve your lost child." When I was little, I loved to talk to anyone, but I really loved to talk to strangers. I wanted to get to know everyone. Long before cell phones, FaceTime, and Apple Tags, I would purposefully get lost and run to the service desk at any store I was at with my parents—just so I could go talk to the service desk clerk.

When we would go out to eat at a restaurant, I would ask to go to the restroom and along the way I would stop at every table, introduce myself, and ask people if they had any kids, where they live, and what they do for a living. If you were to ask my parents, they would tell you that when I was little, I didn't know a stranger. My two brothers would tell you that I was bold, and loud, and thought I was the boss. They liked to tell me those things too.

When I was growing up, I had half-day kindergarten. We went to learn how to follow the rules, play with other kids, and learn our ABC's. I remember very distinctly, that is when things started to change. If you were talking and you weren't supposed to be, you got your name on the board. If you were talking again, you got a check mark, and if you got 2 check marks your parents were called. I got my name on the board just about daily, and my parents were called very regularly. This was the start of feeling like who I was, wasn't good enough. It was one thing that my brothers would tell me I was too much, but when the teacher started telling me too, it really hurt.

At home, our parents loved us, but my mom had her own insecurities that usually looked like making comments about other women's bodies, how they were dressed, and how they were acting, and to my little ears, it sounded like I would never be able to measure up.

I remember going to visit my grandmother and I would run to her bedroom, grab a stack of magazines and go hide behind the sofa. They were *Redbook* magazines and I wasn't supposed to have them because there were naughty words on the front, but I couldn't help staring at Cindy Crawford with her perfect body and wanting that so much. I started my first diet when I was 9 years old and for the next 25 years I was chasing the perfect body.

I spent the next 4 years in 3 different school systems, repeatedly being the new girl. My dad was growing in his career in the corporate world working long hours, traveling, and trying to make a name for himself. My mom stayed home with my brothers and me just trying to keep her head above water. I didn't stay at one school long enough to make any good friends, my older brother was 4 years older than me and didn't want anything to do with me, my little brother was 2 years younger, and we couldn't stand each other at that point in our lives.

I was alone. Not physically, there were people in my house, but I felt completely alone. When we finally settled into our "forever home," I was 13 years old and about to start 8th grade. I moved in next door to a girl who, at that time in my life, was my guardian angel. Kami was in my grade, she knew a lot of people in school, and she was the first friend I had made in 4 years who made me feel like somebody. We spent the whole summer together, I was actually excited to start my new school, I was finally going to be able to be me.

Reality hit when Kami was not in any of my classes, I was just the new girl, again. I began to feel like I had to be in control of everything. I had to conduct myself in a way that was pleasing to others, I had to be who they wanted me to be to fit in, to be loved, to be enough.

This need for control led to a full-blown eating disorder when I was 15 years old that continued for nearly 20 years. I began to seek external validation for my looks, my body, my choices, my career, and nearly everything in my life. I had to be in control of plans and outcomes. I had to have control of everything, I was in control of my destiny.

Control and clarity held me back for so long. Most of my life I wasn't sure If I believed in God. I didn't grow up going to church, and didn't know anything about this man, so I went about my life controlling everything.

I met an amazing faithful man when I was 19 years old who became my husband 4 years later, and although I went to church with him, I had doubts. I went to be with him. I went to make him happy. I went to say I was going. I was in control of my destiny; I had no desire to learn about God.

For the first few years of our relationship, I continued to struggle with disordered eating in silence. In high school, I had been hospitalized, completed outpatient therapy, and been through nutrition counseling, none of it helped. Interestingly, the disordered eating slowly began to improve throughout my relationship with my husband, but I still struggled with thoughts and control. The first time I remember not being completely consumed with thoughts of food, weight, and my body, was when I got pregnant with my first child. However, I again struggled between my two children with the need to return to perfection.

After my daughter was born, I was left with stretch marks, loose skin, diastasis recti (a hole in my abdominal muscles), and a feeling of absolute disgust. I wouldn't wear a bathing suit to play with my kids at the pool, I didn't want to change in front of my husband, I hated getting dressed in the morning because nothing fit my body right, and I hated looking in the mirror. And despite having an incredible job, an awesome husband and 2 beautiful children I found myself completely unfulfilled with life.

I decided to step so far outside my comfort zone and enter a bodybuilding competition, because what better way to obtain that perfect body and be fulfilled, right? Well, I won. I was awarded multiple trophies that told me I had attained the perfect body I had been working 25 years for, and it truly felt like a dream, but not a fairytale dream. A dream like I was living someone else's life, like I was a fraud. It still wasn't enough. That should have been the pinnacle for me, and I couldn't even enjoy it because I didn't feel worthy.

I would look at the trophies that told me I had a great body, but when I looked in the mirror, all I could see were the flaws and how terrible my life was. That's when I knew something had to change.

I spent thousands of dollars on books, courses, coaching, and training, but I realized that what I was missing was God. Three years ago, I slowly started relinquishing control. Three years ago, we moved our family 1000 miles away from the only home our kids had ever known, all our family, and the life we had built.

Looking back now at how everything flowed so smoothly, I know it was God, and it was our first walk of faith. We were supposed to move at the end of the school year together as a family, but my job needed me a little over a month prior to the rest of my family coming. In hindsight God allowed me 40 days to wander in the wilderness, to be uncomfortable, and to start relying on something bigger than myself.

Just one year ago I got extremely intentional with prayer and seeking out the love of God. I accepted Jesus Christ as my Savior and the transformation that has taken place has been nothing less than a miracle. I started reading the Word daily and realized that it is the only self-development book I really ever needed. The Living Word of the Most High King guided me through my day to day struggles.

Accepting Jesus as my Savior allowed me to see that I am never alone. Even when I felt alone as a child, I was never alone. Even when I feel alone now, I'm not. He was always with me, always seeking me, and always pursuing me.

God blessed me with opportunities that have pushed me outside of the self-validating, people-pleasing comfort zone I had built around myself. I've been challenged to get back to my authentic roots, to talk to people, to talk to strangers, to get to know people. The Word of God, the Love of God, and the Grace of God has allowed me to be restored to the people loving, bold, loud, boss babe I was.

Truly I tell you, unless you change and become like little children,
you will never enter the kingdom of heaven.
— Matthew 18:3 (NIV)

This means that we cannot enter into Heaven's Kingdom by defeating all opponents or demonstrating personal accomplishment, but by humbling ourselves and recognizing that, like children, we are powerless over the circumstances of our own lives. Understanding that I am not in control of my own destiny, that I am completely dependent on God to provide what I need and to protect me from harm, was the awakening I needed to start living a new life hand in hand with Christ.

Realizing that I am a child of God, a beautiful daughter of the Most High King, that I am loved and highly favored, and I AM ENOUGH, has allowed me to look at my body in a significantly different way. I can look at my body with all its imperfections and see it for the miracle it is, that it was perfectly made by the Almighty Creator Himself, and He loves me just the way I am.

The way back to the childlike person you are meant to be and the life you desire is through the Lord. You may think you want what society says you should want; the cars, the house, the money, or fame. You may think the way to get to the life you desire and the person you want to be is through control, hustle, and grinding all the way there. However, the peace, the happiness, and the joy you're looking for rests in the Lord. To fully rely on God for counsel, for answers, for vision, for purpose, for your path, and for your plan is what will bring you to what you are truly seeking.

To be restored you have to be completely changed, the version of you that is now, has to be completely transformed to the version that HE has planned out for you. Restored to the child of God you are, to bring you back to HIM!

THINGS TO PONDER...

1. What parts of your life feel broken and need to be restored?

_____

_____

Romans 12:2 (NIV) says, *"Do not be conformed to the patterns of this world but be transformed by the renewing of your mind."*

2. How does this apply to your life?

---

3. Ask the Holy Spirit to come in to reveal and help you remove things that you can't see.

---

4. Write out a prayer for yourself where you can read it aloud.

_____

_____

_____

_____

_____

_____

5. How can you become more childlike?

_____

_____

_____

_____

_____

_____

Darlene Thorne, M. Div.

Darlene Thorne, M. Div., is the CEO of *A Heart After the Father, LLC,* and serves as your caregiver's co-mentor.

Her mission is to influence change to women ministry leaders teaching them how to practice positive personal self-care body, soul and spirit.

As an international speaker, Darlene delivers life-impacting messages at conferences and facilitating workshops and symposiums. Featured on television and radio, Darlene focuses on practicing intentional total self-care and walking in total freedom and authenticity.

As a published author, Darlene has written several books including participating in two anthologies. Each of her books have been a part of her journey in leading others to deepen their relationship with God.

She and her husband, Kevin, serve together as pastors at Renewal Community Church in Clayton, NC. They have two world-changer young adults, Kevin, II and Kennedy Elayne.

linktr.ee/ladydarlene

Day 5

Darlene Thorne, M. Div.

Soul Restoration

Beloved, I pray that you may prosper in all things and be in health,
just as your soul prospers.
— 3 John 2 (NKJV)

In the midst of life's challenges and tribulations, finding restoration for our bodies, minds, and spirits can seem elusive. As Christian believers, we have the opportunity to experience profound restoration through our faith and relationship with God.

The Bible is filled with stories of restoration. We read about individuals who experienced miraculous healing, forgiveness, and redemption. These accounts serve as a testament to God's limitless power to restore broken lives. We too, can open our hearts to the transformative work of the Holy Spirit, who desires to bring restoration to every area of our being.

The Bible teaches us that our physical bodies are temples of the Holy Spirit (1 Corinthians 6:19-20). There is a connection between faith and physical health which emphasizes the importance of balanced nutrition, regular exercise, and adequate rest. This means that our bodies are not our own but belong to God. As such, we have a responsibility to care for them in a way that honors Him.

Caring for our physical bodies is an act of worship. When we eat healthy foods, exercise regularly, and get enough rest, we are not only taking care of our own health, but we are also showing God that we respect and value the temple He has given us.

There is a strong connection between faith and physical health. Studies have shown that people who have a strong faith tend to be healthier than those who do not. This is likely because faith provides a sense of purpose and meaning in life, which can help people cope with stress and make healthy choices. In addition to balanced nutrition, regular exercise, and adequate rest, there are other ways we can promote our physical health.

Prayer and Anointing with Oil

Prayer is a powerful way to connect with God and ask for His help in healing and restoration. When we pray, we are not only asking God to heal us physically, but we are also asking Him to renew our minds and spirits.

That ye put off concerning the former conversation the old man, which is corrupt according to the deceitful lusts; And be renewed in the spirit of your mind; And that ye put on the new man, which after God is created in righteousness and true holiness.
— Ephesians 4:22-24 (KJV)

Anointing with oil is another way to receive God's healing power. In the Bible, oil is often used as a symbol of the Holy Spirit. When we are anointed with oil, we are inviting the Holy Spirit to work in our lives to help heal and restore us.

The Power of Our Mind

The mind is a powerful tool that can either be a source of strength or a breeding ground for anxiety and depression.

Within the intricate tapestry of our being, the mind holds a central and profound position, capable of shaping our experiences and influencing our life trajectories. It possesses the remarkable ability to serve as a source of strength, clarity, and creativity, propelling us towards personal growth and fulfillment. However, the mind can also become a breeding ground for anxiety, depression, and other mental afflictions which lead to emotional distress and hinders our potential. Recognizing the profound impact of the mind, it is important to dive into the transformative power of renewing our minds through the Word of God, meditation, and positive thinking.

At the heart of this transformative process lies the Word of God, a powerful source of truth, wisdom, and hope. By immersing ourselves in the scriptures, we are not only exposed to life-changing principles, but we also encounter the transformative power of the Holy Spirit, who works within us to bring a deeper and lasting change. As we meditate on the Word of God, we begin to internalize its truths, allowing them to shape our thoughts, beliefs, and attitudes. Through this process, our minds are gradually renewed and transformed, enabling us to overcome negative thought patterns and cultivate a healthy mental outlook.

Meditation is another powerful tool for renewing our mind. When we engage in meditation, we intentionally quiet our minds, focus our attention, and connect with our inner selves and God. This practice allows us to access a deeper level of awareness and to observe our thoughts and emotions with greater clarity. Through meditation, we can learn to identify and challenge negative thought patterns, develop a more positive self-image, and cultivate a sense of inner peace and tranquility.

Positive thinking is another essential component of renewing the mind. Our thoughts have a significant impact on our emotions, behavior, and overall well-being. When we choose to focus on positive aspects of life, we create a positive mental climate that promotes emotional resilience and personal growth. Positive thinking involves intentionally directing our attention towards the good, the beautiful, and the hopeful. By practicing gratitude, focusing on our strengths, and surrounding ourselves with positive influences, we can cultivate a more optimistic and hopeful outlook on life.

Negative thinking can become a deeply ingrained habit, but it is not impossible to break free from its grip. By becoming aware of our negative thought patterns, challenging them with evidence, and replacing them with positive alternatives, we can gradually retrain our minds to think in a more positive and constructive way.

A healthy mental outlook involves a balanced perspective on life, a sense of resilience in the face of challenges, and an ability to find meaning and purpose in our experiences. By nurturing a healthy mental outlook, we can cultivate a sense of well-being. We then live more fulfilling lives, and positively impact those around us.

The mind is a powerful tool that can either be a source of strength or a breeding ground for anxiety and depression. By renewing our minds through the Word of God, meditation, and positive thinking, we can overcome negative thought patterns and cultivate a healthy mental outlook. This transformative process empowers us to live more abundant and fulfilling lives, experience greater peace, and positively impact the world around us.

The human soul encompasses our emotions, will, and intellect. When our souls are wounded or broken, it can have a devastating impact on our overall well-being.

Beloved, I wish above all things that thou mayest prosper and be in health, even as thy soul prospereth. — 3 John 2 (KJV)

The human soul is a multifaceted and enigmatic entity that encompasses our emotions, will, and intellect. It is the essence of our being and the source of our identity. When our souls are wounded or broken, it can have a devastating impact on our overall well-being, affecting our relationships, our work, and our physical and mental health.

The good news is that our souls can be restored and healed. This process begins with repentance, acknowledging and confessing our sins to God. When we repent, we ask God for forgiveness and turn away from our sinful ways. This is a necessary step in the process of spiritual restoration, as it allows us to break free from the guilt and shame that can weigh us down.

Forgiveness is another important component of spiritual restoration. When we forgive others who have wronged us, we release them from the burden of their guilt and allow ourselves to move on with our lives. Forgiveness is not always easy, but it is essential for our own healing.

Holy Spirit Involvement

The indwelling presence of the Holy Spirit is also essential for spiritual restoration. The Holy Spirit is the third person of the Trinity and is present in the lives of all believers. The Holy Spirit comforts us, guides us, and gives us strength. When we are filled with the Holy Spirit, we are empowered to live lives that are pleasing to God and to overcome the challenges that come our way.

Spiritual disciplines, such as prayer, fasting, and worship, can also play a vital role in restoring our souls. Prayer is a way of communicating with God and expressing our needs to Him. Fasting is a way of abstaining from food for a period of time in order to focus on God and seek His presence and guidance. Worship is a way of expressing our love and adoration for God. These disciplines can help us grow closer to God and experience His peace and healing.

The process of soul restoration is a journey, not a destination. It takes time and effort, but it is a journey that is worth taking. When our souls are restored, we are able to live lives that are full of joy, peace, and purpose.

Relationships

Healthy relationships are essential for our emotional and spiritual well-being. In the tapestry of life, healthy relationships serve as vibrant threads, intricately woven together to form a resilient and beautiful pattern. They are the foundation upon which our emotional and spiritual well-being rests, providing a sense of belonging, purpose, and love. We are embarking on an exploration of the profound significance of forgiveness, reconciliation, and the cultivation of strong, supportive relationships with others.

As we delve into the transformative power of forgiveness, we not only examine its power, we experience its ability to liberate us from the chains of resentment and bitterness. Forgiveness is not about condoning or excusing harmful behavior, but rather about choosing to release the emotional burden of past hurts. By extending forgiveness, we open ourselves up to healing and growth, creating space for reconciliation and the restoration of broken relationships.

Reconciliation involves acknowledging the pain that has been caused, taking responsibility for our actions, and seeking to make amends. It is a process that requires humility, empathy, and a genuine desire to rebuild trust and connection.

The church has a unique opportunity to offer a safe and supportive environment where individuals can find solace, forgiveness, and the strength to rebuild their lives. Through its ministries, the church can create a space for healing, reconciliation, and the formation of healthy relationships.

As we draw upon wisdom from various sources, including scripture, psychology, and personal experiences, we gain a comprehensive understanding of the importance of healthy relationships and how to cultivate them. By exploring the themes of forgiveness, reconciliation, and building strong relationships, we aim to equip individuals with the tools and insights they need to navigate the complexities of human connections and live more fulfilling lives.

Every human being has a unique purpose and calling on their life. When we are disconnected from our purpose, it can lead to a sense of emptiness and dissatisfaction. Each of us holds a unique brush, destined to paint our own masterpiece on the canvas of existence. When we are disconnected from this divine purpose, it is akin to a ship adrift at sea, lost and without direction. A pervasive sense of emptiness and dissatisfaction gnaws at our hearts, leaving us yearning for something more profound.

Like a compass, discernment steers us toward our authentic path. It empowers us to recognize the subtle voice of our inner wisdom amidst the noisy distractions of daily life. By integrating prayer, meditation, and self-reflection into our routine, we nurture the gift of discernment. This practice illuminates the journey we are meant to undertake, guided by the light of the divine.

Obedience, the handmaiden of discernment, is the bridge that connects our aspirations with reality. It is the act of aligning our actions with our God-given purpose. When we obey the promptings of our hearts, even when they lead us down unfamiliar paths, we open ourselves up to the unfolding of divine blessings.

Perseverance is the fuel that propels us forward, even when the journey seems arduous. It is the unwavering determination to stay the course, despite setbacks and disappointments. By cultivating a spirit of resilience and tenacity, we can overcome the obstacles that inevitably arise on the path to purpose fulfillment.

To Recap

Restoration, a multifaceted journey, encompasses the healing and renewal of our physical beings, our minds, our spirits, our relationships, and our purpose in life. It is a path that begins with surrendering our lives to Christ, embracing His transformative power, and allowing His love to work within us. As we do so, we open ourselves up to the fullness of restoration that He desires for each one of us.

Physical restoration involves the healing of our bodies from illnesses, diseases, and injuries. It also includes the restoration of our physical strength, energy, and vitality. Mental restoration involves the healing of our minds from trauma, anxiety, and depression. It also includes the restoration of our mental clarity, focus, and creativity. Spiritual restoration involves the healing of our spirits from sin, guilt, and shame. It also includes the restoration of our relationship with God and the experience of His peace, joy, and love.

Relationship restoration involves the healing of our relationships with others. It includes the restoration of trust, communication, and intimacy. Purpose restoration involves the discovery or rediscovery of our unique purpose in life. It includes the restoration of our sense of meaning, direction, and fulfillment.

As we seek to live a life of wholeness and abundance in Christ, may this devotional serve as a source of inspiration and motivation. May it remind us of the power of God to restore all things and the hope that we have in Him. May it encourage us to surrender our lives to Christ and to embrace His transformative power fully.

On this journey of restoration, let us not forget that we are not alone. We have the constant companionship of the Holy Spirit, who guides, comforts, and empowers us. We also have the support of a community of believers who are journeying alongside us. Together, we can experience the fullness of restoration that God has for us.

THINGS TO PONDER...

1. How do you integrate the time spent searching the scriptures for passages on healing and restoration into your daily routine, and what insights or personal growth have you experienced through this practice?

_____

_____

_____

_____

_____

_____

2. In what ways has the Holy Spirit guided and influenced your practices and decisions towards achieving better physical and spiritual health, and how has this journey impacted your overall well-being?

_____

_____

_____

_____

_____

_____

3. How do you incorporate the practice of walking in forgiveness into your daily life, and what spiritual disciplines do you maintain to stay receptive and clear in hearing from the Lord?

_____

_____

_____

_____

_____

_____

Ray Lowe

Ray Lowe is a purpose coach, published author, speaker, hope-dealer, and real estate consultant. He is the creator of the *Still Believing* blog.

Ray's passion is to help you awaken, activate, and accentuate your dreams.

He provides personalized guidance and actionable strategies that inspire lasting change. Whether you're seeking clarity in your career, improving personal relationships, or simply striving for personal growth, Ray is committed to supporting you and walking with you every step of the way.

If you're feeling stuck, struggling, or stranded, there is hope for you. Contact Ray for access to his 90-day program to enlighten, encourage, and empower you to find life on the other side of loss. He lives in Nashville, Tennessee.

raylowe1@att.net
stillbelieving.org
facebook.com/ray.lowe.33
x.com/raylowe
linkedin.com/in/ray-lowe1
instagram.com/raylowe1

Day 6

Ray Lowe

Destination

Restoration

The Lord your God, will restore everything you lost; He'll have compassion on you; He'll come back and pick up the pieces from all the places where you were scattered.
— Deuteronomy 30:3 (MSG)

In a world where newness often reigns supreme, there is something profoundly captivating about the beauty of restoration. It can almost be considered an art form or a celebration of history; a process that takes mere refurbishment or rehabilitation to the next level.

Restoration is said to be the action of returning something to a former owner, place, or condition.

Having worked as a residential real estate agent for a number of years, I was privileged to work with several clients who were only interested in purchasing "project" houses. They only wanted the "fixer-uppers," the ones that no one else seemed interested in.

I can remember a particular occasion driving up to a property, grass and weeds near the knees, shutters hanging by a single screw, paint peeling and showing several shades of the original color, and missing windows. I remember the hesitation to even get out of the car, much less walk inside.

Choosing my steps carefully and shuffling across broken boards, I methodically pushed open a door that was now hanging on one hinge, hoping to see something that would capture my attention in a positive way.

The first thing I noticed was a disgusting, musty, foul odor that affirmed the fact that this house had been closed and unused for quite a while.

I was greeted by a torn, dingy carpet that had been stained with anything and everything I could imagine. The walls had holes and cracks that ran from the ceiling to the floor. The blinds were torn and ripped, literally hanging by a thread. The ceiling was sagging so badly that I hesitated to make any sudden moves for fear it could come crashing down.

My Thoughts...

"Who, in their right mind, would even consider buying something like this?"

"There's no way anyone would want this house."
"Just knock it down, level it, and start all over."

I saw reality.

But then I took the client, known as "the investor," and he began to share with me what he saw when he walked in.

His impression was totally different than mine.
"By moving this and shifting that, I could make it work."
"Fresh paint, new carpet, new appliances, new blinds."
"Move this, change that."
"It'll be better than new."

And suddenly, his eyes lit up as if he could see beyond reality and could actually see a glimpse of the future.

Opportunities.
Openings.
Options.

We looked at the same thing, but we did not see the same thing. So often, it's not what we see, but how we process what we see.

A good investor can see what others can't.
A good investor can see potential, possibilities, and promise.

Restoration begins with renovation and ends with transformation. One of the most compelling aspects of restoration is witnessing the transformation unfold.

Often, before the restoration begins, demolition must first take place. Demolition can be dark, dirty, and disgusting. But demolition must precede restoration.

At times, in the demolition process, secrets are uncovered, and treasures are unearthed. Frequently, things that had been covered and forgotten are exposed through the ugly work of the demolition.

Life Restoration

Perhaps, you remember the Mother Goose nursery rhyme:
Humpty Dumpty sat on a wall,
Humpty Dumpty had a great fall;
All the king's horses and all the king's men
Couldn't put Humpty together again.

Restoration happens in a number of things: houses, furniture, automobiles, art, and even human lives. We are all susceptible to experiencing personal seasons of brokenness. It may be trauma, loss, addiction, disappointments, or any number of hardships. Within the depths of those hardships, hope gives the possibility for renewal and restoration.

Life has a way of throwing us curve balls, and often we struggle to just survive. Enjoying the security of peaceful times one day, and suddenly the next we feel, as Humpty Dumpty, that we've fallen and crashed, and our lives seem shattered in a million pieces.

To use the analogy of the "project" houses, we may feel abandoned, forsaken, unwanted, and undesirable.

And for many people viewing our lives, their impressions may be similar to mine when I walked into that house.

Worthless.
Valueless.
Useless.

But God . . .

The Master Investor steps up, and as your original Creator, He knows your worth, your value, your usefulness, and most importantly, your destiny.

God sees what others can't. He sees your potential, your purpose, and His plan. He knows the plans He has for you, plans to prosper you and not to harm you, plans to give you hope and a future. (Jeremiah 29:11)

God thrives on taking on the projects of those who are broken, beaten, and bruised; the fixer-uppers who have been overlooked and undervalued, forgotten, and written off; the lives that no one else believes in.

God Believed in You Before You Believed in Him...

God has placed within you a purpose. A purpose that is beyond what you could ever imagine. A purpose that is bigger than you. While you were in the womb, He placed a plan inside of you to bloom, to achieve that purpose. His desire is that you be fully renewed and restored.

If you feel you are in that rundown, broken, dilapidated state, and have a desire to be restored to fulfill your God-given purpose, you may ask,

"Where do I begin?"

You may question if there's any hope.

You may think you're too broken to be put back together.

You may see no redeeming value in all the broken pieces of your life and may wonder if there is any way back.

There is a way back, and I believe there are three main steps that should be focused on.

1. **Recognize that you are broken.**

   For the restoration to begin, you must acknowledge the reality of your brokenness. It's okay, not to be okay. You must be willing to confront the wounds of the past. You must be willing to peel back the layers of pain and embrace the rawness of your own vulnerability. Too often, our culture celebrates perfection and masks vulnerability. Allow yourself to be transparent, open, and vulnerable. Embrace your brokenness as a part of your journey rather than a mark of your worth.

2. **Realize there is hope.**

   It's been said that a person can live forty days without food, four days without water, four minutes without air, but only four seconds without hope. Realize that beyond the reality of what you see with your natural eyes, there is hope for change. Hope is the active conviction that despair will not have the final word. This is not the end. Your life is not finished.

3. **Reauthorize God to control the process.**

   God is the Master Investor. He delights in taking on unwanted project people. Others may overlook you, but God is looking for you.

In the eyes of the world, you may be just a shattered, broken mess, a fixer upper. But in the eyes of God, He sees nothing that can't be fixed. He sees you restored and whole. But for the restoration to begin, you must release and give God the authorization to take control. As difficult as your life has been, nothing is beyond God's restoration plan.

After you have suffered a little while, the God of all grace, who has called you to His eternal glory in Christ, will Himself restore, confirm, strengthen and establish you. — 1 Peter 5:10 (ESV)

The process of restoration demands a willingness to embrace imperfection and to find beauty in the midst of decay.

Restoration is not merely about fixing what is broken, but more importantly, uncovering the hidden stories and preserving the beauty of the original creation. We must understand that every crack and every blemish, every fault and every flaw, tells a tale of time passed, of a life that was lived, and of the intricate journey that brought you to your present state. Restoration honors those stories.

We must be willing to embrace renovation and undergo transformation to fully allow restoration.

The act of restoration is a labor of love that breathes new life into the old, transforming the forgotten into the cherished. Regardless of how many pieces our lives have been shattered into, God specializes in impossible situations. The number of broken pieces does not matter to God; all He asks is that we release all the pieces, all the brokenness, all the hurt, and all the pain to Him.

God created each of us in His image and in His design. And since He was our original Creator, He has no problem restoring us to our original condition.

God wastes nothing...

He has placed within you potential and a purpose. To maximize that potential and achieve that purpose, His desire is that you be fully restored.

> *Restore to me the joy of Your salvation, and grant me a willing spirit to sustain me.* — *Psalm 51:12 (NIV)*

When we see ruin, God sees redemption.
When we see brokenness, God sees wholeness.

Your destination is restoration!

THINGS TO PONDER...

1. What do you see when you look into a mirror?
    Do you recognize that person?
    Has the toll of life created someone unidentifiable to you?

    _____

    _____

    _____

    _____

    _____

    _____

    _____

2. Do you feel you're too broken, too battered, too bruised to fix?
   Do you feel you're beyond restoration?
   What thing, or things, do you feel is too much for God to restore?

   _____

   _____

   _____

   _____

   _____

   _____

   _____

3. Are you willing to release everything to God?

   Are you willing to let go and let God take control?
   Are you willing to give God all your pieces?

   _____

   _____

   _____

   _____

   _____

   _____

   _____

4. Is hope a part of your vocabulary?
   Are you ready for your next chapter?
   Are you ready to live and dream again?

   _____

   _____

   _____

   _____

   _____

   _____

   _____

   _____

Sandra Krug

As a Christian Life Coach, Sandra helps women grow their success, significance, and legacy. She holds a Bachelor of Ministry (International School of Ministry) and Master of Ministry (Christian Leadership University).

Sandra is a Ziglar Coach, KBA Coach, and a Certified Master Christian Life Coach (International Christian Coaching Institute) with a Transformed Living Coaching Specialization Certification.

She is a Certified Mental Health First Aid Instructor, Certified Human Behavior Consultant, and published author of books and award-winning articles in *Journal for Legal Nurse Consulting*.

Sandra and her husband own an animal rescue ranch in Florida and are on the Board of a sanctuary offering a pet foodbank and children's educational programs. They are ministry partners at their church, involved with food pantry and homeless, children, and missions ministries.

LifeCoachforLadies.com
facebook.com/lifecoachforladies
facebook.com/groups/confidentwomenunite
linkedin.com/company/life-coach-for-ladies
instagram.com/lifecoachforladies
x.com/lifecoachforla1

Day 7

Sandra Krug

Do You Labor to Enter into Rest?

There remaineth therefore a rest to the people of God. For he that is entered into his rest, he also hath ceased from his own works, as God did from his. Let us labour therefore to enter into that rest, lest any man fall after the same example of unbelief.
— Hebrews 4:9-11 (KJV)

Do you usually clean your entire house before leaving for a vacation? It is common for people to do three days' worth of chores in just one day. This could include changing the sheets, doing laundry, mowing the lawn, and so on, all in preparation for the upcoming vacation. But have you ever stopped to think if all this work beforehand is worth it? Are you exhausted before the vacation has even begun?

How can I take time to rest when there is so much to do? Have you ever said that to yourself or others? I used to have that same struggle... all the time... until it almost killed me. I suffered from severe sleep deprivation. One of my neurologists told me that I had gone on this way so long that I was going to have seizures, go into a coma, and die.

I had let the world's lies convince me that my worth came from my work. So... I worked and worked and worked at the cost of my relationships, my body, and even my mind. I had fallen into one of the liar's snares. Does this sound familiar? We often trust God for the "big" things out of our control, yet it can be difficult to trust God for the little, daily things we believe are within our control.

Western culture values hard work and staying busy; however, we often struggle to keep up with all our tasks and responsibilities. It is easy to become overwhelmed and feel like there is no escape from the never-ending rush of everyday life. But there is one source of comfort and restoration we must all turn to in these moments of chaos—God. The importance of rest is also seen in that God made the Sabbath a time of restoration and one of the Ten Commandments.

God's Restoration Covenant

The Sabbath goes hand in hand with the call to always put God first. Amidst our trials and tribulations, God extends a deeply personal invitation to each of us. He calls us to lay down our burdens, step away from the chaos of life, and enter a season of rest. This is not a generic call, but a specific one for each of us tailored to our unique needs and circumstances. The Sabbath is the sign of the covenant between God and His children.

Rest is not a passive state but an active choice. It reflects our trust in God's sovereignty and a commitment to deepen our relationship with Him. In this season of rest, we actively engage with God through reading His Word, prayer, and meditation on His promises. We can find profound peace in the knowledge that we are not alone, and that God's comforting presence is with us every step of the way. God establishes and upholds covenants, and our active rest is a testament to our complete faith in Him.

God, who never sleeps (Psalm 121:2), took a day of rest and integrated it into His creation. He did not do this because He required it, but because WE do! When life feels overwhelming, remember that God is always there for you; He is waiting to extend His loving invitation to enter a season of rest—a time to recharge, refresh, and draw near to Him. The Sabbath covenant conveys the idea of being refreshed on God's terms, a divine invitation always open to us.

His covenants are binding and reveal God's goodness, showing His care and compassion toward us. God says,

> *Come unto me, all ye that labour and are heavy laden, and I will give you rest. Take my yoke upon you, and learn of me; for I am meek and lowly in heart: and ye shall find rest unto your souls. For my yoke is easy, and my burden is light.*
> *— Matthew 11:28-30 (KJV)*

Life can be overwhelming at times, and it is easy to feel alone and unsupported. We must remember that we must not carry life's burdens alone. God invites us to come to Him when we feel tired and weighed down. He offers us a transformative, physical, and spiritual rest beyond mere relaxation. This profound rest rejuvenates our souls and equips us to face life's challenges with renewed energy and hope.

Focus on Him

Communing with God is a potent way to nourish our souls, discover inner peace, and establish a connection with our Creator. When we deliberately set aside time to be with Him, it is crucial to remember that He urges us to be still, calm our hearts, and acknowledge His sovereignty.

> *Be still, and know that I am God: I will be exalted among the heathen, I will be exalted in the earth. — Psalm 46:10 (KJV)*

This necessitates casting aside our worries, distractions, and preoccupations and concentrating on His presence. Doing so enables us to open ourselves to His serene peace and solace.

Being still in God's presence does not mean sitting silently for hours. It means we must create a peaceful environment to focus on Him for restoration. We can do this by finding a quiet spot in our home, walking in nature, or even spending time in church. As we spend time with God, we can pray, read, and meditate on the Bible, or sit silently. Whatever we choose, the most important thing is to open ourselves up to His presence and allow Him to speak to us.

In doing so, we can find the peace and comfort that only He can give and experience the joy of being in His presence.

Truly my soul waiteth upon God: from him cometh my salvation.
— Psalm 62:1 (KJV)

As we seek His presence, we discover He is our source of strength and salvation. In Jesus, we can find true rest for our souls. His loving invitation calls us to lay down our burdens, find peace, and draw near Him.

God's instructions require us to observe a regular weekly break from work so that rest can do its work. Sleep and relaxation are when rest heals our bodies, builds our muscles, restores our minds, and much more. When we rest in the Lord, we experience more than just a physical replenishment of our strength. Our souls are renewed, and we are empowered to face life's challenges without growing weary. We can soar above our circumstances and confidently walk in the guidance of our Lord.

To draw closer to God in this season of rest, I encourage you to take intentional steps. Make it a priority to spend more time with Him in prayer and reading His Word, allowing His wisdom to penetrate your heart and mind. Lay your burdens at His feet, trusting in His sovereignty and care. Claim His divine promises, knowing that He is faithful to fulfill them. God wants to ensure all His children experience complete faith and flourish.

Surrender to Him

As you focus on God through prayer, worship, and meditation on His Word, you will hear His voice speaking to your heart. You will receive comfort for your soul and direction for your life. You will experience peace that surpasses all understanding, even during life's storms. May you find true rest in the Lord, and may His strength and grace sustain you always. May you find solace and peace during this season of rest, and may your spirit be revitalized as you experience spiritual growth and renewal.

We all need some form of restoration in our lives. God desires to fill your heart with His peace and to refresh your soul with His love and grace. Surrender all your burdens to Him and trust His yoke is easy, and His burden is light. Allow Him to guide you through this season, knowing He has a purpose and a plan for every aspect of your life. In His hands, your trials and tribulations can be transformed into opportunities for growth and learning, and your restlessness can be transformed into peace and tranquility.

Work is important, but it is not everything. You can never rest when work establishes your identity because you must always perform. Experiencing the constant pressure to prove yourself through work is overwhelming. You will not achieve the rest God desires until you find that deep rest within your soul involving who and whose you are. Joy, freedom, and peace are obtained in the rest that He has given to all of us.

Taking care of your physical, mental, and emotional health is crucial for success in all life areas. The benefits of prioritizing rest to maintain good health are numerous. Getting enough sleep can help improve your immune system, boost your energy levels, enhance concentration and memory, and reduce stress and anxiety. Regular exercise and a balanced diet can also improve physical and mental health, positively impacting your career and personal life. By exercising complete faith, prioritizing rest, and incorporating it into your daily routine, you can ensure that you are in optimal condition to tackle the challenges that come your way.

This means you will have the energy and mental clarity to perform well at work, engage in meaningful relationships with others, and confidently pursue your goals and aspirations. Remember, taking rest seriously is not a sign of laziness or weakness but part of God's plan; it is essential to a healthy and well-balanced life. Make sure to take care of yourself physically and mentally, and watch your success and happiness grow. Take heart, embrace this season of rest, and allow yourself to be renewed and refreshed in body, soul, and spirit.

Can you identify the specific concerns preventing you from fully embracing a season of rest? Perhaps you are anxious about falling behind in your work or missing out on opportunities. Or maybe you are apprehensive about losing momentum or being judged by others for taking a break. Examining the root source of these fears can help you develop strategies to conquer them and enjoy the many benefits of rest and rejuvenation.

THINGS TO PONDER...

1. How has busyness impacted you and your relationship with God, and what signs indicate that you need rest and restoration?

_____

_____

_____

_____

_____

_____

2. How do you create time for rest in your daily schedule, and what activities bring you joy and relaxation, allowing you to rest in God?

_____

_____

_____

_____

_____

_____

3. How can you share the gift of rest, create a restful atmosphere, set boundaries to protect your rest, and avoid overcommitment?

_____

_____

_____

_____

_____

_____

4. How should loved ones be involved in a season of rest? Do you compare your rest with others or set unnecessary expectations?

_____

_____

_____

_____

_____

_____

5. How can you foster a heart of gratitude and contentment in this season of rest, and what spiritual disciplines can you integrate to deepen your rest in Him?

_____

_____

_____

_____

_____

6. How can you better trust God's timing and provision, and what spiritual truths can you meditate on during a season of rest to deepen your faith?

_____

_____

_____

_____

_____

7. How can you maintain a posture of worship and praise? Will unresolved disputes or unforgiveness hinder your ability to rest in God's grace?

_____

_____

_____

_____

_____

_____

8. How can you let go of perfectionism and embrace grace, and what steps can you take to nurture your physical, emotional, and spiritual well-being?

_____

_____

_____

_____

_____

_____

9. How can you cultivate a deeper intimacy with God? In this season of rest, will you let yourself share struggles with trusted friends?

_____

_____

_____

_____

_____

_____

10. How can you draw nearer to Him in prayer and devotion and acknowledge God's goodness in every circumstance?

_____

_____

_____

_____

_____

Bonus:

How will you bring the blessing of rest into the busyness of everyday life?

_____

_____

_____

_____

_____

Let's pray:

Most Gracious Heavenly Father,

Abba God, I praise You for Your words of assurance in Joshua 1:9 (KJV), which says:

"Have not I commanded thee? Be strong and of a good courage; be not afraid, neither be thou dismayed: for the LORD thy God is with thee whithersoever thou goest."

Life's busyness is overwhelming me. I feel anxious and fearful. I need Your guidance to recognize signs that indicate I need rest. May I find joy in seeking You, and may Your presence fill me with peace and purpose. Please grant me the courage to say no and the wisdom to prioritize.

Help me set healthy boundaries and identify areas where I must take a break. Please grant me the strength to set aside distractions and focus on You. Please show me how to share the gift of rest with others. Let Your rest abound in all I do. With Your help, I can overcome these obstacles and move forward with renewed clarity and purpose. Thank You for Your kindness and understanding.

Like the Psalmist David, I pray you will,

Wash me throughly from mine iniquity, and cleanse me from my sin. — (Psalm 51:2 KJV)

Thank You for this season of rest. You are my refuge, strength, and peace. I pray for guidance on self-care and desire to find true rest in You. Help me trust Your timing and find the courage to be vulnerable with trusted friends and mentors. May my heart be steadfast in worship and praise, acknowledging Your goodness and finding joy in Your presence.

Reveal the dreams You have placed in my heart and guide me to align them with Your plan for my life. Teach me to embrace grace and rest in Your perfect love. As I emerge from this season of rest, help me carry its lessons and blessings into my everyday life. Grant me wisdom to prioritize rest amid busyness, and may Your peace guide my actions. Let this season be a foundation for a balanced and purposeful life in You.

In Your Holy Son Jesus' name, I pray. Amen.

Marla Franks Marcum

Marla is a best-selling Christian author and is presently writing a Christian song with her grandson Alex (14), who lives in California. He and his brother Alan (12) are the sons of Marla's daughter Missy, who went to be with our Lord four years ago. Marla is pleased to be fanning the flame for Christ in her grandsons that their mother started in them.

Marla finds that it is vitally important not only to love the Lord but also to serve him. Living with chronic pain and the loss of a child, she reaches out to those who are suffering. Marla believes that it is never a loss when a loved one goes to Heaven that, in fact, it's a WIN! She resides in Ohio with her feline roommates, Willow and Simon.

facebook.com/marla.troutman.1
instagram.com/marlapierce712
tiktok.com/marlalovesgod3781

Day 8

Marla Franks Marcum

Rest In Me

Yes, my soul, find rest in God; my hope comes from him.
— Psalm 62:5 (NIV)

To me, restoration in Christ means "Rest in Me." I know that I can rest in Jesus's arms at any time, and/or any place I need comfort, strength, or just to feel their love. This gift of unconditional love from God comes from my total surrender to Him. His unconditional love is but one of many gifts that He has given me and all that I had to do was give my all to Him.

Come to me, all who labor and are heavy laden, and I will give
you rest. Take my yoke upon you, and learn from me, for I am
gentle and lowly in heart, and you will find rest for your souls.
For my yoke is easy, and my burden is light.
— Matthew 11:28-30 (NIV)

God has given me complete rest, without worry, and I am so grateful. It is a wonderful thing to be able to face this world without stress and turmoil, knowing that I can give my stress to the Almighty and rest in Him. It wasn't always this way, and I have always believed in God. I just hadn't made the complete transfer of giving myself completely to Him.

*The Lord is my shepherd, I lack nothing. He makes me lie
down in green pastures, he leads me beside quiet waters,
he refreshes my soul. — Psalm 23: 1-3 (NIV)*

The day of my complete restoration was November 5, 2022. Now mind you, I was working in ministry, not as a pastor, but ministering to others at conferences. I was working as the treasurer on a board for a Christian foundation that you would recognize—we even produced a Christian television show. I wholeheartedly believed in Christ and believed that I had given my all to him, but... on November 5, 2022, I was out shopping for Christmas items with family. We were at P. Graham Dunn, in Wooster, OH, and I was still lost in grief over my daughter's passing, as well as the passing of both of my parents.

All three had risen to heaven within 14 months of each other, and I had been my daughter's caregiver in California, as she fought the disease which eventually took her life. I tried to get into the holiday spirit, but was having a very hard time. When we were leaving, I looked toward the little chapel where I knew my father had come to pray for my daughter, his granddaughter, while she was ill.

I headed straight for the chapel, and said, "I need to pray." I was supposed to give a testimony at church the following day, and felt like I couldn't go on, let alone give a testimony. We headed in silence down the short walk to the chapel. This chapel is completely made of wood, and everyone is allowed to write messages to God inside, on everything but the windows and pulpit.

Once we entered, as the other women of my family started examining all of the messages of faith all over the walls, ceiling, benches, and floor, I headed to the front pew and sat in front of the cross. I immediately started to cry my heart out to my God, as He listened. I told Him I couldn't take this emptiness, depression, and loneliness anymore. I asked Him to please fill that hole with light and stewardship for Him. I was crying so hard, I was soaking the front of my shirt.

My family, all women of faith, stayed in the back of the chapel, knowing that I needed to do this on my own, but praying for me as well. I continued praying and God continued listening. I kept repeating my prayer over and over again, asking Father to fill my emptiness with light and stewardship for Him. I felt His light fill me and completely overcome me, until my sadness and depression were gone.

I felt such joy, but also exhaustion. I thanked God for His mercy and everlasting love and felt His arms around me. I was now ready to leave the chapel. I had gone through a complete restoration. As I rejoined my cousin. She said that I looked better, and I told her that I was. My great niece held up a marker and said, "Aunt Marla, we have just the spot here for you to write a message for Aunt Missy," (my daughter).

I wrote a beautiful message to Missy and to God, and then we left. As we walked around the lake, I looked back on the chapel and the most gorgeous light was shining through the chapel window, like God was marking my restoration. I pulled out my phone and took a photo so that day would be immortalized forever. My testimony at church the next day was joyous.

There is a complete difference between giving it all to God and 99% to God. I had given 99% to Him. Once I gave him 100%, my life was majorly changed. I could now talk about my daughter without crying, and I smile when I talked about her. My ministry took on a heavier role in my life as well.

I also realized that restoration is something that God gives us daily in other ways. I had just never realized it before. But when they say that God often works in mysterious ways, well it's true. A little over a year earlier, God had given me a gift of restoration and I didn't even know it. I was out walking with my friend Kim, while she was walking her dog Sophie, and God spoke urgently to me.

He spoke to me and said, "Today I want you to go to The Humane Society and get a cat." I was listening to my friend talk but listening to God. I silently said, "OK" and turned to Kim and said, "What are you doing this afternoon?" She said that she didn't have plans and asked why. I told her that I wanted to get a cat from The Humane Society.

Accept instruction from his mouth and lay up his words
in your heart. — Job 22:22 (NIV)

So after our walk, we went to The Humane Society, all on what God had told me to do. Yes, I had thought about getting a pet, but I had really wanted to get a puppy. However, I had decided that physically I couldn't handle the demands of a dog. I was not prepared for a cat, no litter box, no food, but I was listening to God's instructions.

Once there, I started looking, desiring a kitten. Being very partial to calicos I started looking at the many calicos that needed homes. I jotted down a few names to see which one seemed the best match with me. I had already spoken with the man in charge and he knew that I had a lot of experience with cats, so I was nearly ready to give him my list.

As I was waiting, I looked over at a cage that was holding two long haired black calicos. They had to be sisters and they had to be from the same litter, about four months old. All one had to do was come halfway close to the front of the large cage to realize that this was a wild child. I heard God loudly say, "That's the one for you!" and I actually said, "Are you crazy?" He chuckled and said, "No, my dear, she needs you as much as you need her."

The man was ready for my list, held out his hand and I slid my list in the pocket of my shorts. Kim asked if I had changed my mind about a cat. I said that I still wanted a cat, but I wanted that one, and I pointed at "wild child." Kim asked me if I had lost my mind. The man at The Humane Society told me that he would allow me to try her out. This was only because of the vast experience I had with cats, because she was a handful.

Needless to say, she went home with me and spent the first two days hiding under my couch, with me on the floor with her. It took months until she would sit on my lap, but I restored her faith in people, and she was just what I needed. I decided to name her Willow, and she has been my main emotional support after God. Once I was able to see through her wild hair, I realized she was a Maine Coone, and would be large and busy. Today, two and a half years later, Willow tells me when to go to bed, when to get up, and is the best companion in the world. She knows when I don't feel good, lays on me, and purrs me to sleep. God knew what He was doing when He brought us together.

If you return to the Almighty, you will be restored.
—Job 22:23 (NIV)

As I said, God restores us in many ways. Willow and I finding each other restored each of us. In fact, my first book is centered around Willow. God gave me the idea and as always, I listen to what God tells me to do.

When I need to restore, I listen to contemporary Christian music, garden, video and chat with my grandsons in California. I also love watching Christian movies. Surround yourself with like-minded people. It's hard to maintain friendships with people who don't follow Christ. Sometimes we have to let them go. As the old saying goes, *"you can bring a horse to water but you can't make them drink."* Be of Christ in your life. If you talk the talk—WALK THE WALK!!!

I encourage you to walk with and rest in Christ, my friend. You will find that as you talk the talk – and WALK THE WALK, your restoration is right around the corner.

THINGS TO PONDER...

1. The Lord's Prayer has a new meaning for me now. What does it mean to you?

   _____

   _____

   _____

   _____

   _____

   _____

2. Do you have ways to restore yourself and your faith, when you're feeling weary? What are they?

   _____

   _____

_____

_____

_____

_____

3. Find ways that you can help others to restore when they feel lost or afraid. This is actually a two for one gift. You both find healing and restoration.

_____

_____

_____

_____

_____

_____

Ann Marie Thrives

Ann Marie is a certified human behavioral specialist, coach, speaker, skin care and self-care enthusiast, and best-selling author. She empowers women and entrepreneurs towards confidence, well-being, and purpose to help them become whole from the inside out; to foster courage and strength to accomplish life's purposes.

Who wants to THRIVE—not just survive—in every extension of life? Your wholeness is just a click away.

linktr.ee/wethriveatlife

Day 9

Ann Marie Thrives

Peace In Restoration

Instead of your shame you shall have double honor, and instead of
confusion they shall rejoice in their portion. Therefore in their land
they shall possess double; everlasting joy shall be theirs.
— *Isaiah 61:7 (NKJV)*

One of the first things I think of when I hear the word restoration is wiping the slate clean. I think of do-overs where it looks like the thing that happened never happened. Everything is back to its original state, as if you've gone back in time and erased it from ever taking place.

The ultimate act of restoration took place on the cross when Jesus re-established our broken relationship with the Father. We were redeemed from the sin in the Garden through Him and restored to that initial moment of personal fellowship with God and our intimate relationship with Him. All our sin was wiped clean, and we can now go boldly to the Throne of God for any and everything.

God's restoration is greater than we can ask or think because when God restores, not only does it seem like He's set the clock back, but He also smooths all things out and provides a valuable lesson for us that leaves a beautiful, indelible mark, like a gentle, loving kiss on our cheek.

I have been the recipient of restoration many times in my life. Because of my upbringing, the looking glass of others, and their religious beliefs, I was led to believe in a God that was different from what the Word portrays Him to be.

This caused me to have distorted and warped thought patterns, rooted in immense guilt, that provoked me to go my own way many times in life. Like the Apostle Peter, I had many short bursts of faith. My proclamations were strong one minute, then when faced with struggles or low moments, I turned to my flesh.

The Lord used people, music, and His Word to gently restore my relationship to Him each time I strayed. I am so grateful for the sacrifice of Jesus as this helped me to realize that I am worthy to be restored because of Him.

My most vivid experience with this precious restoration was when I first heard about the veil that was torn in the temple when Jesus exhaled His last breath. Seeing that in the Word showed me that there was no longer anything keeping me from going directly to the Father.

I didn't have to say "x" amount and "types" of prayers to be exonerated and restored to Him. I no longer had to carry the guilt and shame of what my sin had caused because it was taken in by Jesus, exhaled from His breath on the cross, and evaporated in the air. His blood covered every little thing I did and when He said it was finished, it was. There's nothing else for us to do other than go to Him and ask His forgiveness. He is faithful to forgive us.

I used to keep away from God because of the religious belief that I was unworthy to go to Him when I sinned. I was dirty and He was Holy, so I had to go through someone else to get free and even then, there was still a debt owed, and expedition for these sins after death. Jesus made it possible for me to go directly to the Father. I didn't need a mediator because Jesus was that Man. Jesus pulled back that curtain. The veil has been removed, and now I can go directly to God. He sees me through the blood of Jesus, all is forgiven, and I am restored every single time.

One day, in Psalm 103, I saw a list of benefits for the soul that trusts and believes in Him. That His mercies are great towards us, and He has separated us from our sins, as far as the east is from the west. I'm familiar with east and west, but think about it, if you're on the east side of the world and you start heading west, you will continue to go east and never really reach west, you never catch up to it, that is how far He has put our sins away from us. Once He has forgiven them, we never catch up to them again. Selah.

My salvation and sense of redemption did not come easy. I remember sitting in an empty church one day, staring at a crucifix hanging from the ceiling. It was a beautiful, rustic church on the top of a hill, and it was a gray and windy day. No one was there but me and God. The voices of those in my life were so heavy in my heart and mind that I did not know where to turn, so I came here to find refuge.

I remember sitting there, staring up at the cross, listening to the whistling of the wind through the church as I cried out to God for the truth. I just wanted the truth. I wanted what God wanted and to stop the confusion of what others were saying a relationship with Him should be. I looked at the crucifix and I cried in a loud voice spiritually and physically. The only words I could muster were that I wanted Him, His truth, just THE Truth!

Those words, asking for The Truth, soon melted away a veil within my heart. I could feel the power of the Lord overtake the church and permeate my body, my heart, and my mind. The experience is something I will never forget. It was as if the Lord personally came to show me that Jesus was the truth, that all I needed was Him, and that all was well.

The scornful, judgmental voices and the accusatory pointing fingers in my mind were now gone. The torment, shame, and deep oppression my sin had caused was gone. The Holy Spirit took over and there was new life within me. The burdens of the past were no longer on my back and infused in my being.

I had never felt that type of restorative peace before. The Scripture of becoming a new creature rang true for the first time in my life as if new blood was now flowing through my veins. Like a dry-erase board, all the scribbles were wiped away and it was once again white and clean, as if nothing had ever been written against me. I felt one with God, Jesus, and the Holy Spirit. The darkness of my sins and my past was replaced with the light of the Father's fellowship and immense love.

It was difficult to accept this love. I did not understand it. I was not used to it, and I had not seen it before. The love I was used to was clouded by others' pains and life experiences projected onto me. So, this deep and pure love that I was experiencing from God was almost unbelievable.

The Lord is the Master at saving and sparing. He continually saves us and spares us from tragedies even though we may not think it at the time. Looking back, I can see how He was always there for me and was pouring blessings into my life right in the middle of huge and disturbing messes. Like my sweet Jesus, saying "I'm sorry your cake fell to the floor. Here, have a cookie, it tastes better, you'll see."

My favorite stories of restoration in the Bible are of the 10 lepers in Luke 17, Jairus's daughter and the woman with the issue of blood in Mark 5, and of course, the ultimate restoration, Jesus's resurrection. These instances stand out to me the most because of the way they happened and how they relate to my life.

The story of the leper taught me that Jesus restores what is eaten away, and He gives us extra for our gratefulness. He put everything back for that leper. The scripture does not get specific, but what if his fingers, face, nose and who knows what else were missing as a result of the leprosy, and they all grew back as he walked away? Not only would he have the smooth skin of a baby, but he was also made whole because of his gratefulness. There is a difference between healing and wholeness. Healing takes care of what's ailing you, but wholeness, that restores everything in your life and body back to its original form and then some!

There were 10 lepers in that accounting of healing. Only one of the 10 men came back to thank Jesus. Because of this one leper's gratefulness, he was the only one that was made whole.

Jesus even said, *"Were there not ten cleansed? But where are the nine?"* (Luke 17:17 NKJV) To top it off, the one that came back was a *"stranger,"* a *"foreigner," "a Samaritan"* (v.18)! He was not a Jew who had grown up with the scripture promises and in anticipation of a Messiah. He was an outsider with different ways of worship, not of the lineage of Jesus and the chosen people. He said to him, *"Arise, go your way. Your faith has made you well"* (Luke 17:19 NKJV).

As the man went, he saw his healing, and he cried out in a loud voice and glorified God. Then, he ran toward Him, fell at His feet, and thanked Him for his healing. There on the ground, he worshiped the MAN God who had healed him. Jesus, of the line of David, the promised Messiah, took the time to heal a leprous Samaritan. This man had two strikes against him. He was a leper and a Samaritan. Yet Jesus reached out to him, willingly accepted him, and healed him.

Think of what this healing did for this man. He was completely ostracized from society because of this disease. The lepers were standing by the sidelines because they could not be close to people. They were considered unclean, outcasts, and social rejects. The healing and wholeness that Jesus provided restored all those areas of his life. He could now go back to his family, his work, and his life before this disease made him a recluse. As a bonus, he has this awesome experience of meeting the living God to take with him as well.

Then we have the story of Jairus and the woman with the issue of blood. These stories, in particular, have great meaning to me. I have come to realize that, in a sense, I am both Jairus and the woman with the issue of blood. When I read this passage in Scripture, it's like a movie reel starts to play in my head.

I am walking with Jesus and explaining my situation. There are people everywhere and I'm taking a big risk being out here with Him. However, I cannot deny the proof in the Torah of the promise of Him to us. In the middle of our deep conversation, He stops in His tracks and asks who touched Him. He felt the touch of faith drawing on His power and He wanted to know who touched Him with that intensity. She reveals herself. Wait, I know her. She used to come to our synagogue until she was diagnosed with the bleeding and was forced out of community. Stories of her imply that she lost practically everything because of this bleeding and now, Jesus, through her faith, has healed her.

As Jesus is listening to her story, I look over and I see them coming. Their faces do not look good at all, and they bring the news I was dreading. Just as the last words leave their lips, Jesus whirls around as if He can hear the thoughts in my mind and the fear in my heart, his cloak swaying about Him as He turns, His mouth produces a thunderous, yet peaceful voice declaring to me, "fear not, believe only."

He walks me back to my home, passes by the mourners, heading straight for my daughter's room. Shutting everyone out besides me, my wife, and His inner circle of Peter, James, and John, He takes her hand and commands her to rise from her sleep. His words and touch, like electricity through her body, jolt her back to life. She opens her eyes, arises, and walks over to hug me. All the hopes and dreams of a father for his daughter come rushing back to me. Jesus has restored all our lives.

I have been Jairus. I have been face to face with impossible situations that felt as bad as death at the door, because life as I knew it had died. For a good portion of my life and in different instances, I was also that woman with the issue of blood. I was bleeding in so many areas of my life that it seemed like there wasn't enough gauze to plug up the holes to make it stop. No one could give me the triage I needed but Jesus.

There was physical, emotional, and financial bleeding due to a series of incapacities. The bleeding was also spiritual and caused my faith to be like faulty wiring in an old house, flickering on, off, and dim at best. These very experiences had me on the sidelines of life and deep, meaningful fellowship with God.

Only Jesus could redeem the life I had lost and create a new and worthwhile one for me. This bleeding drained every good thing life had to offer and the eternity that awaited me. I smelled. I was weak, broke, and alone. I didn't believe God loved me because I was so ill and that my sins were the cause of it.

I did not fully understand that I could call out to Him and He would rush to me and hug me to Him in a flash. I did not know how to turn to Him, how to call on Him, His Word, or use my authority. I did not even know I had authority and that He had relinquished it to me on the cross. He now lives within me and that puts me on a spiritual plane that only exists when we proclaim our fellowship with Him. Because of Jesus, I have special power to draw closer to God.

Jairus, the woman, and the leper all had special circumstances and, in one way or another, should not have been going to Jesus. Jairus because he was a religious leader, and it was frowned upon by the other Jewish leaders to believe in and be around Jesus. In fact, they carried such hatred toward Him that they plotted to kill Him. Our little woman and the leper had been ostracized and became social outcasts because of their physical conditions. They were both considered of lower class as she was a woman, and the leper was a Samaritan. So, we can add the complications of minority and nationality to their list.

Jesus demonstrated that He was no respecter of persons and rewarded their faith by performing miracles which plugged up the holes in their lives and made them whole again. Raising a beloved daughter from the dead and proving to those who chose to believe that He was the Son of God and He was performing these miracles.

Jesus did not fault the woman for coming forward despite their laws. In fact, He commended her for her faith and acknowledged it in front of her entire community. She was now free to live her life, and all was restored to her. The leper was restored physically by healing and socially, as a Samaritan, was accepted by Jesus.

Not only did God restore them on this earth, He restored them to heaven. His sacrifice tore the veil that was keeping us from an unhindered relationship with God so that we can go straight to His Throne. Our sins and tears have been washed away and we are able to go directly into the Holy of Holies to partake in the Father's fellowship and get the help we need at any time.

Our relationship and right standing with God has been renewed because of Him. We are free to draw higher and closer to God. In my heart, we are in two places, here on this earth and in heavenly places taking full advantage of our blood-bought privileges.

Growing up, I did not know that this sweetness could exist. My understanding of God was warped. He was not a Father or a friend. Now, this new-found restoration allows me the opportunity to live what some call the high life. I am back in the high life again because of Jesus!

There are several Scriptures which refer to our physical, spiritual, emotional, and financial restoration. Some of my other favorites are... Job, where the Lord restored double what he had lost, in Joel the Lord restored the years that were eaten, in Jeremiah He promises to restore our health, in

Isaiah He promises to restore our blessing, our joy, give us a double portion and take away our shame.

Two of my special favorites are John 10:10 and Proverbs 6:31. We know the thief comes to steal and destroy. However, when he is found, he must give back seven times what he has stolen. In essence, I'm too expensive for him to mess with because God has equipped me with His Word and His authority to live an abundant life.

God promises restoration to His church, His people. It is His desire. Like the lepers, Jairus, and the woman with the issue of blood, we can also claim our restoration. With bulldog faith, we can hang on until our miracles come, praising Him for it through our struggles, knowing in our hearts that He is faithful. What He did for others, He will do for us. We can call on Him and get help in our time of need and rise in fellowship with Him here, and eventually rise like Jesus, to heaven in our new and resurrected bodies when we leave this earth. Through belief in Jesus, God promises restoration to us on either side of heaven.

THINGS TO PONDER...

1. Do you feel worthy of the finished works of Jesus on the cross knowing what belongs to you as a child of God?

_____

_____

_____

_____

_____

_____

2. Do you want to be made whole?

_____

_____

_____

_____

_____

3. What do you think it will take to get you there?

_____

_____

_____

_____

_____

4. Are your proclamations strong one minute, and non-existent the next?

_____

_____

_____

_____

_____

_____

5. What Scriptures specific to your situation can you stand on and hang on to in faith until your wholeness comes to fruition.

_____

_____

_____

_____

_____

_____

Guy Morrell–Stinson

Kingdom visionary, best-Selling author, speaker, leadership coach, marketplace servant leader all describe Guy Morrell-Stinson.

He is a visionary Kingdom builder and the founder of multiple Kingdom ministries such as the *Empowered Kingdom, 1 Kingdom Alliance,* and *1 Kingdom TV.* He is an international speaker, author, and empowerment coach.

Guy answered God's call at a very young age. He has dedicated his life to seeking truth and wisdom from the Bible for today. This quest revealed the importance of the Kingdom for Christians in all aspects of life. Guy's mission is to empower Christians in business and ministry to be effective in all aspects of life.

Guy is the founder of the following ministries:

EmpoweredKingdom.com

1KingdomTV.com

1KingdomAlliance.com

Day 10

Guy Morrell–Stinson

Foxholes

He restores my soul; He guides me in the paths of righteousness
for the sake of His name. Even though I walk through the valley
of the shadow of death, I will fear no evil, for You are with me;
Your rod and Your staff, they comfort me.
— Psalm 23:3-4 (BSB)

What can a wounded soldier in a foxhole say about restoration? Restoration is a wonderful title for a book, especially if you are on the restored side of restoration. The horrors of the wars you fought are behind you. Now you can build something new. Restoration is a beautiful thing.

There is the other side of the coin. What if you are not restored? What if you are still in the foxhole? What if you ran out of strength, hope, faith, and energy a long, long time ago? You have nothing left. You are beyond your reserves. In this space, the word restoration is meaningless. It feels like a slap in the face and a punch in the gut. This is where I am. This is where life has been dragging me—mercilessly, and relentlessly for the last forty years. I have given, and given, and given. People have taken, and taken, and taken. Now, I am empty, and have nothing left. In this space, restoration is not a word I want to hear.

At times a hand greater than us grabs our life and will not let go. That hand grabbed Joseph by the scruff of his neck. A few days before the hand came, Joseph's father placed a cloak of many colors on his son. The coat symbolized hope and a future. It spoke of a blessing. At the same time, evil wrapped the hearts of his brothers who plotted his death. As God spoke a blessing, the serpent plotted death.

In a matter of days, Joseph went from hope to a hole. He went from home-cooked meals to a camel dragging his sunburnt body and shredded feet over a furnace of desert sand. One abuse followed another. Yet Joseph maintained his integrity. His character led to recognition, reward, and promotion, not as a free man, but as a slave secretly sorrowing for home. How he longed for restoration.

Then the hand of God stepped in again. Like a fish in a net, Joseph struggled. He walked into a trap set by the lust and fantasies of Potiphar's wife. Joseph chose his integrity. It cost him his reputation, comfort, and freedom. The reward for his integrity was to sit in a dungeon for years.

One day, the unexpected hand grabbed Joseph by the neck and placed Him in front of the most powerful man on earth. A crisis of global proportions was on the way, and only one man was qualified to save and restore the nations of the earth. That man was Joseph. His hell was his training. The dungeon was his schoolmaster.

Joseph's story appears to be a template for people God marks for greater things. We see similar versions of this template in the lives of David hounded by Saul, Moses falling from power, Daniel in the lion's den, Ezekiel despised by religious leaders, the Apostles, and others. It is possible that the epitome of this template is seen in Jesus Christ. The Bible refers to Jesus as a *"Man of Sorrows."* (Isaiah 53:3-4)

Jesus' end was unbelievably horrible. Like a soldier deserted in a foxhole, the cat of nine tails rained explosions of pain all over his body. There was no mercy. This was only the beginning. The cross finalized Jesus' slow miserable death. Where was His restoration?

Then came the resurrection!

Now, we serve a risen Savior! Jesus went to the end. There was no better outcome than crucifixion to look forward to. There was no hope and future on this side of the cross. He had to go through the cross, and He knew it.

The Bible tells of another man, sitting on a heap of ash, covered in open boils. His misery was complete and his wealth destroyed. His family lay dead. He had company. They were three fools, torment, and accusation!

Job's story does end with restoration. God restored his health and wealth. God blessed Job with the most beautiful children in the land.

We may be in a place where we cry out, *"Where is my restoration? Have I not given enough, sacrificed enough, and sorrowed enough?"* Yet, here I am, sitting on a pile of destruction, pain, and sorrows. I have seen satan's naked, vile, hatred. I feel his hot breath. I have fought in the dark hours of the night to fend off wave after wave of satanic assaults. One close to me rallies them. The serpent pursued our family, our health, wealth, and relationships. Death knocked at our door again, and again. Witches and warlocks cast their spells. In the middle of all of this, when I am beyond tired and beyond broken! *Where is my restoration?"*

The circumstances may differ. However, at the root of deep, dark suffering, the cry is the same. Where is my restoration? If the journey is long and arduous, the question becomes, *"So, why bother?"*

I know a man who is a graphic designer. He thinks in pictures. Joseph's father covered Joseph with a beautiful coat made with threads of love. A few days later, the betrayal of brothers and the splattered blood of a dead animal shattered Joseph's life.

The picture of Joseph echoes in the man's mind. He sees a similarity in his and Joseph's journeys. In his mind, at random times, he would see a crown on his head. It was a picture of kingship and anointing.

After decades of blows raining down, the vision of a crown became an epic scene from a movie of a king on a burnt-out battlefield by himself, barely alive. His war-torn garments blackened with soot, and shredded with the stench of blood and smoke. He had no soldiers, friends, kingdom, or horses. They were gone. Nothing was left. The forest was burned. Nothing remained. In that place, the man lay down. The ground was still hot with coals. His face in the ashes. He lay in that field with no rescue, betrayed, shattered, wounded, unable to comprehend how it is possible to still be alive. With all his life gone, he did not have the strength to stand.

Where is his restoration?

Surely, he is too broken, and too empty to be restored!

Lately, a new picture has begun to form in his mind. It looks like someone lifting the outer shell of a man—like a shower curtain on a circular ring. The shell is as thin and wispy as a mosquito net. The outer form of the man is rising slowly, but there is no inner man. The old man who used to live within, is no more. He is gone.

The man stands amazed! He has no strength. He has no inner resources to stand. Yet, he is being lifted up by that great unseen hand. When he looks within, he does not see himself. He looks around, but he is gone. Little by little, a strange transformation is taking place. A surprising whisper of love is flowing through him to others—there was little to none before.

In the place where he knew his strength, another kind of strength that can only be described as the strength of the Savior, is rising up. He has no strength of his own. It is as if a new language, and new understanding filled with immense power and authority is starting to flow into his life.

This is difficult to comprehend or put into words. How do we describe the realization that the old man had to die to be buried with my Savior in order to walk in a newness of life?

Is this restoration, or the beginning of restoration?

Time will tell, because God's hand knows what we do not know.

You may be facing your darkest hour. It may be on a hospital bed. It may be in a trial before corrupt judges. It may be in the form of a country collapsing under dictatorship. Know that the end of that night must come.

I hope that this encourages you in some way. I am writing this because it is a reality that does not seem to fit with the promises from the pulpit or well-wishing Christians who have favorite feel-good verses. When the time comes for your testing in the dark desert place, as it probably will, know that God loves us enough to record the stories of David, Joseph, Moses, and Jesus, to name a few. No matter how dark the night, know that God has not left you. Just stand. When you have nothing left, stand—and rest. That is where you surrender. That is where you are born again.

I believe that our destiny is waiting for us on the other side of this experience. I believe that restoration is part of our destiny.

Last night, the man prayed again. This time a new picture formed in his mind. This time a most beautiful crown and a rich, red, velvet robe was placed at his feet. There was no sign of battle. There was no smell of smoke. The crown was perfectly polished and perfectly restored. It was adorned with gems. There was no sign of battle. The crown was perfect. It was a unique crown. It was unlike all other crowns. The man knew he was not the first owner of the crown.

This crown had been previously worn by a great lion.

Finally, there is laid up for me the crown of righteousness, which the Lord, the righteous Judge, will give to me on that Day, and not to me only but also to all who have loved His appearing.
— 2 Timothy 4:8 (NKJV)

Ephesians 6:8-10 in the Phillips translation is an appropriate close for this chapter.

Be strong—not in yourselves but in the Lord, in the power of his boundless resource. Put on God's complete armor so that you can successfully resist all the devil's methods of attack. For our fight is not against any physical enemy: it is against organizations and powers that are spiritual. We are up against the unseen power that controls this dark world, and spiritual agents from the very headquarters of evil."

Therefore you must wear the whole armor of God that you may be able to resist evil in its day of power, and that even when you have fought to a standstill you may still stand your ground.

Take your stand then with truth as your belt, righteousness your breastplate, the Gospel of peace firmly on your feet, salvation as your helmet and in your hand the sword of the Spirit, the Word of God.

Above all, be sure you take faith as your shield, for it can quench every burning missile the enemy hurls at you. Pray at all times with every kind of spiritual prayer, keeping alert and persistent as you pray for all Christ's men and women.
— Ephesians 6:8-10 (Phillips)

May God restore us in His goodness and mercy.

THINGS TO PONDER...

Here are seven discussion questions that recovery groups can consider during times of great struggle and inner oppression:

1. What are the underlying beliefs or thought patterns contributing to our current struggles?

    • Explore the core beliefs or recurring thoughts that may be fueling feelings of oppression or difficulty.

    • Do these underlying patterns line up with God's Word?

    • If not, what correction is needed?

    _____

    _____

    _____

    _____

    _____

    _____

2. How can we differentiate between constructive self-criticism and destructive self-judgment?

    • Write down strategies for recognizing when self-reflection turns into self-condemnation, and how to nurture a more compassionate inner dialogue.

_____

_____

_____

_____

_____

_____

3. In what ways can we support each other's healing journeys without enabling destructive behaviors?

    • Explore the balance between offering support and maintaining healthy boundaries within the group dynamic.

    _____

    _____

    _____

    _____

    _____

4. What practices or tools have been effective in managing overwhelming emotions or triggers in the past?

    _____

    _____

    _____

_____

_____

_____

5. How does our understanding of self-compassion and forgiveness influence our ability to move forward?

_____

_____

_____

_____

_____

_____

6. What role does gratitude play in shifting our perspective during times of struggle?

• Explore the practice of gratitude and its potential to reframe challenges and enhance resilience.

• How can you walk in gratitude, when there appears to be nothing in your favor, and everything is going wrong?

_____

_____

_____

_____

_____

_____

7. How can we cultivate a sense of hope and purpose when facing seemingly insurmountable obstacles?

• How can you nurture hope and find meaning even in the midst of adversity, drawing upon personal experiences and your faith in God.

_____

_____

_____

_____

_____

_____

8. Is suffering meant to be part of our spiritual 'curriculum,' and pathway to growth?

• What part does suffering play in our spiritual growth?

• Has exploring this question changed your perspective on suffering? If so, how?

• How do you give thanks and praise God when everything is going wrong, and all hope is gone?

• Should we prepare for such experiences in life, and if so, what is the best way to prepare?

_____

_____

_____

_____

_____

_____

_____

Dr. Patricia Y. Oliver, U.N. Ambassador

Dr. Patricia Y. Oliver epitomizes creative empowerment as an esteemed best-selling author, U.N. Ambassador, and global speaker. She weaves leadership and image enhancement through profound relationships. She ignites others, guiding them to transmute adversity into purpose and authority.

Dr. Oliver received her Honorary Doctoral Degree from Trinity International University of Ambassadors. She is the visionary founder of *Life-Turn Foundation,* and the CEO of *Poise and Perfection Imaging Inc.* Dr. Oliver catalyzes societal and business leaders to embrace their authentic selves. As vice-president at *Innovative Global Consulting,* she spearheads corporate negotiations initiatives and fortifies IGC's network. Patricia's strategic acumen influences GEE Entergy and the AWHP International board. She has collaborated with top celebrities, earning the Economic Development G-9 Global Icon Award and The Presidential Lifetime Achievement Award.

patriciaoliver.com
p.mccullough519@outlook.com
linktr.ee/patriciayoliver

Day 11

Dr. Patricia Y. Oliver, U.N. Ambassador

A Journey of Faith and Renewal

*And be not conformed to this world: but be ye transformed by the
renewing of your mind, that ye may prove what is that good,
and acceptable, and perfect, will of God.*
— *Romans 12:2 (KJV)*

Reflecting on my life, I realize it was not as blank as it seemed. Life was elevated, yet it lay in wait within the vast sea—a sea teeming with all kinds of people, some beautiful and evil, friends but enemies, and others murky in the deep blue and black waters. All I knew and ardently believed was that this was my chance for a new beginning, a transformation, unaware of the mysteries lurking in the deep blue sea of mist.

The CEO position I held turned out to be everything it was not meant to be, much like life itself. We see what we desire and become what we aspire to be, only to find the undeniable truth awaiting us at the journey's end. Friendships departed, and partners dissolved, leaving behind the murkiness that permeated my existence, akin to the watery depths that swallowed me in 2010. I found myself spiraling, washed into the sea, with only the wake of an ending, before a new beginning.

We often try to map our lives in our minds, dreams, and emotions, yearning for divine intervention and miraculous transformations. As we forge partnerships and lay the groundwork for our aspirations, we eagerly share our vision with others. Everything seems to align perfectly until it doesn't. The excitement fades, conversations cease, and the company's vision is marred by conflict and discord, leaving me bewildered, wondering if my closest friend and partner at the time had changed. They had, and did change, just as the murky sea does as we rise to the top.

Change is inevitable, and amidst the aftermath, one witnesses everything being washed away, like ripples fading as the boat sails away. Life stands still, without the expected excitement, until the sinister murkiness surfaces. This was my reality in 2010, with the establishment of my Emergency Management firm, which I believed the Lord had blessed me with, only to realize that not everything that glitters turns to gold in the sea's murky depths. A projected $2.8 billion vanished as swiftly as it appeared, leaving me pondering the lessons I was meant to learn from this tumultuous season.

I sought a new beginning and fresh perspective on business and questioned the purpose behind this monumental loss. My journey to restoration had commenced long before my company collapsed. The Lord had been guiding me through a period of solitude, preparing me for the restoration of my new beginnings.

Separation and Relocation: The First Phase

Separation was the first phase, as I distanced myself from my core, feeling a detachment in my spirit and yearning for something more. My spirit was no longer at ease in my inner circle. I relocated to a small town, enrolling my son in a local school and embracing a small church community. During this phase, the depth of darkness began to reveal itself.

As I grappled with the uncertainties, I found solace in the rain hitting the tin roof of a location that would be my safe place, the tranquility of the backyard, and the stillness of my mind. Amid the chaos, I discovered God was revealing my true self, unearthing the years of murkiness and uncertainty.

Isolation: The Crucible of Change

The isolation felt suffocating, yet I emerged from the depths of the murky waters, facing the challenges with renewed strength and determination. Peace washed over me, for I knew I was not alone; the transformational stages had begun, and healing was within reach. What was once a turbulent storm had now transformed into a journey of self-discovery and restoration.

Some additional stages occurred during my restoration period, allowing me to see things through God's eyes. *Elimination:* This stage involved removing certain people and things from my life. *Explanation:* This phase was where I sought and found answers to some of the reasons behind the changes and challenges I faced. Illumination: This period was when things began to improve, bringing clarity and leading towards positive outcomes and celebrations.

As I look back now, I recognize that what I thought was a turbulent awakening in 2010 was, in fact, the beginning of a profound transformation. Life's trials often come disguised as failures, yet these moments are the crucibles in which our true selves are forged.

THE BREAKDOWN OF RESTORATION

Rest: The Destination in the Blurry Sea

Rest is often the first and most elusive part of the restoration process. It was the calm before the storm, the deep, blurry sea that was part of my destination. Finding rest means grounding oneself and stepping back to see the bigger picture amid turmoil and uncertainty. In those quiet moments, we begin to understand that rest is not merely the absence of activity, but a profound state of trust and surrender. It's about finding peace amidst the chaos, knowing that God is at work, even when we can't see it.

Be still, and know that I am God; I will be exalted among the
nations, I will be exalted in the earth. — Psalm 46:10 (NIV)

This was a call to stop striving and to trust in His sovereignty.

Torn: The Painful Ripping Apart

The tearing phase is perhaps the most challenging. The rippling effects of the sea, and the wake, ripped apart and damaged my ego and self-esteem. It felt like everything I had built was collapsing around me. However, it was in this tearing that I found clarity. The tearing apart was necessary to remove the old and broken pieces of my life that no longer serve me. It was painful, yes; but it was also cleansing. This phase resembles a refiner's fire, where the impurities are burned away, leaving something purer and stronger behind. The tearing phase taught me that sometimes, we have to be broken down to be built back up more robust and resilient.

Ration: Daily Portions of Grace

Ration represents the provision of just enough for each day. To supply a portion of what was needed. It was a fixed portion. During this time, I learned to rely on God daily. Matthew 6:34 (NIV) reminds us,

Therefore do not worry about tomorrow, for tomorrow will worry
about itself. Each day has enough trouble of its own.

God provided just what I needed to get through each day, teaching me to trust Him completely. This phase is about learning to live in the present, to find joy and contentment in the daily provisions, no matter how small they seem. It's a lesson in humility and dependence on God's timing and provision.

My Path to Restoration

So really, my ego was ripped apart, and my esteem was torn apart from my self. Here, I was working with three partners, and two were going in their direction. But it was then that I realized the tearing was necessary. It was essential for the removal, but my heart didn't want the damage because of the force of the tear, but it was required for the removal. In life, we want the perfect removal without pain. We want the hurt to stop, but we don't want to go through the tearing of the rest. We want to get straight to the healing and the restoration.

Reflecting on my life, I realize there have been many tears. Some were my decisions, but many were the actions of others. I don't know which was worse; all I know is that all of them came with pain. Restoration came in many forms throughout my life and phases.

As mentioned earlier, there was the separation, the uncomfortable situation, then came the elimination of people, and then the relocation and isolation, which brought about the revelation. It was the revelation that brought further elimination of people and more. Then the illumination, where elevation in my life increased, and much more. Finally, modification still had to change something in 2024.

Restoration was not about returning to what used to be, but stepping into what was meant to be. I went from a place of rest, through a place of tearing, and into the fullness of restoration.

Embracing the New Beginning

In 2024, as my company rose from the ashes, I stand ready to fulfill more contracts with a renewed heart and a vision clearer than ever. The journey through the deep waters, the tearing apart of old ways, and the rationing of daily grace had prepared me for this moment. I was restored, not just in my business but in my spirit. The restoration process is ongoing, and each day brings new challenges and victories. The murky waters of the past have given way to a clear horizon, and I am grateful for the journey. For in every trial, there is a lesson, and in every tear, there is growth. This is why God has promised restoration, a renewed mind, spirit, and purpose.

As I move forward, I do so with faith, knowing that past trials have equipped me for the challenges of the future. My story is one of restoration, God's unwavering faithfulness, and a future filled with promise and hope.

THINGS TO PONDER...

1. Can you recall the precise moment when your heart truly broke, signaling the beginning of your path to healing and restoration?

---

2. Close your eyes and envision the life that was destined for you after a significant loss or change. What does this vision look like, and how do you see God playing a role in your journey to achieve it? Write it down and seek divine guidance for its restoration.

_____

_____

_____

_____

_____

3. In the context of your current life and experiences, what profound significance does the word "RESTORATION" hold for you right now?

_____

_____

_____

_____

_____

_____

Tina Benoit

Tina Benoit is the CFO of *Faith Ventures, Inc.,* a 501c3 Discipleship Training Ministry, the executive director of *Faith Venture Ministries,* and a discipleship pastor.

She is also the director of the PERC (Presbyterian Event & Retreat Center) at the Case Mansion in Auburn, NY.

Tina is a lover of all things Jesus, a "crazy-faith-water-walker", a "life application" teacher, coach, and mentor, a conference speaker, a blogger, vlogger, writer, and an all-around handy ma'am!

She empowers and equips Christians from every walk of life to embrace their giftings, get out of their "boat" and walk in their God-given assignment with authority and power!

Tina has been a pastor, teacher, speaker, and coach since 2005. Her life verse is Philippians 4:13, *I can do all things through Christ!*

www.facebook.com/tina.b.benoit

www.facebook.com/groups/177636594372841

tina.faithventures@gmail.com

Day 12

Tina Benoit

Embrace Redemption

From Failure to Restoration

And after you have suffered a little while, the God of all grace,
who has called you to His eternal glory in Christ, will Himself
restore, establish, and strengthen you.
— 1 Peter 5:10 (RSV)

The Valley of Despair

When I think about acknowledgment of failure, I can't help but reflect on the stories of Adam and Eve, as well as King David. It's like looking into a mirror sometimes and seeing our struggles and shortcomings reflected at us through these ancient narratives.

Take Adam and Eve, for instance. Here they are, in the paradise of the Garden of Eden, surrounded by all this beauty and goodness. Then they make that one fatal mistake—eating from the forbidden tree. It's like they had everything they could ever want, but it still wasn't enough. Sound familiar?

What really gets me is their reaction afterward. Instead of owning up to their mistake, they try to hide from God, like a couple of kids caught with their hands in the cookie jar. Eventually, they come clean, acknowledging their guilt and shame. You know what? That's the first step towards restoration right there.

Then there's King David, *"a man after God's own heart"* (1 Samuel 13:14). Even he wasn't immune to temptation and sin. His affair with Bathsheba and the murder of Uriah is some pretty heavy stuff. Yet, when confronted by the prophet Nathan, David doesn't try to weasel his way out of it or shift the blame onto someone else. No, he owns up to his mistakes, confessing his sins before God and man.

Do you know what's really amazing? Despite all their flaws and failings, Adam, Eve, and King David were able to find redemption—eventually. It wasn't easy, and it certainly didn't happen overnight. However, their willingness to acknowledge their failures and seek forgiveness paved the way for their restoration.

It is a powerful reminder that none of us are perfect. We're all going to mess up from time to time. It is just part of being human. It's what we do afterward that really matters. Do we try to cover it up and pretend like it never happened? Or do we own up to our mistakes, seek forgiveness, and take steps toward making things right?

For me, the choice is clear. I may not always get it right, but I'm committed to acknowledging my failures, seeking forgiveness, and moving forward with humility and grace. After all, if Adam, Eve, and King David could find redemption, then surely there's hope for the rest of us too.

A Ray of Hope

Now, there comes that point when you're knee-deep in the muck and mire of your own mistakes, that it feels like there's no way out. I've been there, staring into the abyss of my own failures, wondering if redemption was just a pipe dream. However, just when I thought all hope was lost, a ray of light pierced through the darkness, illuminating the path ahead.

It's like that moment when you are stumbling through a pitch-black room, fumbling for the light switch, and suddenly, there it is—the warm glow of illumination, banishing the shadows and showing you the way forward. That is what it felt like for me when I stumbled upon the stories of David and Peter in the Bible.

Here were two men who had messed up in some pretty big ways. David, with his affair with Bathsheba and the whole Uriah debacle (2 Samuel 11:1-12:9). Then we see Peter, denying Jesus not once, not twice, but three times. Talk about hitting rock bottom (Luke 22:55-62).

The really amazing thing to me is, despite their colossal failures, both David and Peter were able to find redemption. It required major loads of "humility" on both their parts. However, it is through the transformative power of repentance and the boundless nature of God's grace, they were able to pick themselves up, dust themselves off, and start again.

For me, that was a game-changer. It showed me that no matter how far I had fallen, no matter how deep the pit I had dug for myself, there was always hope. Hope for forgiveness, hope for redemption, hope for a second chance.

A ray of hope is a pretty powerful thing to hold onto. It's like a lifeline amid a stormy sea, keeping you afloat when everything else seems to be dragging you under. When I think about that ray of hope piercing through the darkness, I cannot help but feel grateful. Grateful for the chance to start again, to make things right, and to walk in the light of God's grace.

The Journey of Repentance

Have you ever had one of those moments where you just know you have messed up so bad you feel like, *"God will never forgive me for this one?"* Yeah, I've been there. It's like this heavy weight in your chest that just won't go away, reminding you of all the ways you've fallen short. You know what?

It's also a wake-up call—a reminder that maybe it's time to own up to your mistakes and make things right.

So, with a heart heavy with remorse, I did just that. I embarked on the journey of repentance, humbly acknowledging my shortcomings before my Loving, Heavenly Father. It wasn't easy, baring my soul like that, but I knew it was necessary if I ever wanted to find peace.

It reminds me of the story of the prodigal son. You know, the one who squandered his inheritance and ended up eating with pigs? Yeah, that guy. Even in his lowest moment, he found the courage to turn his gaze towards home, yearning for reconciliation and restoration.

His father didn't meet him with anger or judgment. No, he ran out to meet him, wrapping him in a warm embrace and welcoming him back with open arms (Luke 15:11-32). That's the kind of love and forgiveness we all long for—a love that sees past our mistakes and embraces us just as we are.

So, armed with nothing but a heavy heart and a glimmer of hope, I set out on my own journey of repentance. It wasn't easy, facing up to all the ways I had fallen short. However, with each step forward, I felt the burden lift a little more, replaced by a sense of peace and freedom.

Here is the thing about repentance—it's not just about saying, *"I am sorry."* and moving on. It's about truly turning away from your old ways and embracing a new way of living. It's about surrendering your pride and ego and opening yourself up to the transformative power of grace.

Let me tell you, it's worth it. When you finally lay down your burdens at the feet of Jesus, you find a love and acceptance beyond anything you could ever imagine. So yeah, if you ever find yourself weighed down by your mistakes, just remember—the journey of repentance may be tough, but the rewards are beyond measure.

Surrender and Submission

Then there are those days when life throws you curveballs that you just didn't see coming! Yeah, I've been there too. It's like you're sailing along on this smooth sea of certainty, and then bam! Out of nowhere, you hit this storm that threatens to capsize your boat.

That is what happened to me when I hit rock bottom. I was clinging to the wreckage of my own mistakes, desperately trying to steer my ship back on course. No matter how hard I tried, it felt like I was just spinning my wheels.

It wasn't until I reached the point of utter exhaustion when I finally let go of the reins and surrendered control, that things started to change. In the crucible of surrender, I relinquished my pride and surrendered my will to God, finally! It wasn't easy, handing over the keys to my kingdom like that, but I knew deep down that it was the only way forward.

It reminds me of the story of Job. Here's a guy who had everything, wealth, health, and a loving family. Then, in the blink of an eye, it was all ripped away from him. Talk about a gut punch. Yet even amid his suffering, Job never lost faith. He said,

> *Though He slay me, yet will I trust Him.*
> *— Job 13:15 (KJV)*

That's the kind of trust I aspire to have. It's not blind faith or wishful thinking—it's a deep-seated conviction that no matter what happens, everything will be okay in the end. It's about trusting in a higher power, even when the storms of life threaten to overwhelm us.

Here's the thing about surrender—it's not about giving up or throwing in the towel. It's about acknowledging that sometimes, we're not in control of our circumstances. It's about letting go of our need to have all the answers and trusting that there's a bigger plan at work.

When you finally surrender to God, you'll find a sense of peace and clarity that you never thought possible. It's like lifting a weight off your shoulders and stepping into a whole new world of possibility.

So, if you ever find yourself caught in the eye of life's storms, just remember, the path to peace begins with surrender. Who knows? You might just find yourself sailing into calmer waters than you ever thought possible.

THINGS TO PONDER...

1. Have you ever had an experience where you felt like giving in or throwing in the towel - and you actually did? What happened?

   _____

   _____

   _____

   _____

   _____

   _____

2. Did you have an experience where you wanted to give in and throw in the towel but you decided to surrender instead? What happened?

   _____

_____

_____

_____

_____

_____

_____

3. What life storm's do you still need to deal with?

_____

_____

_____

_____

_____

4. Can you pray and ask God for wisdom and discernment?

_____

_____

_____

_____

_____

5. Can you surrender to Him in regard to these storms?

_____

_____

_____

_____

_____

_____

Day 13

Tina Benoit

Restoration Through Forgiveness
The Journey to Healing and Renewal

Be kind to one another, tenderhearted, forgiving one another,
as God in Christ forgave you.
— Ephesians 4:32 (NRSVUE)

Embracing Forgiveness

In this chapter you will see that forgiveness is different than surrender. In fact, forgiveness is a funny thing. For a long time, I struggled to wrap my head around it. I mean, how do you forgive someone who's hurt you so deeply? Perhaps even more challenging, how do you forgive yourself?

I wrestled with those questions for what felt like an eternity, weighed down by the burden of my own mistakes and shortcomings. However, in a moment of clarity, it hit me like a ton of bricks. Forgiveness isn't about letting someone off the hook or pretending like nothing ever happened. It's about setting yourself free from the chains of resentment and bitterness, allowing yourself to move forward with grace and compassion.

So, with tears of remorse streaming down my face, I finally let go of the anger and resentment that had been eating away at my soul. I sought forgiveness—not just from others, but from myself as well. It was a humbling experience, to lay bare my heart and soul before God, but it was also incredibly liberating.

I remember reading about Joseph in the Bible—the guy who was betrayed by his own brothers and sold into slavery. Talk about a raw deal. Yet even amid his suffering, Joseph found it in his heart to forgive his brothers.

You meant evil against me, but God meant it for good.
— (Genesis 50:20 ESV)

That's the kind of grace and forgiveness I aspire to have.

Then there's Jesus, who forgave those who crucified Him even as He hung on the cross. I mean, talk about next-level forgiveness. It's a reminder that forgiveness isn't about deserving or earning, it's about extending grace and compassion to others, even when they least deserve it.

When you finally embrace the liberating power of forgiveness, you'll find a sense of peace and freedom that you never thought possible. It's like a weight being lifted off your shoulders, allowing you to step into a new chapter of your life with hope and joy.

So, if you ever find yourself weighed down by the burden of unforgiveness, embrace the truth that the path to freedom begins with forgiveness. You might just find yourself walking on air before you know it.

The Miracle of Restoration

"Wow, how did I get here?" That's how I felt when I looked back on my journey of restoration. It was like watching a sunrise after a long, dark night—the dawn breaking upon the horizon, casting its golden light over everything in its path.

Here I was, broken and battered by life's storms, wondering if I'd ever find my way back to solid ground. But then, little by little, I started to see the pieces coming together. It was like watching a puzzle being assembled right before my eyes, each piece fitting perfectly into place. It was even more amazing the day I realized that God was the "Puzzle Master" who held all the pieces to my life!

Yes, indeed! It was a miracle—a miracle of restoration unfolding before my very eyes. It's like the stories of Jacob reconciling with Esau or the rebuilding of the Temple in Jerusalem—testaments to the transformative power of God's redeeming love.

First, let's look at the story of Jacob and Esau. Here were two brothers torn apart by jealousy and deceit, each harboring resentment towards the other. But then, in a moment of divine intervention, they were able to set aside their differences and embrace one another as brothers once more. (Genesis 33:4-10) It's a reminder that no matter how far we've strayed or how deep the divide is, God's love has the power to bridge even the widest chasms.

In addition, there's the rebuilding of the Temple in Jerusalem, a symbol of hope and restoration for the people of Israel. Despite the devastation of exile and the destruction of their sacred place of worship, they never lost faith that God would one day restore what had been lost. Sure enough, He did. He brought them back to their homeland and rebuilt the Temple even more glorious than before (Ezra 5 & 6).

For me, my journey of restoration is a testament to that same hope and faith. It's a reminder that no matter how broken or lost we may feel, God's love has the power to heal and restore us. As I stand here, basking in the warmth of His grace, I can't help but feel grateful for the miracle of restoration unfolding before my eyes.

Failure is Never Final in the Restorative Hands of a Loving God:

Do you ever feel like you are walking on air? That's how I feel these days, walking in the light of redemption. It's like every step forward is bathed in this warm glow of hope and possibility, guiding me towards a brighter tomorrow.

I mean, don't get me wrong, it hasn't been easy. There have been plenty of bumps along the way, moments where I have stumbled and fallen flat on my face. Yet with each setback, it only made me stronger, and more resilient. It's like I'm walking through fire and coming out the other side unscathed, thanks to the power of redemption and restoration.

Let me tell you, this is a journey fueled by faith and hope.

1) Faith that God has a plan for me, even when I cannot see it for myself.

2) Hope that no matter how dark the night may seem, dawn is just around the corner, ready to chase away the shadows.

It reminds me of the promise of restoration proclaimed throughout the Scriptures:

Behold, I make all things new.
—Isaiah 43:19/Revelation 21:5

It's like God's way of saying, *"Hey, no matter how broken or battered you may feel, I'm here to make things right again."* Let me tell you, that is a promise worth holding onto with all my heart.

So, with each step forward, I walk in the light of redemption, knowing that no matter what challenges lie ahead, God has my back. It's like I'm walking hand in hand with my Heavenly Daddy, with His love lighting the way and His grace guiding my every step.

The most amazing thing to me is, it is not just about me, it's about all of us. When we surrender to God's plan for our lives and walk in the redemption that only He can administer, we become beacons of hope for those around us, shining the light of God's love into even the darkest corners of the world, as He so lovingly restores us to better than we ever were before.

So, if you ever find yourself feeling lost or broken, just remember—the path to redemption is always open. All you have to do is take that first step forward, and before you know it, you will be walking in the light of God's love, fueled by faith and hope because failure is never final in the restorative hands of a loving God.

THINGS TO PONDER...

1. Forgiveness plays a significant role in the process of restoration. Can you think of a time when you struggled to forgive either yourself or someone else? How did you ultimately find the strength to extend grace and move forward?

---

2. Surrendering to a higher power and trusting in God's plan were highlighted as essential steps in the journey of redemption. How do you cultivate trust and surrender in your own life, especially during challenging times?

_____

_____

_____

_____

_____

_____

3. The chapter concludes with a reflection on walking in redemption and embracing the promise of restoration found throughout Scripture. How does this message resonate with you personally, and what steps do you take to walk in the light of redemption in your daily life?

_____

_____

_____

_____

_____

_____

Denise Bender McCluney, R.D.H., B.A.

Denise is a prophetic worship dancer, intercessor, and Stephen Minister.

She began dancing at age 3 and became a professional dancer by 14. She chose not to become a ballerina but rather a prophetic worship dancer.

At age 32 she had a transformational experience that changed the trajectory of her life. She fully surrendered her life to Christ and her new life mission was to help women recognize their identity as a daughter of the King.

She later discovered she had breast cancer, but God gave her the strategy for her healing in a "sacrifice of praise" expressed in worship dance. Through God's revelation she overcame the works of darkness and created a holistic approach to wellness that she offers to others.

She loves traveling, any outdoor activity, and spoiling her three small grandchildren.

Day 14

Denise Bender McCluney, R.D.H., B.A.

A Story of Redemption

The Lord is my shepherd; I have all that I need. He lets me rest
in green meadows; He leads me beside peaceful streams. He renews
my strength, He guides me along right paths, bringing honor to
His name. Even when I walk through the darkest valley,
I will not be afraid, for you are close beside me. Your rod
and your staff protect and comfort me.
— Psalm 23:1-4 (NLT)

I never dreamed that I could be restored mentally, physically, emotionally and spiritually from all the trauma I've endured thus far. But God... the process has been long and hard, climbing many mountains and walking through many death valleys; but God has always been faithful every step of the way.

The first major valley for me was when my children were 8 and 11; the doctor confirmed that the lump on my breast was malignant. The nurse promptly suggested that I get "my affairs in order."

You never forget where you were or what you were doing at that moment of impact. The trajectory of my life was forever changed; a bomb had gone off and now it was time to deal with the fallout from it. God brought an army of praying Momma bears to walk alongside me through this season. They fasted, prayed, cooked, cleaned, and took care of my children while I endured the grueling season of chemotherapy.

As I asked God for His battle plan and strategy, He made it known to me that my healing would come through worship. I had been a dancer from the age of 3 with professional training at the age of 14. My Father was a professional ballroom dancing teacher that was eager to share his love for dancing with me. I didn't really appreciate it as a teenager, but later learned to love our common interest.

I knew how to move gracefully to music, but God taught me how to worship Him as a sacrifice of praise in the beauty of holiness. There was always a profound exchange as I gave my body and spirit to the Lord in worship. The scripture that came to my mind back then, and still does today while dancing is Isaiah 61:1-3 NLT which says,

> *The Spirit of the Sovereign Lord is upon me, for the Lord has anointed me to bring good news to the poor. He has sent me to comfort the brokenhearted and to proclaim that captives will be released, and prisoners will be freed. He has sent me to tell those who mourn that the time of the Lord's favor has come, and with it the day of God's anger against their enemies. To all who mourn in Israel, He will give a crown of beauty for ashes, a joyous blessing instead of despair. In their righteousness, they will be like great oaks that the Lord has planted for his own glory.*
> *— Isaiah 61:1-3 NLT*

When I dance, I feel the presence of the Lord, throughout my entire being. I Praise God, He did heal me! I can rejoice that after 25 years, I have had no recurrence of cancer! He taught me how to overcome. I am Restored! I not only have lived to see my children grown, but am enjoying their beautiful babies!

My faith walk was not always easy, but as I held the hand of Jesus, I trusted every step of the way.

For every child of God defeats this evil world, and we achieve this victory through our faith. And who can win this battle against the world? Only those who believe that Jesus is the Son of God.
— 1 John 5:4-5 NLT

This Scripture was one of many that I held onto throughout my journey through the valley. I won the battle against the world by believing in my Jesus, the Son of God.

The next major valley I walked through was having to end my 30-year marriage. I lived on an emotional rollercoaster with him from the onset. Way too many deal breakers, but I was determined to make it work, as I did not believe in divorce. However, when someone wants out of the marriage, there isn't much recourse except to comply.

After one and a half years of trying everything to hold it together, I knew that God was asking me to divorce my husband. His (God's) statement to me was that he (my husband), had plenty of time to repent and that He (God), would not tolerate how he was treating "MY DAUGHTER." He said, *"Do you trust Me?"* Of course, Lord.

The unearthing of a 30-year marriage along with caring for my elderly parents was daunting! Again, God brought an army of my Godly girlfriends to help me move, pray, encourage, and tend to my every need. There were many other things happening in my life simultaneously that were almost as stressful as my marital situation.

A month after my divorce was final, my Father passed away and nine months later my Mom passed away. I had no time to mourn any of it; instead, I had to spring into action and get rid of a lifelong bevy of stuff that my hoarding Father had collected while doing the same with my marital house. I also worked full-time and did all of this by myself. Another bomb had gone off and I was left to forge through the rubble quickly. The fallout was extensive, even though my children were out of the house.

Yet, I clung to my Jesus and many Scriptures, including 1 Corinthians 15:57 NLT which reminded me,

> *But thank God! He gives us victory over sin and death through our Lord Jesus Christ.* — *Corinthians 15:57 NLT*

True to form, God sent an army to handle every single detail. It was truly miraculous how and where these people just appeared as I needed them for whatever task at hand. I have learned that God is always leading me through whatever valley experience I may be walking in at the moment. I only need to abide under the shadow of the Almighty. As I trust in Him and acknowledge Him, He directs my path.

During my faith journey, I journaled often as it helped me to stay centered. It is very important to journal and remember God's faithfulness.

> *But then I recall all you have done, O Lord; I remember your wonderful deeds of long ago. They are constantly in my thoughts. I cannot stop thinking about Your mighty works.*
> — *Psalm 77:11-12 (NLT)*

Remembering is a real faith builder. Yet, journalling gives us something to go back to and read from our own hand, then remember all that God had done for us surrounding that situation.

Fast forward 10 years; my family has been restored and redeemed. My ex-husband and I have a very good relationship with our children and each other. We honor and respect one another as a brother and sister in Christ. Our children are happily married with beautiful grandchildren. My health has been restored, I am in a church that has honored and "made room for my gift of dance," and my blessings are endless. I am truly living my best life now. I now realize that through the valley of the shadow of death, God brought me to the life He had planned for me.

Through this process I have learned that we often settle for the low hanging fruit, but He protects us from settling and staying in that place if we cooperate with Him. I have learned to embrace the process of walking alongside Him when He says stay, I stay. When He says move, I move. I remain always in the glory cloud knowing that ABBA knows best. I never fear evil because I know I am more than a conqueror in Christ Jesus. Restored and redeemed.

THINGS TO PONDER...

1. What is your "but God story?"

_____

_____

_____

_____

_____

_____

2. Do you often offer God a sacrifice of praise? (It is life changing.)

_____

_____

_____

_____

_____

_____

3. If so, what is your sacrifice of praise?

_____

_____

_____

_____

_____

4. Do you really understand the truth you are standing under; that God's will is for you to be triumphant in all you do?

_____

_____

_____

_____

_____

5. Where in your life have you been triumphant

_____

_____

_____

_____

_____

_____

6. What things do you want to triumph over now?

_____

_____

_____

_____

_____

_____

Mark and Christine Zimmerman

Christine Zimmerman is a visionary leader dedicated to serving others through faith, education, and healthcare. Christine, an inspiring author, established *Hearts of Healing Grace Ministry* and the *Embrace of Grace Healing Retreat Center,* providing both spiritual and emotional support.

Mark Zimmerman, a devoted servant of the Lord, began his healing journey with Christine 14 years ago. Co-founding the *Hearts of Healing Grace Ministry* and the *Embrace of Grace Healing Retreat Center,* Mark focuses on spiritual and emotional healing. An accomplished woodworker and leader, Mark fully committed to ministry after retiring, offering guidance and support to those in need. Together, they also serve as leaders and marriage mentors, helping couples strengthen their relationships.

facebook.com/cris.crannie

facebook.com/groups/460762034028881

instagram.com/czim402

christinecrannie@yahoo.com

EmbraceofGraceRetreat.com

Day 15

Mark and Christine Zimmerman

Soul Wounds

A Journey of Love and Faith

He heals the brokenhearted and bandages their wounds.
— Psalms 147:3 (NLT)

Healing Together: A Journey of Love and Faith

Our healing journeys began shortly after meeting. Both of us had endured significant heartbreaks in our lives, including broken marriages before meeting each other. Yet, we were both certain the Lord brought us together.

Mark was the answer to years of prayers Christine had offered during her first marriage. As they transitioned from friends to partners, it became evident that their union was an answered prayer, with Ephesians 3:17-18 (NLT) serving as a guiding scripture:

Then Christ will make his home in your hearts as you trust
in him. Your roots will grow down into God's love and keep
you strong. And may you have the power to understand,
as all God's people should, how wide, how long,
how high, and how deep his love is.
— Ephesians 3:17-18 (NLT)

Mark's unconditional love profoundly impacted not just Christine, but also her children. Their daughter often remarks on the unconditional love of a father that she had never experienced before. During their journey, Mark supported Christine through her divorce, while she walked alongside him in his grief over the loss of his mother, who had passed away just a month before they met.

Their shared experiences deepened their bond, and they resolved to heal because they cherished the divine union they felt God had orchestrated. Though their journey holds much backstory and depth, they are compelled to share it in a book they are writing together. Their purpose is to encourage anyone undergoing their own healing process, assuring them that God has a grander plan for their story.

Healing Scars:
Letting Go of Pain and Embracing Restoration

The narrative for this chapter began unfolding when Mark spent time with God, who revealed to him that they were meant to co-author a book on healing soul wounds. This revelation reminded Mark of a story he had heard years ago about a father and his son. The father instructed the son to hammer a nail into a wooden fence every time he experienced an outburst of anger. Over time, as the son's outbursts diminished, the father directed him to remove the nails, one by one, day by day, for each day that he did not lose his temper.

After all of the nails were removed, the young boy noticed that the fence was full of holes. The holes left behind served as a poignant metaphor for the scars and wounds caused by uncontrolled anger and hurtful words. These wounds, unseen but impactful, weaken us and create openings for negative influences. God desires to heal these wounds, preventing further damage and fortifying us against the enemy's schemes.

Mark's revelation from God highlighted that seeking Jesus for healing transforms our wounds into mere scars, carrying no more pain, only the memory of their origins. This genuine forgiveness and pursuit of Jesus for healing exemplify the transformative power of His grace. These wounds are traumatizing whether stemming from loss, betrayal, rejection, bitterness, molestation, unforgiveness, guilt, shame, or other sources. They then often linger into adulthood, shaping our emotional landscape.

When delving into the concept of soul wounds, it's crucial to understand their profound impact on one's spiritual and emotional well-being. They are not mere emotional scars but disruptions in the delicate balance of the soul, often stemming from traumatic experiences or prolonged neglect.

Addressing these wounds requires a multifaceted approach to soul care, involving introspection and seeking external guidance for emotional healing. To truly heal, one must uncover the roots of their pain, understanding where it originates and how it has intertwined within their being.

Like a tree with deep roots, merely cutting it down does not eliminate it; the roots must be unearthed to prevent further growth. This process of uprooting requires diligence and a willingness to confront the deepest sources of pain, allowing for genuine healing and restoration.

Soul Wounds in Scripture: Lessons from Imperfect Heroes

In the Bible, numerous figures grappled with profound soul wounds. David was burdened by guilt after his affair with Bathsheba and the murder of her husband Uriah. Job endured the loss of his wealth and family. Joseph was betrayed and sold into slavery by his brothers. Jacob deceived his brother Esau for his birthright, and then Jacob was manipulated by Laban to work seven years for his wife Rachel.

Scripture unequivocally states that we must not hold onto grievances against others. Despite walking closely with the Lord, even the faithful were vulnerable to pain inflicted by the enemy. Even those intimately connected to Jesus experienced soul wounds. Some disciples harbored jealousy, and Peter denied knowing Jesus out of fear.

These examples underscore that no one is exempt from such wounds, but all can find solace in the merciful Father, who aids in growth and healing. Judas stands as a poignant example; his betrayal of Jesus cost him dearly, highlighting the importance of choosing healing and forgiveness for restoration. Jesus Himself exemplified this on the cross, praying for forgiveness for His persecutors. *"Then Jesus said, 'Father, forgive them, for they know not what they do'"* (Luke 23:34 (a) NKJV). Yet, forgiveness isn't facile, especially for those deeply wounded. It may seem to absolve wrongdoers, but in reality, it entrusts them to the Father's transformative grace.

Forgiveness:
A Path of Mercy and Redemption

In ministering to others, we've witnessed the struggle to forgive profound injustices. Yet, forgiveness isn't about excusing wrongdoing; it's about entrusting offenders to God's redemptive work. We've all erred, but through God's mercy, we've been forgiven. This same grace extends to those who've wronged us, offering hope for healing and restoration. Shouldn't we have mercy on our fellow servant, just as God had mercy on us?

Then the angry king sent the man to prison to be tortured until he had paid his entire debt. That's what my heavenly Father will do to you if you refuse to forgive your brothers and sisters from your heart. — Matthew 18:34-35 NLT

We've encountered situations where we've had to pause our work with individuals until they're ready to embrace forgiveness. Sometimes, it requires a deliberate act of will, saying, *"Lord, by the act of my will, I choose to forgive."* At times the feelings aren't there initially, and the process might need to be repeated several times. We've learned that delving into the core of those hurt feelings, confronting the pain head-on, often leads to the deepest healing.

The liberation found in embracing forgiveness is truly transformative. For Mark, it was not just transformative but lifesaving. When faced with a debilitating diagnosis in 2015, his prognosis seemed bleak. Yet, by 2020, his specialist at Duke University deemed him a miracle, a testament to his resilience. What the doctor didn't know was that alongside conventional treatments, Mark had also sought alternative therapies at a spiritual retreat center. There, he underwent profound inner healing and forgiveness, shedding burdens he hadn't even been conscious of carrying.

Mark received a diagnosis of dermatomyositis, an autoimmune disease, along with interstitial lung disease. His health rapidly deteriorated, revealing a condition deeply rooted in self-hatred, guilt, and shame—burdens he hadn't recognized until seeking help at the retreat. His specialist initially gave grim odds, stating that they could only hope to slow or halt the disease's progression, as there was no cure.

Later, the specialist asked Mark if he believed he was cured. Mark's response reflected his faith: *"I didn't think that was an option, but we knew this could only be God."* Mark could have chosen to remain in unforgiveness, but as God doesn't coerce forgiveness, He also recognizes its necessity for our well-being. Scientifically, it's understood that physical ailments often stem from internal emotional burdens, such as bitterness. How much more so, when we come to realize the fullness of who God created us to be.

Recently, during a study, Christine came across the story of Rachel hiding her father's household idols underneath her on her camel's saddle. This narrative deeply resonated with her, shedding light on the things we cling to, not being ready to release them.

These idols, which we allow to take the place of God, compel us to attempt to deceive even our Heavenly Father. They can take various forms, such as control, pride, or gossip, each hindering our spiritual growth.

Christine grappled with control, reluctant to relinquish aspects of her life that she believed she could manage on her own. It was through prayer and introspection that she realized her struggle stemmed from deep-seated trust issues, cultivated by years of disappointment and betrayal. Her reluctance to trust extended even to her relationship with God, as she sought to project an image of strength and self-reliance. Yet, upon closer examination, she discovered that many of these tendencies were inherited, passed down through generations as familial "idols" and generational curses.

Consulting resources like *The Divinity Code to Understanding Your Dreams and Visions* deepened her understanding of these spiritual dynamics, revealing underlying yearnings for unity and struggles with self-righteousness and shame. Recognizing the roots of her insecurities and fears, she humbled herself before the Lord, crying out for the ability to trust Him completely.

She acknowledged the ways in which pride had exerted control over various aspects of her life, hindering her spiritual growth and emotional well-being. While the journey toward healing is marked by pain, sacrifice, and surrender, it is ultimately fulfilling and transformative. To deepen our relationship with the Father, we must be willing to let go of anything that hinders our walk with Him, surrendering ourselves entirely to His divine guidance and grace.

Navigating Indicators of Healing and Spiritual Growth

How do you know if you are still struggling with soul wounds? There are several indicators that reveal ongoing struggles, but perhaps the most telling is found in Galatians 5:22-23 (a) (NLT),

But the Holy Spirit produces this kind of fruit in our lives: love, joy, peace, patience, kindness, goodness, faithfulness, gentleness, and self-control. — Galatians 5:22-23 (a) (NLT)

If we find ourselves lacking in any of these areas, it's likely that soul wounds are hindering our ability to manifest the fruit of the Spirit.

A more significant sign is if we still yield to the desires of our sinful nature. As outlined in Galatians 5:19-21, this includes behaviors such as sexual immorality, impurity, lustful pleasures, idolatry, sorcery, hostility, quarreling, jealousy, outbursts of anger, selfish ambition, dissension, division, envy, drunkenness, wild parties, and other sins like these. It's uncommon for Christians not to have wrestled with at least one, if not several, of these areas.

It's essential to note that this list isn't exhaustive, as it concludes with "other sins like these." God diligently works within us to address these issues until we experience healing in every aspect of our lives, allowing the fruit of the Spirit to flourish. As believers, we should earnestly desire to overcome the tendencies of our sinful nature. Healing soul wounds facilitates restoration in areas where we struggle to manifest the fruit of the Spirit.

Contemplating the contrast between the fruit of the Spirit and the inclinations of our sinful nature, it becomes evident that the former offer a far more desirable path. Who wouldn't prefer joy, love, and peace over the discord and envy associated with indulging our fleshly desires? These virtues are within reach for all of us, representing the restoration our Father longs to bestow upon each of His children.

Overcoming Barriers to Spiritual Healing: Insights and Scriptures

There are numerous factors that can impede our journey towards healing with the Lord. Unforgiveness stands as a significant barrier, often halting our spiritual progress. Scripture strongly emphasizes the importance of forgiveness.

> *For if you forgive others their trespasses, your heavenly Father will also forgive you, but if you do not forgive others their trespasses, neither will your Father forgive your trespasses.*
> *— Matthew 6:14-15 (ESV)*

This highlights that failure to forgive others can hinder our own forgiveness from the heavenly Father. Another common hindrance is a lack of knowledge of the Word, as Hosea 4:6 warns that people perish due to a lack of understanding. Additionally, a deficiency in faith can stifle our advancement towards complete freedom in Christ. Expecting God to heal on our terms is yet another stumbling block.

Frequently, we impose conditions on our healing, thereby limiting God's work in our lives. Similarly, seeking solutions from human sources rather than trusting in God's intervention can obstruct our spiritual healing. Transparency and honesty play pivotal roles in receiving healing yet fear and pride often hinder our ability to be vulnerable.

The power of confession and prayer in the healing process is explained in James 5:16 (ESV),

*Therefore, confess your sins to one another and pray for one
another, that you may be healed. The prayer of a righteous person
has great power as it is working. —James 5:16 (ESV)*

Flagrant or habitual sin poses a significant barrier to healing.
Continually engaging in sinful behavior without repentance contradicts
our commitment to God's will (Romans 6:1-2).

Speaking against God's anointed leaders is another area of concern,
as it opens us up to spiritual attack (1 Chronicles 16:22). Furthermore,
various other factors such as neglecting tithes and offerings, generational
curses, and involvement in occult practices can impede our healing journey.

Embracing the Refiner's Fire:
Finding Purpose in our Struggles Through Faith

Not long ago Christine had been having a very difficult week at work
and she was discouraged when she came home. I was trying to encourage
her and lovingly told her that when I had a really bad day, I'd ask the Father
what exactly is it that He wants me to learn from it.

Of course, in that moment, Christine didn't receive that word very
well, but later she let it sink in, and she realized the profound truth in it.
If we could all grasp that everything we go through is the Father trying to
work things out of us that grieve Him, then we have to allow Him to take
us through the refiner's fire, if we want to be who He created us to be. We
must allow Him to work in us, or we will continue to face the same struggles
until we finally come to the end of ourselves.

A prayer that we often pray is Psalm 139:23 (ESV), *"Search me, O
God, and know my heart! Try me and know my thoughts!"*

In conclusion, we encourage you to persist in your healing journey by seeking the Father's guidance in all areas of your life. Be open to His revelation and allow Him to work in your heart. Even in challenging times, remember that every experience serves a purpose in refining and shaping us into the image of Christ. Trust in God's process, and you will ultimately find the freedom and restoration you seek.

We hope this chapter encourages you to continue in your healing journey.

THINGS TO PONDER...

1. Seek the Father in all areas of your life. Ask Him to show you if there are any areas of your life that He wants to heal. He is faithful. He will show you what it is that is hindering you, if you genuinely seek His touch.

    _____

    _____

    _____

    _____

    _____

    _____

2. Then, write down what He is bringing to your mind.

    _____

    _____

    _____

_____

_____

_____

3. Ask Him the healing steps He wants you to take.

_____

_____

_____

_____

_____

4. Take those steps needed to begin your healing process.

_____

_____

_____

_____

_____

We pray that this is the start to a great restoration journey for you!

Maria Mitchell Crane

Artist, Best Selling Author, Coach, Solution-ary, Speaker, Teacher, Pastor

Maria loves people and enjoys connecting with others to creatively solve problems. She helps people identify limiting beliefs and replace them with powerful personal declarations so they can live out their true identity in freedom and joy.

Maria enjoys creating beauty through various artistic mediums and writing music. Participating in missions, traveling, and hiking are other favorite pastimes.

She lives in Santa Rosa, California with her husband. She looks forward to helping you *"RENEW YOUR MIND, REPAIR YOUR HEART, AND RESTORE YOUR HEALTH!"*

CraneTransformationCoaching.com

MariaCrane.com

Day 16

Maria Mitchell Crane

The Sacred Shift
How Prayer Transforms History

*If my people, who are called by my name, will humble
themselves and pray and seek my face and turn from their
wicked ways, then will I hear from heaven and will forgive
their sin and will heal their land.*
— 2 Chronicles 7:14 (NIV)

The Power and Privilege of Prayer

The Lord has given us the incredible gift of prayer to bring heaven's presence to earth and advance the Kingdom of God. What an amazing privilege! God designed our prayers to be the means of bringing Heaven to earth and to allow us to co-labor with Him! When we learn and operate in this very simple, but powerful gift, we see restoration in our lives, the lives around us, and in the nations.

Prayer is one of the most effective tools to war against the devil's destructive schemes and takes us on a great adventure with the Lord. He designed our world to work through prayer, and there is a wonderful power available to us not only when we pray individually, but also when we join with others in unified prayer that activates our legal authority as Kingdom builders.

Global prophetic prayer movements have shifted history and made

His powerful name known throughout the earth. When we participate in these prophetic prayer movements, we too can change history and thereby participate in global restoration. Our Heavenly Father extends an open invitation to each of us to be involved in these life-changing prayer adventures.

Some people still ask: If God can do everything and anything He desires without us, why does He ask us to pray? As evident in Genesis chapter one, He wants us to exercise our God-given authority and dominion over the earth on behalf of the Kingdom of God. John Wesley said: "Without God, man cannot; without man, God will not." When we pray according to His will and in Jesus' name, we are legally authorizing and releasing the resources stored in Heaven for earth's benefit. He does it through people who are willing to intercede and enter the Courts of Heaven to be His conduits and Kingdom vessels.

Effective Personal Prayer Movements

1. Consistent Private Prayer Life

Our individual private prayer lives, and time spent in the Lord's presence provides the wisdom and power we need in life. Jesus prioritized prayer and modeled it faithfully when He went to places of solitude to talk with His Father. These times strengthened Him for His earthly assignment and will do the same for us as we pray consistently.

Very early in the morning, while it was still dark, Jesus got up, left the house, and went off to a solitary place, where he prayed.
— Mark 1:35 (NIV)

But Jesus often withdrew to lonely places and prayed.
— Luke 5:16 NIV

The Lord wants us to go up higher and enter His courts with praise. Too many Christians live a mediocre life and never ascend the Holy Hill of the Lord. In the book of Revelation, the Lord tells us:

Come up here, and I will show you what must take place
after this. — Revelation 4:1 (NIV)

From these places of elevation in the Spirit, the Lord can speak to us prophetically and reveal His plans and secrets to us, but we must be willing to spend time in His presence to go there. In addition to strengthening His relationship with His Father when Jesus went up on the mountain to pray, He received wisdom about what to pray for and how to impact lives and draw people to His Father. We will too, as we seek the Lord in prayer.

2. Clean Hearts and Lifestyle of Repentance

When the disciples asked Jesus to teach them how to pray, He taught this powerful 5-lined prayer:

"When you pray, say:

Father, hallowed be your name, (Holy is Your Name)
Your kingdom come, Your will be done on earth, as it is in heaven.

Give us each day our daily bread.

Forgive us our sins as we forgive those who sin against us.
Lead us not into temptation, and deliver us from evil. "
— Luke 11:1-4 (NIV) (emphasis mine)

The Lord's prayer perfectly highlights the desired result of bringing God's Kingdom to earth and warns us about things that can hinder our prayers:

My temple will be called a house of prayer for all nations,
but you were changing God's house into a hideout for robbers.
— Mark 11:17 (NIV)

God wants us to pray from a place of purity, free from sin and unforgiveness. Our heart's condition needs to be right. May we prayerfully echo David in the Psalms:

Search me, God, and know my heart: test me and know my
anxious thoughts. See if there is any offensive way in me,
and lead me in your way everlasting.
— Psalm 139: 23-24 (NIV)

Blot out my transgressions, Wash away all my iniquity, and
cleanse me from my sin. For I know my transgressions and my sin
is always before me. Against you and you only, have I sinned
and done what is evil in your sight.
— Psalm 51:1-4 (NIV)

Psalm 66 clearly warns us:

If you regard iniquity in your heart, I will not hear your prayers.
— Psalm 66:18 (NIV)

We cannot have unconfessed sin in our hearts and expect the Lord to answer our prayers. He wants us to be in the right relationship with others too.

Therefore I want people everywhere to pray, lifting up
holy hands without anger or disputing.
— 1 Timothy 2:8 (NIV)

When you stand praying, if you hold anything against anyone,
forgive them so your Father in heaven may forgive your sins.
— Mark 11:25 (NIV)

Make every effort to mend the holes in our nets by being reconciled with others so the enemy doesn't have a foothold and our personal prayers aren't in vain.

When we pray from a penitent humble heart our prayers are answered. Nehemiah tangibly demonstrates this when he cries out to the Lord in repentance:

*LORD, the God of heaven, the great and awesome God, who
keeps his covenant of love with those who love him and obey his
commandments, let your ear be attentive and your eyes open to
hear the prayer your servant is praying before you day
and night for your servants, the people of Israel.*

*I confess the sins we Israelites, including myself and my father's
family, have committed against you.*

*We have acted very wickedly toward you. We have not
obeyed the commands, decrees and laws you gave
your servant Moses.*

*Remember the instruction you gave your servant Moses, saying,
"If you are unfaithful, I will scatter you among the nations,
but if you return to me and obey my commands, then even
if your exiled people are at the farthest horizon, I will gather
them from there and bring them to the place I have
chosen as a dwelling for my Name."*
— Nehemiah 1:5-9 (NIV)

When Nehemiah learned that his people were suffering back in Judah.
He mourned, wept, fasted, and prayed. He knew that his unconfessed sins
would hinder his prayers and that he needed to repent not only for his sins
but for the sins of his family. After his repentance, God gave Nehemiah
favor with King Artaxerxes and answered his prayer to rebuild the wall.

We see Daniel make a similar plea:

*So I turned to the Lord God and pleaded with him in prayer
and petition, in fasting, and in sackcloth and ashes. I prayed
to the Lord my God and confessed: "Lord, the great and
awesome God, who keeps his covenant of love with those
who love him and keep his commandments,
we have sinned and done wrong.*

*We have been wicked and have rebelled; we have turned
away from your commands and laws. We have not listened
to your servants the prophets, who spoke in your name to
our kings, our princes, and our ancestors, and to
all the people of the land.*

*Lord, you are righteous, but this day we are covered with
shame—the people of Judah and the inhabitants of Jerusalem
and all Israel, both near and far, in all the countries where
you have scattered us because of our unfaithfulness to you."*
— Daniel 9:3-7 (NIV)

God hears the cry of a humble heart that has been cleansed through
the tears of repentance. Our tears become liquid prayers of intercession.

Are you willing to stand in the gap and confess your sins and the sins
and idols of your family, city, and nation? The Lord is searching for those
who are ready to build up the wall of intercession.

I looked for someone among them who would build up the wall
and stand before me in the gap on behalf of the land so I would
not have to destroy it, but I found no one.
— Ezekiel 22:30 (NIV)

God gives us the prescription for restoring our land:

If my people, who are called by my name, will humble themselves
and pray and seek my face and turn from their wicked ways,
then I will hear from heaven, and I will forgive their sin
and will heal their land. Now my eyes will be open and
my ears attentive to the prayers offered in this place.
— 2 Chronicles 7:14-15 (NIV)

The Lord heals our land as we humble ourselves, pray, seek Him, and pray.

3. Faith Fueled Prayers

We have a legal mandate to go into the Courts of Heaven and be faithful servants who steward heaven's resources. In addition, when we gather to intervene on behalf of our cities and nations we must pray with faith-filled prayers.

No matter which version of the Bible we read, or which Gospel we read it in, Jesus tells us: *"If you have faith, you can say to this mountain 'Fall into the sea.' If you have no doubts in your mind and believe what you say, it will happen, God will do it for you, so I tell you to believe that you've received the things you have asked for in prayer and God will give them to you."* — Matthew 17:20, Mark 11:23, Luke 17:6 (NIV)

WOW! What an incredible promise! I often ask the Lord to strengthen my faith and remove any doubts before launching into these bold types of prayers. James 5:16 states that the prayers of a righteous person are powerful and effective. When we are in right standing with God (by placing our faith and full trust in Him) He loves to answer our prayers.

4. Scriptural Prayers and the Holy Spirit's Guidance

Scriptural exhortations to pray for cities and nations often focus on seeking guidance, peace, and blessings for the community and are revealed through the Holy Spirit. These three examples demonstrate this:

*Also, seek the peace and prosperity of the city to which
I have sent you into exile. Pray to the Lord for it,
because if it prospers, you too will prosper.*
—Jeremiah 29:7 (NIV).

Here the Lord links prayer with the prosperity of a city and exhorts Jeremiah to pray for Babylon, the very city he is exiled to, because his welfare will be tied to its welfare.

Paul also urges us to pray for the leaders and people in a region to promote peace and holiness.

*I urge, then, first of all, that petitions, prayers, intercession
and thanksgivings be made for all people—for kings and
all those in authority, that we may live peaceful and
quiet lives in all godliness and holiness.*
— 1 Timothy 2:1-2 (NIV)

The Lord wants us to pray for leaders as well as for places because they are filled with the people He loves. Especially now while Israel is at war with Hamas let's faithfully honor His request.

Pray for the peace of Jerusalem: may those who love you be secure.
—Psalm 122:6 (NIV)

When we approach prayer with humility, acknowledge the limitations of human understanding, and remain open to receiving prophetic insights and guidance from the Holy Spirit, our prayers are powerful and transformative. It is in this space Christ's presence is magnified.

5. Spiritual Warfare Strategies

It is critical to remember that we are not battling flesh and blood.

For our struggle is not against flesh and blood, but against
the rulers, against the authorities, against the powers of this
dark world and against the spiritual forces of evil in the
heavenly realms. — Ephesians 6:12 (NIV)

Often corporate times of prayer and fasting are needed to break certain strongholds. As the Gospel of Mark states, the disciples asked Jesus privately why they could not cast out a certain demon.

After Jesus had gone indoors, his disciples asked him privately,
"Why couldn't we drive it out?" He replied, "This kind
can come out only by prayer.
— Mark 9:28-29 (NIV)

We want to put on the full armor of God (Ephesians 6:10-16) and declare and personalize the promises in His Word because it has power and never returns void. For example, we pray for our city inserting the name of our city in Scripture like this:

No weapon formed against us here in Santa Rosa (name your town/ city) can stand Isaiah 54:17 NIV.

Our Father, Who Art in Heaven, Hallowed Be Your Name. Your kingdom comes to Santa Rosa (name your city), Your will be done here in California (name your city and region.) Luke 11:2-4 KJV.

6. Unified Prayer With Others

Again, truly I tell you that if two of you on earth agree
about anything they ask for, it will be done for them by my
Father in heaven. For where two or three gather
in my name, there I am with them.
— Matthew 18:19-20 (NIV)

Global prophetic prayer movements, where individuals and communities worldwide come together to engage in prayer, often have a prophetic focus, relayed by the Holy Spirit. These movements emphasize seeking God's guidance, revelation, and spiritual insight.

Many prayer movements started with one or two individuals, who were willing to stand in the gap and commit to persistent intercession.

For instance, in 1727 the Moravian Church experienced a powerful revival marked by continuous 24 hour prayer that lasted for 100 years and inspired many to be missionaries and live out the great commission. The

Moravian Church first came to America in 1735 and had a great impact on John Wesley. There were also the First and Second Great Awakenings (18th and 19th centuries).

We can read about many other prayer movements like the Walsh Revival (1904-1905), Revival in Korea (early 20th century), Latter Rain Movement (1940-1950), Charismatic Renewal (1960-1970), and the 24/7 prayer movement in 1999. All these prayer movements shifted the trajectory of their atmosphere, and the world.

Our Own 2020 Grassroots Prayer Movement: PACT

When the pandemic started in March of 2020, we could sense the severity of the situation. In response, our church, The Promise Center, began to lead daily Facebook live prayer sessions. I was asked to be one of the leaders and drew tremendous encouragement in coming together via Zoom to pray daily for the needs of individuals, our community, and our nation.

Five months later, the Holy Spirit prompted me to move prayer from the comforts of our homes into the heart of downtown Santa Rosa square to pray in person. We started on July 4th, 2020, with just a few of us who had similar hearts for intercession. By the grace of God, we have continued for over three and a half years.

What a joy and honor it has been to co-labor with Him in this way and display His Kingdom in the heart of Santa Rosa, the city where I was born and raised! We named our grassroots local prayer time PACT because "Prayer Always Changes Things."

What an awesome reality of the double power of prayer! Not only will our prayers accomplish things on earth, by bringing heaven down; they will be part of the worship that will break out in heaven at the wedding feast of the lamb:

And when he had taken it (the Scroll), the four living creatures and the twenty-four elders fell down before the Lamb. Each one had a harp and they were holding golden bowls full of incense, which are the prayers of God's people.
— Revelation 5:8 (NIV) (emphasis mine)

May we never underestimate the power of prayer to bring Heaven to earth and be found faithfully filling the bowls in heaven for His honor and glory. Our prayers show we are taking authority by taking dominion and positioning ourselves to help bring restoration to ourselves and the nation.

Closing Prayer: Lord Jesus, remind us that prayer always changes things and moves the heart of God. Teach us to pray with clean hands and pure hearts. May we enjoy the privilege of prayer and the great adventure of establishing Your Kingdom here on earth. Holy Spirit guide us as we pray and trust we are filling the golden bowls of incense with our prayers. Connect us with other like-minded individuals who want to live out 2 Chronicles 7:14 and practice the unity of Psalm 133. And when we stand before you, King of kings and Lord of lords, let us hear:

Well done good and faithful servant. Enter into My kingdom.
— Matthew 25:21 (NIV) (emphasis mine)

THINGS TO PONDER...

1. Lord, is there any unconfessed sin in me that would hinder my prayers?

   _____

   _____

   _____

   _____

   _____

   _____

2. Lord, what is on your heart today that you want me to intercede for?

   _____

   _____

   _____

   _____

   _____

3. Are there any spirits that we need to bind on earth in this region? (Matthew 18)

   _____

   _____

_____

_____

_____

_____

4. If so, Lord, what are those specific spirits?

_____

_____

_____

_____

_____

5. Show me how long to persist in praying for this, and when my assignment is over.

_____

_____

_____

_____

_____

Kelly Williams Hale

Kelly Williams Hale is a speaker, author, and life coach. She is passionate about Jesus and encourages others to deepen their personal relationship with Him. Her teaching and online courses help Christian women walk in their unique calling to bring God glory. Partnering with the Holy Spirit, Kelly teaches women how be courageous and confident in Christ.

Her speaking topics include spiritual growth, emotional resilience, and leadership. Kelly is living proof that our mess truly becomes our message and past mistakes don't define future success.

She is happily married (third time's a charm!), a mom of three—each born a decade apart— delivering her youngest at 44 years old.

When she's not encouraging women in her Facebook group, *Sisters Who Shine,* she can often be found singing and dancing to anything by the band *For King & Country.*

Visit thebebravelife.com for more information.

Day 17

Kelly Williams Hale

True Transformation

Let Go, Let God

Do not conform to the pattern of this world, but be transformed by the renewing of your mind. Then you will be able to test and approve what God's will is—his good, pleasing and perfect will.
— *Romans 12:2 (NIV)*

There's a meme going around the internet that I absolutely love. It's a picture of a young girl holding tightly to a small teddy bear. Kneeling in front of her is Jesus. His outstretched hand is inviting her to hand over her precious stuffed animal while his other hand is holding a much bigger teddy bear behind his back. *"But I love it,"* the little girl says. To which Jesus replies, *"Trust me."*

Such a powerful message wrapped up in a small digital image. If I'm honest, I've been that little girl. I think we all have. We hold tight to what we know. Often what we've come to love. The ideas, plans, and many times the people that are comfortable or familiar. We can settle for a small version of what we think we want, not realizing that Jesus has so much more for us.

I'm the oldest of four siblings and the only girl. I may or may not have been a bit bossy growing up! Looking back, I can see how God was cultivating leadership in my spirit. But for many years I attributed my resilience to basic survival skills. Dysfunction is present in many families. Mine was no exception.

My parents married young and had four kids by the time they were 25. My dad was a Vietnam vet and witnessed situations and scenarios no 19-year-old should ever encounter. My mom did the best she could: caring for an emotionally unavailable husband and keeping us kids fed, clothed, and safe. I learned—at a very young age—to fly under the radar, not cause trouble, and do what I could to keep the peace. This often meant helping my mom or instructing my brothers to behave. It was my responsibility to take care of everyone.

This sense of responsibility followed me into adulthood. I became known as the friend everyone could count on. I often heard, *"You are so easy to talk to,"* and *"I can tell you anything."* My superpower was understanding. It was a beautiful trait to have. Admirable even. Until it wasn't.

I was in a relationship with my second husband for years before we got married. We broke up, got back together, broke up again. It was an unhealthy cycle... and then I got pregnant. *Well, we must get married,* I thought. I grew up in the church and good Christian girls do not get pregnant out of wedlock and most certainly don't have a baby outside of matrimony. And this was my second husband! I had traveled this road before. *Did I not learn **anything**?*

My son was 18 months old when I realized there was a serious problem in our marriage. Remember, I'm the one who is responsible for everyone else. I took care of everything at home and when things weren't "just right," my husband did not hesitate to convey his displeasure. There wasn't any physical abuse, but I would soon realize that emotional abuse can be more damaging.

I was holding onto my own "small teddy bear." I was operating from a worldly perspective of "I can take care of this." My human mind could only see what my reality was currently. For years, I desperately wanted safety. But I was blinded by familiarity and held tightly to what felt comfortable. I was clutching "my way" rather than believing God had a better plan for my life.

It was during this time that I began to cry out to the Lord. I couldn't do this on my own anymore. Isn't that what we do? We put God in a little box and pull Him out only when life gets difficult. But thankfully, He meets us right where we are. I'm reminded of the prodigal son we read about in Luke chapter 15. The son who demanded his inheritance, left his family, and basically went along his merry way. He spent years in the world, doing what he wanted, selfishly satisfying his desires, and basically living the good life. Until he wasn't.

A few days later this younger son packed all his belongings and moved to a distant land, and there he wasted all his money in wild living. About the time his money ran out, a great famine swept over the land, and he began to starve.
— Luke 15:13-14 (NLT)

When this young man finally came to his senses, he decided to go home.

*"So he returned home to his father. And while he was still a long way off, his father saw him coming. Filled with love and compassion, **he ran to his son, embraced him, and kissed him.**"*
— Luke 15:20 (emphasis mine).

Like the prodigal son's father, God welcomed me with open arms. He was patiently waiting. So, I began digging into God's Word. The Scriptures spoke to me in a fresh new way, and I started to truly believe what He says. Jesus loves me. I am redeemed. I am a daughter of the Most High God.

I also discovered Jeremiah 29:11 (NIV) and declared it as my life verse.

For I know the plans I have for you, declares the Lord,
plans to prosper you and not to harm you,
plans to give you hope and a future.

That was over 20 years ago. I came to know Jehovah-Rapha, the Healer. Jesus healed that part of me that felt unworthy. He provided the safety I craved and tried so diligently to control by taking care of everyone else. I had finally surrendered to God's plan for me.

But... the story doesn't end there! Read on, dear friend.

God has done incredible things in my life. My second husband and I did divorce, and I became a single mom (again) at the age of 33. I continued to seek the Lord and received blessings upon blessing in my life. I met a man (at 40) who was a direct answer to prayer and married (again!) a year later. We welcomed our son, Austin, when I was 44! God is so good.

My marriage is strong. My children are healthy. I'm an author, a speaker, and a life coach. God has blessed me with the gift of encouragement, and I give Him all the glory as I help other women understand who they are in Christ.

These are all beautiful, wonderful things. But God showed me recently that He's got a "bigger teddy bear" for me. He pointed out that I've become comfortable and familiar with what I have. He's showing me the subtle ways that I still feel responsible for other people, including: in my family, my ministry, and my online platform. He revealed to me how I will hesitate to share something—the truth—because I'm worried how other people will respond.

God told me that I need to hand over my fear. He directed me to:

Call to Me, and I will answer you, and show you great and mighty things, which you do not know. — *Jeremiah 3:33 (NKJV)*

Despite my best efforts, I realized I had picked up the old patterns of people-pleasing. I've been operating from my own strength. I've been subtly leaning on my own understanding, placing my value on what I have accomplished, and relying on "what I know".

Over the years, I realized I prayed more that God would bless the plans I made rather than asking Him to show me His plan. There have been many times I thought if only I tried harder, or did more, or maybe if I'd just pray harder, then maybe I'd be farther along on my journey. Please don't get me wrong, God has opened many doors for me. And I'm extremely grateful. In hindsight, I can see the areas where I put more certainty in my own abilities instead of being fully surrendered to God's will.

Maybe you've heard the saying: "If it's going to be, it's up to me." I believed this lie. I got caught up in the hustle culture. Do more. Work harder. Go. Go. Go. I believed that I needed to make things happen. We can also believe that good is good enough. It's a tactic of the enemy that keeps us from the "best" that God has for us.

The thief comes only to steal and kill and destroy.
I came that they may have life and have it abundantly.
— John 10:10 (ESV)

As Christians, we are called to become more like Christ. When we accept Jesus as our Lord and Savior, we are given the "mind of Christ" (1 Corinthians 2:16). Yet we still live in a fallen world. We want to follow Jesus, but we have habits and patterns of thinking that can challenge (at best) our pursuit of Him.

We destroy arguments and every lofty opinion
raised against the knowledge of God, and take
every thought captive to obey Christ."
— 1 Corinthians 10:5 (ESV)

We are instructed to literally take these thoughts prisoner, lock them up and throw away the key!

Another tactic satan uses to separate us from God is comparison. We have only to look at social media to begin comparing ourselves with others. I fell for this lie as well. As I was building my business and ministry, I found myself looking at other women in business and thinking, She seems so successful, maybe I should do what she's doing?

It's so easy to forget that God has a plan specifically assigned to us. He created us with our unique fingerprint so that we can make a mark in the world—for His glory.

Renewing our mind is not a one and done deal. It's a daily practice. Transformation takes time. It's a process. Both can often look like one step forward, three steps back. Thankfully God uses our mishaps, mistakes, and even our momentum. He takes our forward and backward steps and will work things out for our good.

And we know that in all things God works for the good of those
who love him, who have been called according to his purpose.
—Romans 8:28 (NIV)

Nothing is wasted!

How do we know what God's purpose is? First and foremost, we were created to glorify God. We do that when we believe and fully accept who we are in Christ, set aside our human need to control, and keep our eyes fixed on Jesus. The gateway to our purpose is opened when we fully surrender and confess, not my will Lord, but Yours.

I've been asking God to show me what I need to hand over. He's telling me to surrender my fear of being perceived as bossy. My assignment is to share the message God has given me, with authority. Audacious authority. God gave me the gift of encouragement *and* leadership skills. He planted the seed when I was a young girl (as a bossy big sis!) and unbeknownst to me, He's been watering it for years.

Because of my previous doubts and insecurities, I downplayed these gifts. I wanted to make everyone feel comfortable which meant dimming my own light. The enemy used fear to keep me from fully accepting that,

I am fearfully and wonderfully made. — Psalm 139:14 (NIV)

God has a path of destiny for each of us that includes the traits that we deem weird, quirky, or just plain wrong—when we look at ourselves through a world lens. When we look through a Kingdom lens, we see that we are called to be bold and brave.

Assessing our feelings and learning not to react to them is another skill we can cultivate. Renewing our mind daily is a choice. We get to decide which lens we will look through: the world's view or God's. He gave us the Holy Spirit to guide and instruct us along the way. We're never alone. Will we default to our human response, or will we trust Jesus? God says trust and obey. Obedience is simply belief.

Do we believe what God says?
Do we believe we are who God says we are?

Maybe you're wondering, *"What is my 'bigger teddy bear'"?* As believers, we know our purpose is to glorify God. How we do that is directly related to our gifts, talents, and life experience. When we are seeking His will for our lives, He will plant a desire in our heart that only He can water. His only requirement: *believe.*

Satan plants seeds as well. He will plant the seed of doubt and remind us of our mistakes. He will plant a seed of fear and show us where we've tried before and failed. He'll plant a seed of comparison and have us believe we don't have what it takes.

We have direct access to everything God has for us through the Holy Spirit. All that we need to fulfill His plan for our life is available supernaturally: *the provision, the abundance, the hope, and our future* (Jeremiah 29:11).

The word reformation is very similar to the word transformation. Reformation is a noun and defined as the action or process of reforming. Reforming is a verb and is defined to make changes in (something, typically a social, political, or economic institution or practice in order to improve it).

We are all in a constant state of change. The Bible tells us to grow in the grace and knowledge of Jesus (1 Peter 3:18). But often the idea of change, let alone the actual making of change, can be daunting.

What are the practices in your life that need to be reformed? What behaviors contradict the Word of God? When we say, *"This is who I am."* or think, *"This is as good as it gets."* We agree with the idea that we can't grow.

Becoming the person God created us to be requires us to set aside our familiar habits and behaviors. This is often uncomfortable. It may hurt. I remember my nephew complaining about how his legs and knees ached when he was about 14. These are literally growing pains.

I'm going to reference another meme I've seen on social media. Bear with me! There's a drawing of a basic stick man on the left and a very colorful, vibrant drawing of a stick man on the right. The basic stick man says to his friend, *"You've changed."* The colorful, vibrantly illustrated stick man says, *"We're supposed to."*

Our transformation can be physically, emotionally and/or spiritually uncomfortable. God may ask us to make changes that will upset other people. We may get pushbacks when we decide to step into our assignment and purpose. Our transformation can be uncomfortable for others. Your friends and family may not understand what's happening or why you're different. They are used to the old you, but you are growing into the person God created you to be.

The Bible says we will have haters. But we get to count it all joy when we experience these trials and hardships, knowing that we've placed God at the center of our lives, where He rightly belongs. We get to be an example to others, giving God glory in all things. The joy of the Lord is our strength.

As we travel the road of being transformed, the journey is marked with daily reminders to surrender. Letting go of what we know, or thought we knew! And trusting that His "bigger teddy bear" is coming. We get to replace the question *"What do I do next?"* with *"What do you have for me today, Lord?"*

We get to decide. We've all made decisions we're not proud of. I know I have! And most likely, we have witnesses or evidence of those choices. (Can I just say I'm so glad we didn't have social media when I was in my 20s?!) The world may judge us for what we've done in the past, but we are not defined by our mistakes.

We are defined by who God says we are!

So how do we let go of what we hold dear (our plans) so we can receive the "bigger teddy bear" (God's plan) that He promises us?

First, we acknowledge that He is God, and we are not. We praise Him for giving us life. We thank Him that we are *fearfully and wonderfully made,* (Psalm 139:14). Second, we repent. We admit that we've allowed fear to keep us from our divine destiny because we've not fully trusted Him. Third, we hand over our will and our way and simply ask Him to show us what the next move is—for today.

God has a plan for our life. A good plan. As we transform and intentionally seek out God's will for our lives, we will see miracles occur. When we renew our mind daily and surrender, He will bless us. My favorite translation of Ephesians 3:20 comes from The Passion Translation.

Never doubt God's mighty power to work in you and accomplish all this. He will achieve infinitely more than your greatest request, your most unbelievable dream, and exceed your wildest imagination! He will outdo them all, for his miraculous power constantly energizes you. — Ephesians 3:20 (TPT)

My faith walk has been filled with potholes, unexpected exits, twists and turns, detours and the occasional re-routing. If I'm honest, there's been more than the occasional re-routing! My faith walk has also been filled with joy, love, and grace.

> *But he said to me, "My grace is sufficient for you, for my power is made perfect in weakness." Therefore I will boast all the more gladly about my weaknesses, so that Christ's power may rest on me.*
> *— 2 Corinthians 12:9 (NIV)*

Some of the most powerful lessons happened when I was at my weakest. I found the promise of Jesus when I was in the fire. He's with us—always—and through Him, we receive life. Our life is God's gift to us. What we do with it is our gift back to Him.

Dear reader, you are chosen. You have an assignment. God has planted desires in your heart that only you can fulfill. His will for you is to be unapologetically who He created you to be. You are a masterpiece. You have gifts and talents that God will use to advance His Kingdom. You are an ambassador for Christ.

When we show up authentically as ourselves, we can change the world. You were made for impact and influence. People so desperately need the hope of Jesus. They need someone who is real and raw and can say, *"When I surrendered control of my life to Jesus, I discovered freedom."*

I believe in **you!**

THINGS TO PONDER...

1. What is God asking you to surrender?

_____

_____

_____

_____

_____

_____

2. What does it mean to you when God says, *I have a plan for you?*

_____

_____

_____

_____

_____

_____

3. What areas in your life have you struggled with the most? Financial? Health? Relationships? Purpose?

_____

_____

_____

_____

_____

_____

4. Do you believe you are *fearfully and wonderfully made?*

_____

_____

_____

_____

_____

As you journal the answers to the questions above, invite the Holy Spirit to guide you. I'd also love to support you on your journey. Visit kellywilliamshale.com or email me at thebebravelife@gmail.com for more information.

Peggy A. Grimes

Peggy A. Grimes is a best-selling author, public speaker, spiritual coach, and mentor. Her greatest passion is helping women succeed on their emotional healing journey, empowering them to become Kingdom Women who can take back their marriage, children, families, and communities for the Kingdom of God. She served as CEO of the Montana Food Bank Network prior to moving to her current home in Jacksonville, North Carolina.

Peggy has been featured on various episodes of *The Kingdom View* TV Show, *1Kingdom TV,* and *The Renegade Women* and *Women Rise Up!* Podcasts. She is prophetic and a woman's leader in her church, the current board chair of *White Raiment Ministries, Inc.,* and a course leader for *Kingdom Women Rising,* a nonprofit ministry for women suffering from deep traumatic wounds.

KingdomWomenRising.org
facebook.com/TheKingdomLifeCoach
instagram.com/KingdomWomenRising
KingdomWomenRising@gmail.com

Day 18

Peggy A. Grimes

Restoration

God's Precious Gift

He restores my soul. He leads me in paths of righteousness
for His name's sake.
— Psalm 23:3 (NIV)

My story begins many years ago when I lived in overwhelming trauma. The trauma of a daily nature! Trauma from a place it should never come! My world consisted of putting my needs and the desire of God's heart aside just to survive.

But God...

He is truly the "Restorer of the Breach." My breach was with who I was and who I longed to be; the person God created me to be with a beautiful plan for my life! This was something I could only dream of and hope for. In my trauma, I had broken my close relationship with God. Then came restoration!

God, in the person of Jesus Christ, rescued me after 43 years of torture in a horrible marriage. Not only did He rescue me, but He also rescued my husband from his prison as an abuser and then took him to his heavenly home—the culmination of "his" restoration. I was now free to live the life I was destined to live. I could now truly follow the plan God had for me.

After my husband's transition to Heaven, healed, and delivered, I began to focus my attention on becoming what God had determined for my life. I have turned my trauma into a powerful testimony of restoration. Holy Spirit has imparted such wisdom for me to not only receive healing for myself, but to help so many other women receive their healing as well. God, in His goodness, leaves no stone unturned. The work of Holy Spirit in and through us is a marvel to behold.

But I will restore health to you and heal your wounds,
declares the Lord, "because you are called an outcast,
Zion for whom no one cares."
— Jeremiah 30:17 (NIV)

During my years of trauma, I truly felt like an outcast, hiding my pain and misery from everyone, even my family. I was ashamed to mention to anyone what I was going through, and I longed to have a confidant who could share my feelings, frustrations, hurt, and pain. Don't get me wrong, I loved my husband; however, living in trauma for so many years will change who you are. You become the "trauma person," and identify as such.

My physical appearance had changed; I began to look way older than my years! I was no longer interested in caring for my appearance or my physical health. For over forty years I cried out to the Lord to release me from the person I had become; from this life of trauma.

Finally, I repented for letting my trauma rule my life and for my part in how I negatively dealt with my situation. I knew God heard my prayer and would rescue me from the hell I was living in. How could I have known the beautiful plan God had for me? He was creating a powerful testimony in me through my trauma. Now, I was free to walk in that testimony! It wasn't easy, but it was freeing, and it gave me hope for a better future with God as my rock and Holy Spirit as my guide.

For seven years, I walked in God's goodness. His testimony through me reached into the souls of so many others. I was made whole! I was no longer a "trauma person." Now I was blessed and walking in the fullness of God. I was RESTORED!

During these blessed years, I walked in the power and authority of Jesus Christ. I was blessed and able to be a blessing to many. My life was peaceful, and I began to learn the mysteries of God and Heaven, a desire fulfilled. I became debt-free, started a ministry and a business, plus I was active in my church, which was something my husband would not allow. I felt I was living with a double portion of God's blessings.

Instead of your shame you will receive a double portion,
and instead of disgrace you will rejoice in your inheritance.
And so you will inherit a double portion in your land,
and everlasting joy will be yours.
— Isaiah 61:7 (NIV)

In my years of trauma, I was so focused on just keeping one foot in front of the other that I did not see the trauma my children were suffering. They suffered because I had shut down my emotions, which included the inability to see their need for my emotional care and support. For years, I never saw how they suffered. I never realized how much they needed me. I was so focused on just making it through each day, each hour, that I was blinded to their emotional needs.

I tried to make sure all of their physical needs were met, but that very important component of a mother's love was not there for them. My lack of empathy and compassion made me look like a cruel taskmaster to them. My children are now grown and carry their own scars. My most devout prayer is to see them set free from the trauma of their childhood. This is what happens in so many families. Children watch us as parents very closely. Their lives are formed by what they see and hear from their parents. It's so hard when we're in the midst of our situation to see the damage we are doing to those we love the most.

> *Father God, I thank You in Jesus' name for always loving us, even amidst our mess. I thank You that it is not Your intention that we remain there. You always see the best in us, Lord God, and Your will is that we have an abundant life, filled with the knowledge of You and Your great blessings.*

> *Unfortunately, Father God, this is not always the reality for many of us; for many families. My prayer today is that because I know Your heart is to seek the lost—those lost without a relationship with You, and those who are lost in their circumstances. You have been merciful to me; to restore me! You can and long to do the same for anyone who reaches out to You asking for help in their pain, in their sin, in their sorrow, and their trauma. Step into their situation, Lord God, as only You can, and lift them to You. Comfort their hearts with the words they need to hear to let them know You see them and You care.*

> *Holy Spirit, be their guide. Show them how to endure and help them know that their pain does have an end. You God are the Restorer, the one who makes things new. You did it for me when I cried out, and You will do it for them. Amen.*

Then it happened...

During those seven years of grace and powerful testimony, I thought I'd been healed and would never have to suffer as I had for 43 years. Not so! Remember I told you my children had suffered trauma along with me? Well, their trauma became my trauma and once again I was brought back to "trauma person."

This year I went through about four months of reliving my past trauma with one of my children. I was confused. I was distraught at the fact that I could fall right back into being a "trauma person." How could this happen? I had been living a life of blessing. My ministry was growing; I was debt-free; I lived in peace, rest, and joy! How could the Lord let this happen again?

During these very difficult months, I realized there was still something in me that Satan had a right to use against me, but I could not identify what it was. After a few months of once again living as "trauma person," I cried out to God asking what I had done wrong. The heavens were closed. I could not hear from God, but I desperately wanted to get out of this situation.

As the months went by, I saw myself falling further into that "trauma person," acting the same as I had with my husband. I became so distraught that I allowed myself to be that person again. How could that happen? I was walking in the blessing of God with a growing ministry and here I was back at the same place...allowing myself to step back from the time and structure I was used to in my daily walk with God. I stepped back from my ministry and from spending time with my friends. I was starting to fall into depression... something that had become so foreign to me!

Once again, I cried out to God! He didn't answer right away... I heard nothing.

Finally, God opened a door for my release. A door that would take total trust in His ways to walk through. I knew God was making a way for me to be restored to where I was. Once I gave my sin over and let God take the wheel, I knew restoration was coming.

A week later, as I was spending time in prayer, God spoke these words to me: "I have now removed the "root of enabling" from your life. As I thought about it, I was a bit confused. How was I enabling my husband or my children? Then God spoke "you allowed them to make you a victim.

You allowed them to pull you from Me. I finally understood! I had enabled them.

I enabled my husband to treat me as he did; to insist on being God in our family; to be our teacher of the Word! I enabled him to speak disrespectfully to me and treat me with disdain and I continued that behavior in my life. So, the first thing I had to do was repent! God had given me several previous opportunities to allow Him to remove this "root," but I was blinded to it.

Finally, the root was gone! I was set free! Once again, RESTORED!

I will repay you for the years the locusts have eaten—the great locust and the young locust, the other locusts and the locust swarm—my great army that I sent among you. You will have plenty to eat, until you are full, and you will praise the name of the Lord your God, who has worked wonders for you; never again will my people be shamed.
—Joel 2:25-26 (NIV)

Once again, my life is back on track. Once again, the blessings are flowing. My ministry is thriving, and I am helping others through their trauma! God is so good! His love cannot be measured! It is greater, higher, and more powerful than anything we can think or imagine.

My story is not unique or unusual. So many of us have a "Restoration" story; a story of the love of God who reached down to draw us out of our past, our wounds, our sorrow. Not only does He restore us to Him, but He restores our testimony of who He is and what He longs to do in and through us. He first sent me the autumn rains of restoration from my trauma with my husband. Now I'm walking in the spring rains of restoration from the "root of enabling" that held me captive for so many years.

> *Be glad, people of Zion, rejoice in the Lord your God, for He has*
> *given you the autumn rains because He is faithful. He sends you*
> *abundant showers, both autumn and spring rains, as before.*
> *—Joel 2:23 (NIV)*

If you are still living in your trauma, still waiting for your "restoration," take heart! God has heard your prayers, and He will be your way of escape. Not only will He see you through your trauma, but He will create such a powerful testimony in you that will reach many others who need to hear your story. Again, I say, "Take heart!" Forty-three years was a long time for me, as it was for the children of Israel on their desert journey. However, just as the joy they had when they finally reached their Promised Land, I can assure you my joy was equal to theirs, and yours will be as well. There is no one like our God.

Even in our mess, God always has the answer; He always has the plan of escape! I encourage you to open your heart to God and let Him heal you. You don't have to be a "trauma person!" You can be restored!

My encouragement for anyone reading this chapter still suffering in their circumstances is to first repent for any hurt you may have caused in your trauma, then forgive yourself and those who participated in causing your trauma. Finally, reach out to someone you can share with in confidence. Please don't do as I did and try to bear it alone. Ask God to send someone to help you; to walk alongside you and be an intercessor for you.

If you have no one to rely on, please reach out to me. I've been there, I understand, I would love to walk alongside you and be a guide in your restoration!

THINGS TO PONDER...

1. Are you a "Trauma Person," or a "Restoration Seeker?"

   _____

   _____

   _____

   _____

   _____

2. Are you ready to be healed?

   _____

   _____

   _____

   _____

   _____

3. Do you want to learn how to forgive those who hurt and/or abused you?

   _____

   _____

   _____

_____

_____

_____

_____

4. Are you ready to walk in the plan of God for your life?

_____

_____

_____

_____

_____

If you stated you are a Restoration Seeker, ready to be healed, desiring to learn to forgive and to walk in God's plan, don't be afraid to reach out! Your time is now, the door of opportunity is open! Your healing is waiting... Restoration IS His name!

Dorease Rioux

Dorease Rioux is a kingdom-minded entrepreneur, #1 International best-selling author, and an inspirational speaker with dynamic messages. She's known as a *"Cheerleader for dream chasers and dream do-ers."*

After leaving her plane-hopping, award-winning career as a corporate executive, Dorease founded *Crowned for Purpose Enterprises.*

As "The Victory for Purpose" Coach, Dorease empowers Christian women to achieve break-through from hurts that hinder... so they can step into their purpose and fulfill their destiny story with confidence and courage.

As hobby homesteaders in the land of Goshen, Dorease and Tim enjoy their rural-country lifestyle with seven beloved dogs, and a myriad of other delightsome creatures great and small. Dorease tends well to their Rioux Zioux with lots of TLC, singing, and camera clicks as a wonder-seeking shutterbug.

facebook.com/groups/529654824795621
daughters-united-network.mn.co/spaces/13938599/discovery
youtube.com/@dorease
linkedin.com/in/dorease-rioux-a013938
CrownedForPurpose.com

Day 19

Dorease Rioux

A Grudge in the Garden

Flourish in the Fragrant Fruitfulness of Forgiveness

... console those who mourn in Zion, give them beauty for ashes,
the oil of joy instead of mourning, praise instead of despair.
For the LORD has planted them like strong and graceful oaks
for His own glory.
— Isaiah 61:3-4 (NLT)

Roots and Renewal

With trepidation and high hopes, my husband and I made a bittersweet decision: to leave our remote mountain-top haven with its spectacular views and move near my beloved parents in the Deep South.

After fifteen years of loving life in the Rocky Mountains, we sold our high-country ranch, cradled in the wilderness wildlands, and relocated near my historically lovely hometown. Despite having lived away for over thirty years, the call of my southern roots had beckoned... and I had answered "yes."

Our new house was a modest mid-century American home nestled in a pastoral setting, with wildflower meadows, hemmed in by forests. This quaint homestead exuded a vintage charm with towering, flowering old plantings that serenaded the arrival of spring with a dramatic floral symphony of fragrant colors.

A Trail of Thorny Tangles

One cool, spring morning, I joined my husband outdoors as he tackled some late season pruning of trees in a shady garden beside our house. As he went about the task with his usual strength and stamina, I trailed along to cheer him on.

The farm had proven to be an ongoing battlefield against nature's encroachment. Poison ivy, like sinuous serpents, wrapped around and fastened onto tree trunks and branches, threatening the life and purpose of the once-bountiful hardwoods and our hopes for a fruitful harvest.

Our mission became clear—free our trees from the poison ivy shackles and restore them to their former glory. One by one, over many days, the elderly trees were liberated from their leafy captors. Thankfully, the fig and pear trees, despite their age and injury, still stood stately with promise, a testament to their hardy resilience.

However, a once-lush peach tree had fallen prey to the poison ivy's sinister grip. Its neglect and demise triggered some unresolved hurts and disappointments buried inside. On the farm, our fight was far from over, but with every dead branch pruned, every inch of clinging corruption cleared away, actual progress was being made.

There was one last tree to assess—a scraggly old plum barely clinging to survival. After it was tenderly groomed, we agreed in a prayer for its recovery.

For some inexplicable reason, this frail fruit tree's restoration story mattered to me. So, I made the decrepit old hardwood my focal point in the garden, became its keeper, and believed it still had a fruitful purpose to fulfill. Thus, with expectancy over the weeks ahead, I felt the moving of waters in my soul... and I washed the old tree with the water of God's Word as I spoke blessings over it.

Each day as I prayed, I envisioned the tree free of shackles, standing stately in the garden, growing strong in the sunlight, and flowering to bear good fruit. Within the garden of my own heart, this tree became a symbolic marker of hope for me.

> *For there is hope for a tree, if it be cut down, that it will sprout again, and that its shoots will not cease. Though its root grow old in the earth, and its stump die in the soil, yet at the scent of water it will bud and put out branches like a young plant.*
> *— Job 14:7-9 (ESV).*

Hurt, Hindered, and Held Back

Over the decades, through serving others as a Ministry Leader, RN, Corporate Executive, and Life Coach... I've observed that there are various hindrances that seem to impede spiritual growth, psychological health, and fruitfulness in the lives of many believers.

One major hindrance tops the list!

- This one sly thing will hamper your intimacy with the Lord... and... with others.
- It'll handcuff your prayers... block God's blessings... and keep you limping along in the wilderness.
- It'll hold you back so you cannot fulfill your God-given calling and purpose to any great degree.
- It's so significant that it'll prevent you from being forgiven by God... and from experiencing restoration and a lifestyle of freedom with peace, joy, and fulfillment.
- Furthermore, this serious heart issue opens the door to the demonic.

What would you guess tops the list of hindrances?

The Answer: **_Unforgiveness._**

Do we want our lives marked by the rotting reek of bitterness… or… by the heavenly perfume of forgiveness?

If we cave in to coddle a perceived wrong, the foul stench of bitterness will set in. It'll hold us captive, defile others, and hinder various areas of our lives.

However, if we prefer the heavenly perfume that comes with the blooming buds of good fruit, then, we must grow our roots down into good soil. In particular, we flourish and thrive as we *guard our hearts* from offense and meditate on God's Word every day. This nourishes the soil within and keeps it fertile. Thus, we can be assured that it's much easier to let go of offense and hard feelings when we tend well to the soil of our hearts every day.

A Grudge in the Garden

As we unearthed the destructive roots of poison ivy that were inhibiting our fruit trees, the Holy Spirit nudged me about the garden of my own heart being neglected. This stark realization prompted a sobering confrontation with some tainted feelings buried deep inside.

That very day I bowed before the Lord. With the Holy Spirit's guidance, I experienced a breakthrough and stepped onto the path toward healing and restoration.

Admittedly, I had felt warranted to justify some hard feelings about wrongs carried out against me, thus, I had embraced offense, and permitted my wounds to fester in the underground which had led to a stronghold of unforgiveness in my soul.

Hence, I've come to believe when we fail to dismiss offense early on, it can gradually burgeon down into a seething grudge of unforgiveness, resentment, and bitterness—it's what I refer to as *"the toxic trio."* When those clinging shoots and roots take hold, they're not easy to get rid of.

On the other hand, when we consciously choose to forgive, in spite of how we feel, the path is cleared for inner healing to begin. Heart restoration literally starts once we relinquish the right to harbor a grudge that we perceived as warranted.

It should be noted that our decision to forgive will be in opposition to our feelings, and if we don't control our emotions, they'll control us. I do believe we can accept how we feel without letting our emotions dictate our decisions. Thus, we must stand firm in our commitment to forgive because it's an act of obedience that pleases God (Matthew 6: 14-15).

Of course, it may defy logic to pardon those who we perceive have wronged us. However, when we don't, or we won't, "we" suffer... and, when we justify unforgiveness, "we" pay twice. Here's why... in Matthew 6:15, Jesus warns if we refuse to forgive others, neither will our Father forgive us. So, regardless of our feelings, we are instructed to forgive as the Lord freely forgives us (Colossians 3:13).

And, even if a wrongdoer "gets by with it," "never apologizes," and "never changes," our decision to let it go doesn't absolve what they did, but it unshackles us from the choking grip of "the toxic trio."

Furthermore, since we're all capable of wrongdoing, it's wise to swiftly cast aside pride, and extend forgiveness, even when it seems undeserved, because God has graciously forgiven the inexcusable in us.

Clearly, the overall cost of forgiving the inexcusable in another person pales in comparison to the burden of limping along in the wilderness ourselves, weighed down by the baggage of resentment! Indeed, it's not about the offender deserving our forgiveness, but about the degree of freedom we desire for ourselves.

Also, the pathway of forgiveness empowers us to release our expectations and any need for restitution or an apology. It further frees us so we can confidently dwell in the secret place of the Most High, experience His presence, and partake in His peace.

In keeping with that, my mother taught that a lifestyle of forgiveness keeps us *"under the spout where the glory comes out!"* Doris Haltom also said, *"When wronged, you face a choice: GROW BETTER... or... turn bitter."* She still reminds me today that *"Forgiveness is a GIFT we give ourselves."* These practical truths have influenced my life since girlhood.

Overall, regardless of the injury, it's imperative to embrace the forgiveness process, uproot bitter entanglements, and dismantle strongholds that shackle our hearts. It's definitely a priceless gift we give ourselves. Yet, conversely, it's self-destructive and foolish when we allow "the toxic trio" to take root and spread its purulent poison... that's akin to letting poison ivy wreak havoc in the garden of our hearts.

So, it is empowering for us to realize that our decision to forgive won't change the past, but it will pave the way for a better future.

Flourish in the Fragrant Fruitfulness of Forgiveness

I was born as a merciful encourager. It's still my greatest joy to bless, build, and empower others. However, I grieved the beautiful Holy Spirit, hurt myself, and disappointed others when I justified my feelings to embrace offense.

As a result, I found myself ensnared in a back-and-forth figure-eight. This meant my innate gifts, calling, and purpose were hindered and held back... and my God-ordained destiny story was delayed in a kirkyard of decay. The worst part was... grappling onto those hard feelings was a distraction that hampered intimacy with my Abba Father.

As I learned to tend well to the garden of my heart, I discovered that *forgiveness* is a heartwarming and holy pathway... and... *freedom* is its ultimate reward!

Next, I'll unveil secrets as succulent as ripe fruit. These powerful principles equipped me to swiftly toss offense over the fence... and to break free from unforgiveness that had slipped through and taken root.

The Healing Tree

Forgiveness is a decisive act of obedience that flows from a strong and grateful heart. I have learned that inner healing done God's way is the best way. Generally, it begins with forgiveness. In my *"Crowned for Purpose"* coaching course, I help Kingdom women achieve breakthrough from hurts that hinder and hold them back, so they can move forward to fulfill their God-given purpose.

After the commitment is made to forgive, then comes the process to carry it out. Depending on the severity of the perceived offense, there may be grief to process through, as well, but that's a topic for another time.

Personally, I've learned that *inner healing done God's way is the best way...* generally, it begins with forgiveness.

Here are some *life-application gardening tools* to take with you. They're how I navigate the forgiveness process after I make a conscious commitment:

1. **Yield, Surrender, and Submit to the Holy Spirit**

   • Repent for my part in the situation, receive Father's forgiveness, and forgive myself.

- Invite the Holy Spirit's help in the forgiveness process toward the offender(s).

- Every day, praise and pray in the spirit.

2. **Be Accountable**

- Take responsibility for my part without defensiveness or excuses.

- If warranted, apologize and ask for forgiveness.

- Place any blame appropriately, without speaking poorly of others.

3. **Navigate Loss and Grief**

- While advancing through forgiveness, allow myself to experience a separate grief process if needed (Note: healthy grief includes anger).

- When hurtful memories arise, I briskly reframe them. For example: I say aloud, *"I will not go there because I gave up my right to be offended. I lay myself down and declare 'more of YOU Lord Jesus... less of me!'"*

4. **Immerse in God's Word**

Decree Scripture. Each time a negative thought returns, I cast it down, and decree aloud some personalized and previously memorized scriptures such as... *Lamentations 3:22, Psalm 51:10, Colossians 1:10, 3:12-15, and Romans 5:5.*

5. **Fruit of the Spirit**

- With intention, I stir up and cultivate the 'Fruit of the Spirit' each day (Galatians 5:22-23).

6. **Love and Boundaries**

- Choose to love and bless the offender(s), and if the Holy Spirit leads, do it from a safer emotional distance with healthy boundaries in place.

7. Goal: to Please God

• Every day, make it my aim to please the Lord... and... focus on using my God-given gifts, calling, and purpose to serve others, advance God's Kingdom, and bring Him glory.

I'm occasionally asked about reconciliation. While I tend to prioritize it due to having a high *Emotional IQ* score, I recognize that reconciliation is a distinct process from forgiveness. Reconciliation isn't always essential, particularly when physical or emotional safety is at risk, and when faced with ongoing manipulation and/or opposition.

Furthermore, forgiveness doesn't mean we forget. Memories may persist, but they can serve as meaningful life lessons.

Trees of Righteousness

That spring, the old plum tree bloomed in the garden on our homestead, its heavenly fragrance was a healing balm for my heart. The vintage sugarplum queen gifted us with seven crisp, sweet plums that first summer, heralding a season toward restoration for the tree... and me.

It has been a few years, but this restoration story inspires me to be like *the trees who clap their hands and praise Him*... to daily partake in the *washing of the water by the Word*... to keep my eyes on the Son... to maintain a clean and pure heart... to get rid of offenses quickly... to cultivate growth of *spiritual fruit*... and to please my Heavenly Father so I'll be counted among His *"Strong and Graceful Oaks of Righteousness."*

What about you, *mighty oaks?* Will you guard and cultivate a heart that forgives? Doing so will ensure you make significant strides toward a restored lifestyle of freedom... fragrant and fruitful with peace, joy, and a deep sense of fulfillment.

As we depart a *restored garden* today, I invite you to personalize and decree Psalm 1:3 (TPT) with me:

> *I am standing firm like a flourishing tree planted*
> *by God's design, deeply rooted by the brooks of bliss, bearing*
> *fruit in every season of life. I'm never dry, never fainting,*
> *ever blessed, ever prosperous. — Psalm 1:3 (TPT)*

Dorease Rioux ~ *Keeper of the Garden of My Heart*

THINGS TO PONDER...

1. Why do you think God wants you to forgive others?

   _____

   _____

   _____

   _____

   _____

   _____

2. From *"A Grudge in the Garden,"* what insights will you take and apply?

   _____

   _____

_____

_____

_____

_____

3. Growing up, what did you learn from your caregivers about forgiveness?

_____

_____

_____

_____

_____

4. As an adult, who has influenced you to take forgiveness seriously? How can you help others learn how to break free from this hindrance?

_____

_____

_____

_____

_____

_____

5. Will you find me online and share your personal story of forgiveness?

_____

_____

_____

_____

_____

_____

I'll be delighted to hear about how you achieved a breakthrough.

Linette Rainville

Linette Rainville is a compassionate sister-survivor who is a mentor, coach, leader and speaker. Her greatest passion is to help women recognize, rise up, and run with her gifts, helping them build ministries from the ground up.

As the founder of *Daughters United* and *Mission Builders Academy*, she equips Kingdom women to dream bigger, build stronger, and launch impactful missions that support the fabric of the family.

This ministry is training up an Army of Esthers who are becoming movement leaders, making a difference, right where they are, with what they already have in their hands. Their mission is to MEET, MENTOR & MOBILIZE... so that others can be equipped to GATHER, GO & GROW!

Linette@DaughtersUnited.org

linetterainville.com/free-gift

calendly.com/linetterainville/discovery_call

daughtersunited.org

Day 20

Linette Rainville

Turning Pain into Purpose

*You intended to harm me, but God intended it all for good. He
brought me to this position so I could save the lives of many people.*
— *Genesis 50:20 (NLT)*

❝ *I don't believe we are ever fully RESTORED until we learn how to
REPURPOSE our PAIN.*❞—Linette Rainville

Within the ranks of our *Daughters United* sisterhood, there lives a
strong bond of camaraderie because we all have a story. Each one of us has
been on the battleground of life and we've lived to talk about it. Our stories
are all different, but similar. Each precious sister has walked through her
own unique storms and "lifequakes", and now she's decided to partner with
God to turn her pain into purpose.

If you're there right now, sitting right in the middle of your hot mess,
I want you to know that you are not alone! You are going to get through
this.

Our Heavenly Father loves us way too much to leave us abandoned,
even if it's us who's been doing the running.

Believe it or not, He actually chases after us! Remember Jesus who
left the 99 to go after the 1? You might be thinking, hmmm..., ok Linette,
but you don't know my situation... it is utterly impossible.

Well dear one, can I just say this.

It certainly looked IMPOSSIBLE for God's people who were trapped between the Red Sea and Pharaoh's chariot army didn't it?

The winds came, the sea split, the wall of fire appeared, and God's people fled to safety on dry ground!

Wasn't it utterly IMPOSSIBLE for a young VIRGIN girl from an itty bitty town to become the mother of the most important person to ever walk the earth?

Angels appeared. Mary pondered. Joseph believed. Elizabeth heard. John leapt. Shepherds quaked. Wise men came. Jesus grew. Blind eyes saw. Deaf ears heard. Lame legs danced. Disciples learned.

Then...

A thorny crown was worn.
The rugged cross was borne.
Innocent blood was shed.
The holy veil was torn.
The earth was under storm.
A guarded stone was rolled.
Bewildered soldiers feared.
The Resurrected ONE revealed.
The Holy Spirit filled.
Tongues of fire fell.
Disciples ran to go and tell.

The rest is HIStory!

Isn't it mind blowing that modern time has been "marked" for the last 2000 years with the terms B.C. (Before Christ) and A.D. (Anno Domini-the "year of the Lord") all because of one "man"—JESUS CHRIST.

IMPOSSIBLE you say?

Okay, by now you get my point.

The big blessing for you and me is that our Father GOD is still in the business of turning the impossibly bad, into the incredibly GOOD.

One of my most favorite underdog stories comes from the life of Joseph, and the punchline of his entire saga is summed up at the very end of the Genesis story.

> *You intended to harm me, but God intended it all for good. He brought me to this **position** so I could save the lives of many people. — Genesis 50:20 (NLT) (emphasis mine)*

Hmmm...

This sounds remarkably familiar to the words spoken to Queen Esther, one of my heroines of the faith. Her uncle Mordecai, poured bravery into her heart when he challenged her by saying:

> *For if you remain silent at this time, relief and deliverance for the Jews will arise from another place, but you and your father's family will perish. And who knows but that you have come to your royal position for such a time as this? — Esther 4:14 (NIV)*

And "who knows" that you have "come to" or rather "survived through" your **position** so that you could also save the lives of many people.

I know your wounds might be way too fresh in this moment to think that you'll ever be able to use your story for the saving of many lives, but trust me, your story can have a powerful ending.

When we place the broken pieces of our lives into the masterful hands of our loving Father, the work of art that He creates is nothing short of miraculous!

You may be familiar with this saying from Luke 1:37 (KJV),

For with God nothing will be impossible.

Let's take a 360 view of this truth from a few translations:

*"For no word **from God** will ever fail."*
New International Version (emphasis mine)

*"For the word of God will **never fail**."*
New Living Translation (emphasis mine)

*"For there is **nothing that God cannot do**."*
Good News Translation (emphasis mine)

*"For **no word** from God shall be **void of power**."*
American Standard Version (emphasis mine)

*"Because **nothing is difficult** for God."*
Aramaic Bible in Plain English (emphasis mine)

*"Because **nothing shall be impossible** with God."*
Young's Literal Translation (emphasis mine)

What words stood out to you as you re-read these scriptures?

How can you apply this promise to your own life and situation?

While God may not answer our prayers exactly how or when we want, be sure of this, God does hear you, and He will answer you too, it just might sound or look a little different than you'd expect.

Because we are human, we all want to run away from pain at all costs. We all want "drive through" miracles. However, God in His wisdom and mercy, prepares for us a "slow roasted" family style dinner that includes a generous side helping of character formation.

I get it. Just like some of you reading this:

I never want to live in poverty again.
I don't ever want to be a child of domestic violence, again.
I pray I won't ever have to go through major surgery, again.
Or left abandoned after 30 years of marriage, ever again.

But you know what? All of those things shaped me into the woman I am today.

I didn't allow these circumstances to make me bitter, but these things taught me how to become better.

Each trial made my heart keenly aware of the needs of others... and have impassioned me to do something about it. This is why I say, "I don't believe we are ever fully RESTORED until we learn how to REPURPOSE our PAIN." You see, GOD never wastes our pain. He REPURPOSES it.

My heart is thrilled as I watch our mentoring mission mobilized. A common statement I hear from many is this: *"The things I thought would break me, are the very things God has used to make me!"*

God has called modern day Esthers and Davids to become beautiful examples of how to repackage their pain... in partnership with Him.

It thrills my heart to see men and women trailblazers become prayer warriors, mentors, ministers and ministry midwives who have not just settled for survival but are actually becoming change agents for REVIVAL.

These Kingdom soldiers are using their experiences to become the heart, the hands, and the feet of Jesus on earth.

I love seeing this scripture from Psalm 40:2 (NLT) coming to life in real time:

> *He lifted me out of the pit of despair, out of the mud and the mire.*
> *He set my feet on solid ground and steadied me as I walked along.*

On a daily basis I encounter these resilient soldiers who are developing new ways to help heal, train, and equip others.

These ministry mentors reach out their hands to others stuck in a pit or the valley, and share a lifeline of hope, saying...

"Let me pull you up."
"Let me walk with you for a while."
"Let me help you through the process."
"I've been right where you are."
"I know the way through."
"I can show you what helped me to heal, rebuild and grow."

This is how we give the enemy a black eye. This is how we repurpose our pain. We must rise to the call to become Spiritual Mothers, Spiritual Fathers, and Mentors for the next generation.

In this hour, the LORD is calling His modern day Esthers, Deborahs, Abigails, Gideons, Josephs and Joshuas to ARISE.

So, ARISE we MUST! Our children, grandchildren, and great grands depend on us! Even amidst our pain, our wounds and our scars, can we dare to believe that God can use us right where we are; with what we already have in our hands?

After a tremendously difficult 2023, walking my Mama through the end of life, clearing out her apartment, and undergoing a total hip replacement, I was in one of those "bone weary" seasons.

New Years Eve, December 31st, 2023, I put on some instrumental worship music and snuggled in close before the LORD. With notebook and pen in hand I longed to hear what HE would say to me for the upcoming year.

In those precious, intimate moments I was "wrecked" in His presence. He began to pour a deep message into my soul. His words cascaded from my heart and flowed onto the paper as I scribed what my spirit heard my LORD speak.

I want to give you a peek inside my journal right here, as I pray these may be right "on time" words for many in the body of Christ, not just myself. I hope these words move you, as they did me that night. They left me saying YES LORD, your WILL, your WAY.

My Conversation with the Lord

Me:
Here I am Lord.
Speak to me.
Teach me.
I'm listening.

I hear the Lord saying to stop running.
To pull up a cushion and sit at His feet.

He is saying... *"I want to make you UNSHAKABLE."*

"O Daughter, how I long to be with you.

How I long for you to come and sit under the shadow of my presence.

I want for you to spend quality time with me.

Stop running **TO** the things of this world but run **INTO** my waiting arms.

Let my everlasting, never failing love embrace you.
For I myself will calm you and carry you.

My big strong arms will break away every fear and you will hear me rejoice over you with a love song.

As we embrace, you will feel my strength.
You will hear my tender whisper in your ear saying,
I LOVE YOU.
I GOT YOU.
I AM WITH YOU.

As you gaze into the deep sea of my eyes, my love will refresh you.

You will hear my voice echo into your soul.
'Deep calls to Deep.'

As I hold you closer, you'll hear me say... *'Your sad days are over.'*

YOUR STRONG GOD is clearing a way through the wilderness.

I am making a straight path for you through this desert.

And as we sit together, I will intently listen to all your plans, dreams and ideas.

We are all here with you, daughter.
The Father, Son, and Spirit are all here, sitting at this table with you.

We will unroll the scroll.
We are giving you a pen to write the vision and make it plain.

In this blueprint, you will begin to understand how your Heavenly Father intends to fill those valleys, level the hills, smooth those ruts and clear the rocks in your way.

As Our counsel envelops you, you will begin to embrace the dream that we placed on the inside of you.

O how you fit perfectly into My plan and perfect hour.
Let this be the moment of your knowing.
Open your heart.

Prepare to be moved by the BIG LOVE of your Father God.

I want you to GET IT.

To finally realize how BIG, how WIDE, how HIGH, how VAST My love for you really is.

Beloved one, how I long for you to partner with me on this mission.

How I long to use the gifts that I've placed inside of you.

I had a plan in mind as I was weaving you in your mother's womb.

Before you ever breathed your first breath or took your first step, I had your purpose in mind.

But like all children do, you tend to run ahead of Me, instead of running to Me.

So many times you have tried to *make things happen* in your own strength or you've sought after man's plan instead of seeking your Father's wisdom.

Don't you know that I know the way?

How I long to share these scrolls of direction, wisdom and guidance with you!

Seek ye first the Kingdom... and all these things shall be added unto you! — Matthew 6:33 (KJV)

Again, I say, I am shaking in this hour and only the unshakable things will remain.

In this last season, people and circumstances and even your own insecurities, have attached labels onto your destiny.

As you sit in My presence, there will be a magnetic shaking.
I will pull away every misspoken label that has ever attached itself to you.

Right here and now I am taking you in My arms, and holding you close to My chest.

LISTEN close and hear as My heart calls... as DEEP calls to DEEP.

You ARE My beloved, My very own treasured possession.
Listen as I lovingly whisper in your ear...

My yoke is easy.
My burden is light.
Take MY yoke upon you.

Right here, right now I am clothing you with a custom-made mantle.

Suddenly everything that you've been doing will pale in comparison to this divine call and anointing that I have placed over your life.

In this moment, be filled with new strength.

As you sit with Me,
I will renew your strength.

I will restore your vision.

I will reinstate your mantle.

I will replenish your passion.

After the shaking, you will have a great PEACE.

One that passes understanding.

This will be for you a HOPE and an ANCHOR that cannot be moved."

Prayer

O precious child of God, sit a little longer with Me as I cover you right now with a mantle releasing prayer...

Father,

Be close to this precious heart who is reading these words right now. They have gone through some really hard things. Not one minute were they ever out of Your sight.

You were there watching, waiting, catching, and saving them at every turn. And now they are coming to you with their war-torn soul to become fully RESTORED.

Holy Spirit, do what only you can do to release them from the memories, lies and wasted years of pain. REMOVE the strongman of isolation, intimidation, and imposter syndrome from their life.

Precious Jesus, wrap Your massive arms around your child in this moment. Shower them with Your unconditional love and healing balm.

Place Your healing hands inside their soul and take away any shame, blame, anger, or regret. They are RESTORED NOW in JESUS' MIGHTY NAME! In this sacred moment, begin filling Your child with creative ideas to repurpose their pain.

Give them a VISION.
Reveal to them their MISSION.
Clothe them with their MANTLE.
Embolden their VOICE to share their story.

Help them envision the 10's, 100's and 1000's you have CALLED them to reach.

Thank you for downloading a BLUEPRINT that they will be able to follow.

Give them YOUR GODFIDENCE to BUILD it and WALK it out...

For Such A Time As This!
I BOLDLY ask all this in Your mighty, powerful name, Jesus.
AMEN and AMEN!

Things to Ponder...

1. What healing did you experience as you were reading this?

_____

_____

_____

_____

_____

_____

2. List the things you felt the Lord released you from.

    _____

    _____

    _____

    _____

    _____

    _____

3. When I prayed for your Vision, Mission, and Mantle what did you
    see?

    _____

    _____

    _____

    _____

    _____

    _____

4. Write down any images that flashed through your mind.

    _____

    _____

    _____

    _____

_____

_____

5. Brainstorm some ways God might be wanting to use your story to
    help others. Write these ideas down.

    _____

    _____

    _____

    _____

    _____

    _____

Sharon Baker

Sharon Baker, founder of *Embracing Abundance Life Coaching,* has profoundly impacted the personal and professional growth sectors throughout her 25-year career. A certified business professional, life coach, speaker, and Best-Selling Author. Sharon began her professional journey in the corporate world, emphasizing forward-thinking leadership, development, and employee engagement. Her coaching platform combines her deep business knowledge with innovative coaching techniques, helping clients unlock their passions and achieve their goals.

Overcoming personal limiting beliefs has equipped Sharon with special insights into defeating scarcity mindsets. Beyond individual coaching, she collaborates with corporations to boost workforce potential and resilience, frequently speaks at major events, and has authored best-selling books. Sharon is also a Presidential Lifetime Achievement Award recipient, honored for her significant contributions to societal advancement.

embracingabundancelifecoaching.com
facebook.com/sharon.baker.50552
linkedin.com/in/sharon-y-baker
instagram.com/embracingabundancellc

Day 21

Sharon Baker

The Shepherd's Soul Work

He restores my soul. He guides me in paths of righteousness
for His name's sake. — Psalm 23:3 (KJV)

Remembering the Shepherd

As a child, I learned many scriptures, but I can't recall the exact moment I memorized the entire 23rd Psalm. I was likely nine or ten. The only shepherds I knew were those in the Christmas Nativity scene. How different were they from the one mentioned in the Psalm? The first verse, *"The Lord is my shepherd; I shall not want,"* was both intriguing and puzzling. As a child, I thought, *"Want what?"*

Back then, I didn't fully grasp the context of this scripture, but it resonated with me. I loved flipping through our large family Bible, captivated by the images of Bible characters and the essence of God and His Son, Jesus Christ. Over the years, as I began to understand the power of scripture and the importance of reading and meditating on it, this passage became a source of comfort and a reminder of God's love.

King David describes God as a shepherd who provides everything necessary: rest, nourishment, and guidance toward righteousness. Even in perilous situations like *"the valley of the shadow of death,"* David trusts God to protect and comfort him, akin to a shepherd with his flock. Despite facing adversaries, God abundantly blesses David with a prepared feast, an overflowing cup, and anointing. David remains confident that God's kindness and mercy will follow him all his life, always finding a home in God's presence.

Reflecting on the Good Shepherd, I ponder some of the many names of God. The first verse prompts reflections on Jehovah Jireh, our provider, adept at managing our needs. But when considering the workings of the soul, I think of God's role as Jehovah Rapha, our healer, who impacts all dimensions of our being. With Him, we can experience healing in body, soul, and spirit. Finally, Jehovah Shalom, who provides peace—a soul existing in peace is a soul that has been restored. In reviewing these intricacies, it behooves us to examine our human element. By understanding our composition, we can experience God in a transformative way.

We Are Also Three

Humans are unique in nature and disposition, but we also share many similarities. Just as we worship a Triune God (Father, Son, and Holy Spirit), there are three parts to the human condition. In 1 Thessalonians 5:23 (NIV) it confirms, *"May God himself, the God of peace, sanctify you through and through. May your whole spirit, soul, and body be kept blameless at the coming of our Lord Jesus Christ."* We are indeed three-dimensional.

Like astronauts wear a spacesuit to venture into space, we have an "Earth suit"—our body. Our body, the first component of our humanity, covers both our soul and spirit, allowing us to live out our purpose on earth.

Our soul, comprised of our mind, emotions, and will, enables us to experience feelings like joy, love, sadness, anger, relief, and compassion. It also allows us to think, reason, reflect, remember, and contemplate, as stated in Genesis 2:7 (KJV), *"And the Lord God formed man of the dust of the ground and breathed into his nostrils the breath of life; and man became a living soul."*

Our spirit is the deepest aspect of our being. Through this innermost dimension, we connect with God on a spiritual level. John 4:24 (NIV) states, *"God is spirit, and his worshipers must worship in the Spirit and in truth."* Each component is essential: our physical senses reside in the body, our personhood is rooted in the soul, and our connection with God through the spirit.

Moving forward, we will delve into the third verse of this well-known passage and explore its implications for our souls and the paths we follow under the care of the Shepherd. This is soul work at its finest.

The Undoing (In a Good Way)

The lives we lead are filled with adversity and hardship. As humans, we endure trials and tribulations that can manifest as betrayal, loss, sadness, brokenness, defeat, and hurt, affecting us mentally, emotionally, and spiritually. Forgetting our intrinsic value can lead us to question our worth, often spiraling into self-hatred—the most destructive form of hatred. This state can bring about feelings of worthlessness, remorse, and depression, pushing us into profound brokenness.

Recall a time when you endured a painful event; looking back, it might be hard to understand how you survived. Perhaps it was the death of a loved one, a personal illness, the loss of a job, or infidelity in your marriage. During such times, God is especially close to us. Psalm 34:18 (NIV), reassures us,

The LORD is close to the brokenhearted and saves those who are crushed in spirit. — Psalm 34:18 (NIV)

The term "undo" means to cancel or reverse the effects of a previous action. This concept is central to what God does when He restores us—undoing the negative to bring about something positive. In this context, undoing acts as a counterattack against whatever adversities we have faced. When King David speaks of God restoring his soul, he refers to God's ability to repair, refresh, and return it to its original state. As our Creator, only God truly understands what we need for genuine renewal and is uniquely capable of completely restoring our souls.

In the restoration process, we experience God's deep love, forgiveness, redemption, mercy, and healing. Remember, only God can truly undo harm and restore. Restoration is yet another expression of God's grace. The Scriptures remind us that God is a compassionate and loving Father, actively working to mend our brokenness and reconcile humanity to Himself, demonstrated by sending His Son, Jesus, to atone for our sins, affirming our worth. Yes, you are worth it!

The Value of the Soul

Even our adversary, Satan, recognizes the importance and power of our souls, continually striving to wreak havoc and claim as many as possible. Our souls are the ultimate prize because they are valued immensely by God. As expressed in Ezekiel 18:4 (KJV),

Behold, all souls are mine; as the soul of the father, so also the soul of the son is mine: the soul that sinneth, it shall die.
— Ezekiel 18:4(KJV)

However, weary souls are vulnerable, necessitating protection at all costs. Proverbs 4:23 (NIV) emphasizes this, stating, *"Above all else, guard your heart, for everything you do flows from it."* This passage refers not to the physical heart but to the core of our being—our soul.

Consider what restoration feels like physically. Perhaps you've been extremely tired, overwhelmed by a hectic life, and living in what feels like a constant state of busyness. When you finally get the chance to rest, and sleep for what seems like days, you awaken refreshed and renewed, unable to recall the sensation of being sleep-deprived. Your mind is clear, your body rested, and your focus sharp, ready to tackle the world anew.

A similar transformation occurs when God restores our soul. He delves into our inner dynamics to ensure that each restoration is uniquely tailored. I refer to this as customized restoration. What it takes to restore one person may differ from another. While life's unexpected events ("life happens" scenarios) can be challenging, it is our active and deliberate participation in sin that often necessitates a deeper level of restoration, typically preceded by confession, repentance, and recommitment.

God is acutely aware of our human frailties and stands ready to meet our needs. He invites us to ask for all that we require in life. Proverbs 4:5 (NIV) encourages us to *"acknowledge Him in all our ways, and He will direct our paths."* As our soul's experience brokenness, it is through His Spirit and our spirit that we find renewal.

Roadblocks to True Restoration

What prevents us from achieving complete restoration? Although God will never force restoration, there are three primary obstacles that often hinder our experience of true restoration.

• *Failure to Acknowledge the Need:* Surprisingly, some people believe they don't need God, despite acknowledging His existence. They feel in control of their lives. However, experiencing a traumatic event or drifting away from God invariably impacts the soul, which encompasses our emotions, will, and mind. Denying this need only exacerbates the distance between us and true healing.

• **_Reluctance to Commit to God:_** Does this mean restoration is impossible without commitment to God? Not necessarily. Restoration spans a broad spectrum and can manifest in many forms. However, a full commitment can deepen and accelerate the process, inviting more profound changes.

• **_Feeling Unworthy:_** Previously, I mentioned that restoration is a form of God's grace. Unfortunately, some individuals feel their past actions make them unworthy of God's love, complicating their ability to accept this gift. Overcoming these feelings of unworthiness is crucial for accepting the full spectrum of God's grace.

To navigate these mental traps, we must embrace the truth. Proverbs 1:7 states, _"The fear of the Lord is the beginning of knowledge, but fools despise wisdom and instruction."_ Engaging with scripture and prayer allows us to build a relationship with God and embark on a genuine journey of renewal.

Several years ago, during a particularly rough patch in my life—questioning my work, relationships, and general circumstances—I found myself overwhelmed and distraught. Late one night, too broken to speak, my heart communicated what my voice could not.

At that moment, I felt the Lord's comforting presence envelop me like a warm blanket. Even though I was unable to articulate my needs, God knew them and intervened. This is the kind of God we serve—one who understands our needs and meets us exactly where we are.

God is ready to remove the roadblocks, but we must be open to embracing Him. The impact of His restoration can be profound, and if we are fortunate, we will experience it multiple times throughout our lives. Once touched by God's restoration, the experience is indescribable, uniquely felt by each individual. God is ready to welcome all who are willing. As Matthew 11:28 (NIV) invites, _"Come to me, all who are weary and burdened, and I will give you rest."_ The Shepherd is waiting; are you ready?

Steps to Renewal

True renewal with God requires mutual engagement. Our omniscient, loving, and omnipotent Creator desires the rejuvenation of our soul. While many associate the need for renewal with extreme trauma or life-altering events, the truth is that daily challenges and the constant struggle against our fleshly desires necessitate regular restoration.

By committing to these five actions, we meet God halfway. Psalm 55:22 reinforces this commitment: *"Cast your cares on the Lord and he will sustain you; he will never let the righteous be shaken."*

• *Stay Tuned in Through Prayer:* Prayers stir the heart of God and pave the way for accelerated rejuvenation. Regular engagement in prayer deepens our connection with God, central to the restoration of the soul. This practice fosters peace, clarity, and strength, realigning us with God's desires and serving as a spiritual discipline that enhances moral and spiritual growth.

• *Cement the Word in Your Heart:* Through Scriptures, we absorb and repeat God's words, which He honors and responds to. Immersing ourselves in The Word is a vital method for restoring the soul, as it provides correction, encouragement, and wisdom, essential for spiritual growth and resilience.

• *Seek Out the Holy Spirit:* The Holy Spirit plays an integral role in our spiritual renewal and restoration, offering continuous guidance, comfort, and strength to overcome adversities. Actively inviting the Holy Spirit into our daily lives enhances our sensitivity to divine promptings and enriches our decision-making.

• *Make True Worship a Priority:* Regular worship grounds us in our faith, serving as a powerful reminder of God's sovereignty and love. True worship extends beyond church services, influencing how we live and interact with others, embodying a lifestyle that honors God in every action.

• ***Acknowledge Him as Lord and Savior:*** Acknowledging God as Lord and Savior opens us to complete restoration. Surrendering to Him is not a one-time event but a lifelong journey of forsaking our will for His. This process gradually purifies and restores our souls, enabling us to reflect His love and grace in our daily lives.

By embracing these steps, we prepare ourselves for the Shepherd's guidance and care, ready to experience the profound benefits of soul work, as promised in the teachings of Psalm 23 and exemplified in our lives.

THE "WE'S"–WIN: BENEFITS OF THE SOUL WORK

We Embrace Our Identity

Restoration by God helps us embrace our true identity as His children. This recognition comes with an understanding of the inherent value and purpose that God places on each life. When God restores a person, He often clarifies and reaffirms their calling and the unique gift's He has bestowed upon them. This newfound identity can inspire confidence and a sense of divine mission, encouraging individuals to live out their lives with purpose and dedication according to God's plan.

We Become More Compassionate

Being restored by God can profoundly increase compassion in an individual's heart. Experiencing God's mercy and grace firsthand often makes people more empathetic towards others' struggles and pain. This empathy can lead to a more loving and service-oriented lifestyle, as restored individuals are motivated to extend the same kindness and forgiveness that they received from God. This compassion is not only a reflection of their personal transformation but also a testament to the transformative power of divine love in their lives.

We Get to Know Our Creator

Being restored by God often leads to a closer relationship with Him. This closeness manifests as a deeper understanding and appreciation of God's nature and His will for our lives.

Restoration removes the barriers of sin and guilt that can distance us from God, allowing for a more intimate connection. As believers feel God's healing and forgiveness, they often find themselves more inclined to seek His presence through prayer, worship, and scripture, experiencing a renewed sense of faith and trust in His guidance.

Mustering of the Sheep

The entire chapter of Psalm 23 is an anthem honoring the Good Shepherd. In this epic text, David shares how important God is to him by expressing his thankfulness. But venturing over to Matthew 18:13-14, we see how important the sheep are to the Master. It suggests that He will leave the ninety-nine to search for the one lost sheep. Scripture states,

> *And if he finds it, truly I tell you, he is happier about that one sheep than about the ninety-nine that did not wander off. In the same way your Father in heaven is not willing that any of these little ones should perish. — Matthew 18:12 (NIV)*

Our souls are important to Him and restoring them is high on His agenda.

The Shepherd's Soul Work is Vital to Our Being

In essence, the restoration of the soul is about returning to a life that reflects spiritual health, vitality, and a deep connection with God. This process is unique to each individual and involves various aspects of their faith and practices. As referenced in Psalms 23:3, not only does He restore us, but He will also lead us down the right path.

Psalm 23:6 ends so graciously, letting us know what we will experience if we allow ourselves to be led by the Shepherd. David exclaims,

Surely goodness and mercy shall follow me all the days of my life:
and I will dwell in the house of the Lord forever.
— Psalm 23:6 (NKJV)

As mentioned above, God is ready to welcome all who are willing. As Matthew 11:28 (NIV) invites, *"Come to me, all who are weary and burdened, and I will give you rest."*

THINGS TO PONDER...

1. The Shepherd is waiting; are you ready to look within?

_____

_____

_____

_____

_____

_____

2. Are you willing to repent and forgive so Jesus can restore?

_____

_____

_____

_____

_____

_____

3. If so, ask Him now.

_____

_____

_____

_____

_____

_____

4. How have you felt God's provision, healing, or peace lately? Has there been a moment where you've clearly seen Him as Jehovah Jireh, Jehovah Rapha, or Jehovah Shalom?

_____

_____

_____

_____

_____

_____

5. Can you think of a time when you truly felt your soul was being refreshed by God? What was that like, and what did it teach you about how God is present in your life?

_____

_____

_____

_____

_____

_____

Day 22

Sharon Baker

Return to Me, Your First Love

*Yet I hold this against you: You have forsaken the love you had
at first. Consider how far you have fallen! Repent
and do the things you did at first.*
— Revelation 2:4 (NIV)

What About Love?

From my earliest memories as a child, I felt a divine pull on my heart, which led me to accept Christ at the tender age of ten. However, as the years rolled by, I drifted away from the faith until I recommitted myself to Christ as an adult in 1991. I will never forget sitting in church with my six-month-old daughter and hearing the voice of God urging me to return to Him. Despite recognizing my need for God, I did not fully comprehend the depth of His love for me; I did not truly grasp the profound impact of agape love. I do not think that most Christians do, and this is how we fail.

Prior to COVID, I lived a life of busyness. There was work, church, and community stuff. I did not realize that I was checking the boxes, but I was. When COVID hit in 2020, it changed everything—not just for me, but for the world. I was able to slow down and rekindle my relationship with God. Because, although I had been attending church regularly for 30 years, heavily involved in the children's ministry, had taught Sunday School and Bible Study, and held many positions in the church, I had lost something with the Lord. My prayer time had been rushed, and I was unable to truly focus as I reviewed Scripture.

During this time of solitude that COVID so graciously provided, I was able to pray more, study more, begin to see things differently, and reconnect with God. This insight resulted in me leaving a church that I had been a part of for over 30 years, and retiring from my job of over 22 years. We will always experience breakthroughs, revelations, and clarity when He becomes our focus. But as the activity picked up again, I found myself again in a "busy land," and once again sacrificing my relationship with my Savior. It is a vicious cycle.

When most individuals come to Christ, they enter what is referred to as the "honeymoon phase," where they have fallen in love with Christ and are eager to know Him. They faithfully work in the church and attend services excited and elated. These new believers find themselves dedicating their time to prayer and reading scripture, but over time, the newness wears off. Many believers go through the phase of being disconnected, but still serve. This lack of intentionality and focus impacts them in one way or another. They may choose to continue in formality, losing their true connection with Christ, or for others, they may leave the fellowship altogether. Neither route is good for the body of Christ.

Why does this happen? How can individuals with the best intentions drift off course and lose their connection with God? Although Jesus mentions the Ephesian Christians in Revelation 2:4, this is a timely message for churches and believers today. These words serve as a call to people to turn once more to God's love and to remember what first drew us to Jesus in the first place. Matthew 22:37–38 (NIV) states,

Love the Lord your God with all your heart, with all your soul, and with all your mind. This is the first and greatest commandment.
— Matthew 22:37–38 (NIV)

It appears that our first love has been replaced by self-love and our own agenda.

The Pew Research Center provides some interesting but startling data relating to Christianity and the unchurched. According to a 2019 report, since 2007, the percentage of adults who say they are atheists, agnostics, or "nothing in particular" has grown from 16% to 29%. During this time, the share of U.S. adults who identify as Christians has fallen from 78% to 63%. There are many factors that have contributed to the shift in these numbers, but more so, it serves as a confirmation of the prophecy spoken of many years ago.

Changes in Lifestyles and Values

Times have changed, and it is reflected in much of what we do. As alluded to earlier, our focus has shifted, and we have subscribed to the world of busyness, organized chaos, and instant gratification. We live in a world that is driven by one dopamine fix after another. So much so that even if we try to commune with God, we are unable to focus for an extended period. We are often engulfed in our cell phones, social media, jobs, and all sorts of activities and commitments.

Because of this pace, our spiritual life becomes a source for microwave prayers, half-hearted fasting attempts, and adhering to a schedule of formality where we are simply checking the boxes. What once was a relationship that was so pure is now simply, religion. Furthermore, we buy into the fallacy that there is not enough time to commune with our God, giving Him our leftovers at our own discretion. Lord, help us!

It should be noted that the Christians in Ephesus were not doing everything wrong as many churches today. In fact, Jesus praises them for their numerous efforts and honorable deeds, and how they overcame adversity and persisted without tiring. In particular, the Ephesians' ability to discern false teaching was highlighted. What God wants us to realize is that true fellowship and intimacy with him are non-negotiable.

The Reconciliation: The Way Back to the Father

To get back to the Father we must be willing to be vulnerable, humble, obedient, and, most of all, available. As we move toward reconciliation, it will be beneficial to examine five key areas. These include examining your heart, understanding His purpose, leveraging spiritual saturation, leaving the zone, and rededicating daily. Making a commitment to focus on these areas in partnership with the Holy Spirit will allow us to reclaim our first love.

Examine Your Heart

Let us start with the basics and ask God for His guidance. King David expressed it best in Psalm 139:23–24 (NIV) when he expressed,

Search me, God, and know my heart; test me and know my anxious thoughts. See if there is any offensive way in me and lead me in the way everlasting. — Psalm 139:23–24 (NIV)

As David did, we must go before the Lord and ask Him to reveal things about ourselves that we cannot see. Unveiling and addressing our true motives will allow us to make God a priority again. As we examine our hearts, let us truly and deliberately meditate on Scripture so it can integrate into our spirit. Allowing the word to penetrate deeply is how we will see our best results. David validates this practice when he confesses,

I have hidden your word in my heart that I might not sin against you. — Psalm 119:11 (NIV)

Make sure that repentance is included in this process because God requires it.

Put into Action: Ask God to search your heart and be prepared to repent.

Understand His Purpose

In Rick Warren's (2002) book, *The Purpose-Driven Life,* he states, *"Focusing on ourselves will never reveal our life's purpose."* Still, many individuals and Christians think that their purpose is about them. Warren takes this a little further by abdicating the following: *"You were made by God for God, and until you understand that life will never make sense."*

We must seek and impress upon the Lord to help us identify our purpose and understand how it supports His purpose and plan. When we remind ourselves of this truth, everything else takes a back seat, because our lives will revolve around God's will and not our own. As believers, we often get caught up in living here on Earth without preparing for the next life. This does not mean that we should not enjoy our lives, but we should integrate God into all aspects of them. Remembering our true purpose will remind us that this planet is not our home and that our bodies are living sacrifices, on-loan vessels, commissioned to do God's work.

Put into Action: Ask God to reveal his purpose for your life. It is never too late.

Leverage Spiritual Saturation

The state of being completely immersed and involved in one's spiritual path is known as spiritual saturation. This means that from the beginning of our day to the end of our day, our focus is on God. This requires incorporating more Godly things, improving the quality of those things, and "checking" those things that, although not classified as sinful, can corrupt our spirit. Maximizing "God Time" with prayer, fasting, and worship foundations can only be accomplished through surrender.

Surrendering these areas will allow God to bring us to a genuine place. Effective saturation requires that we take it a step further. It challenges the things that we are focused on outside of "God Time," because these things are more prone to manipulation. This means analyzing and being more selective about what we watch, listen to, and engage in, such as movies, music, television shows, literary works, and even the news.

Although I am not completely opposed to all secular music or shows, I do not think it benefits believers to have these things as a primary source of entertainment. What we must ask ourselves is whether this thing is bringing us closer to God or taking us away from God.

To ensure balance, I would recommend listening to and reading more Scripture, and engaging in more praise and worship music, whether we are awake or asleep. There is nothing better than waking up to God's Word after listening to it all night; it puts us in a different head space. Proverbs 4:23 (NIV) affirms,

Above all else, guard your heart, for everything you do flows from it. — Proverbs 4:23 (NIV)

Put into action: Increase godly influences and minimize secular activities.

Leave The Zone

As we continue to move through reconciliation, we must understand that this process requires sacrifice, and will take us out of our comfort zone. As we "leave the zone," be prepared to trust God by exercising our faith in more ways by doing things that defy logic and are beyond our understanding.

Fasting is an area in which we gain more if done correctly. It is giving up something good to gain something better. Intense and structured fasting can strengthen our relationship, but it is not just about not eating or not doing something; it is a spiritual exchange that happens when we are abstaining.

There may be other instances when God is requiring a sacrifice of what we deem to be a physical need, or even a psychological need. Specifically, God may want to share a word in the midnight hour, and we must become sensitive to His call. This does not mean that God does not want us to get our sleep; it means we must show God that we are willing to sacrifice our time, whenever it may be.

The need to sacrifice sleep is outlined in Jesus' warning to His disciples. He asked them to keep watch in the Garden of Gethsemane as He prayed to God. This was a tense time for Jesus, as He approached God three times regarding His upcoming fate. Each time, Jesus would return and find the disciples sleeping. He said,

Stay awake and pray that you won't be tempted. You want to do what's right, but you're weak. — Matthew 26:41 (NIV)

This statement looks beyond the physical aspects of sleep and warns us about the value of sacrifice as an avenue for strengthening us spiritually.

Put into action: Get comfortable with being uncomfortable. List ways to leave your zone.

Rededicate Daily

I love weddings, vow renewals, baby dedications, and baptisms. These ceremonies are particularly enjoyable because they are God-based and tied to commitment. In celebration of my 30-year anniversary, I have decided to have a vow renewal ceremony and celebration. I am doing this for two reasons: first, because I think that it honors God and the institution of marriage. This action says that I am committed to both my husband and my God.

The second is that I have never had a wedding. Back then, we chose the cleaner, cheaper route and exchanged vows at the local courthouse, but a wedding was always in my heart. It is a woman's thing; apart from that, the ceremony means something.

As we return to the Father, let us do it with celebration and ceremony to remind God of our commitment to Him.

Do your best to present yourself to God as one approved,
a worker who has no need to be ashamed, rightly handling
the word of truth. — 2 Timothy 2:15 (NIV)

This should be a big deal. Invite your friends and family so that they can witness your rededication. But to make it the most effective, do not limit it to just one day; celebrate it every day. As we arise with gratitude, remind God with prayer, praise, and verbal affirmation of your rededication. Our thought process should be that it is a new day with a new dedication.

Put into action: Create your rededication affirmation and communicate it daily.

The Love You Save May Be Your Own

God's love is amazing. Even in all our human frailties, He continues to love us. One day, it is my prayer that we will all understand the gravity of His love. 1 John 4:9–10 (NIV) reminds us,

> *This is how God showed his love among us: He sent his one*
> *and only Son into the world that we might live through him.*
> *This is love: not that we loved God, but that he loved us*
> *and sent his Son as an atoning sacrifice for our sins. He loved us*
> *first and expects the same in return. Is that truly too much to ask?*
> *— 1 John 4:9–10 (NIV)*

Returning to the Father requires commitment, focus, and the Holy Spirit. I am convinced that those who heed Jesus' warning to return to their first love will experience intimacy with God like never before. There is a special anointing waiting to be released and an open heaven waiting to be established. God tells us in Amos 3:7 (NIV),

> *Surely the sovereign LORD does nothing without revealing his*
> *plan to his servants, the prophets. — Amos 3:7 (NIV)*

God is waiting for those who will diligently seek Him, sit at His feet, and then walk in obedience.

THINGS TO PONDER...

1. How would you categorize your relationship with God?

2. How would you like it to be?

3. Are you regularly attending church and serving?

_____

_____

4. Do you know your purpose, your reason for being here?

_____

_____

_____

_____

_____

5. Is fasting a part of Christian Walk?

_____

_____

_____

_____

_____

6. Have you been baptized in the Holy Spirit?

_____

_____

_____

_____

_____

_____

7. Do you believe that God loves you?

_____

_____

_____

_____

_____

_____

8. If so, why? If not, why?

_____

_____

_____

_____

_____

_____

Misty Dawn Allen

Misty Dawn is a Best Selling Author, and entrepreneur with compassion and a heart for encouraging, uplifting and inspiring others. She is actively pursuing her purpose in ministry and Kingdom business for such a time as this, while possessing great courage, and trusting God with faith and endurance. She is a graceful example of turning pain into purpose. God gets all the glory!

Misty is also a U.S. Marine Corps Veteran who is now Retired from the Civilian Federal Government where she served in Executive positions and a counselor to her peers. Her governmental background is part of God's plan for her life, purpose and ministry. She is now using her gifts to build a God-inspired brand as a riter and Creative Designer for the Kingdom.

facebook.com/dawn.allen.351
instagram.com/lighthands

Day 23

Misty Dawn Allen

Renewed by Grace

Embracing God's Restoration Power

*"The Lord is my Shepherd [to feed, guide, and shield me],
I shall not lack.*

*He makes me lie down in [fresh, tender] green pastures;
He leads me beside the still and restful waters.*

*He refreshes and restores my life (my self); He leads me in the paths
of righteousness [uprightness and right standing with Him—not
for my earning it, but] for His name's sake.*

*Yes, though I walk through the [deep, sunless] valley of the shadow
of death, I will fear or dread no evil, for You are with me; Your rod
[to protect] and Your staff [to guide], they comfort me.*

*You prepare a table before me in the presence of my enemies.
You anoint my head with oil; you fill my [brimming] cup runs over.*

*Surely or only goodness, mercy, and unfailing love shall follow me
all the days of my life, and through the length of my days the house
of the Lord [and His presence] shall be my dwelling place.*
— Psalm 23 (AMPC)

*And He who sits on the throne said, "Behold, I am making all things
new." Also He said, "Write, for these words are faithful and true [they are
accurate, incorruptible, and trustworthy]." — Revelation 21:5 (AMP)*

In the grand scheme of the Bible, one of the most exciting themes are those of restoration. From Genesis to Revelation, we see a divine thread woven throughout history, depicting God's relentless pursuit to restore His creation to His intended glory. Therefore, let's explore the profound and manifold nature of God's restoration, and take a look at key stories and Scripture references that speak to His eternal promise.

The story of restoration begins in Genesis in the Garden of Eden. When Adam and Eve sinned, the perfect relationship between God and humanity was fractured. However, even in the midst of judgment, God did give clues of a future restoration. In Genesis 3:15 (NIV), God spoke to the serpent saying,

And I will put enmity between you and the woman,
and between your offspring and hers; he will crush your head,
and you will strike his heel. — Genesis 3:15 (NIV)

This verse is a prophecy which foretold the coming of Christ, the ultimate restorer who would defeat satan and redeem humanity. Next we have the story of Noah that further illustrates God's desire for restoration. After the flood, God established a covenant with Noah, promising never to destroy the earth with a flood again. (Genesis 9:11)

The rainbow serves as a sign of this covenant, a reminder of God's faithfulness and His commitment to restoring creation and fulfilling his promises. Hallelujah!

God's restoration plan continued with His covenant with Abraham. In Genesis 12:2-3 (NIV), God promises Abraham, *I will make you into a great nation, and I will bless you; I will make your name great, and you will be a blessing. I will bless those who bless you, and whoever curses you I will curse; and all peoples on earth will be blessed through you.*

This covenant not only promised personal blessings to Abraham but also foreshadowed the ultimate universal blessing that would come through his lineage... Jesus Christ our redeemer!

The story of Abraham's descendants, the Israelites, is a testament to God's restorative power. Despite their repeated disobedience, God continually sought to restore them. The "Exodus" from Egypt is a vivid show of this. God heard the cries of His people and delivered them out of slavery, and into the Promised Land (Exodus 3:7-8).

Another well-known example of God's restorative work is found in the story of the prodigal son (Luke 15:11-32). This story illustrates God's readiness to restore those who have strayed. Luke speaks of a father who joyously receives his repentant son, complete with a robe, a ring, and a feast! All of this symbolizes the abundance of God's grace and His eagerness to restore our broken relationship with Him. Jesus awaits us in the same way!

God also spoke about restoration through the Prophets. Many prophetic books of the Old Testament are filled with promises of restoration. The prophets spoke of a time when God would restore Israel, not just physically, but spiritually. In Isaiah 61:1-3 (NIV), this prophet declares, *"The Spirit of the Sovereign Lord is on me, because the Lord has anointed me to proclaim good news to the poor. He has sent me to bind up the brokenhearted, to proclaim freedom for the captives and release from darkness for the prisoners, to proclaim the year of the Lord's favor and the day of vengeance of our God, to comfort all who mourn... To grant to those who mourn in Zion; to give them a beautiful headdress (**crown**) instead of ashes, the oil of joy (**gladness**) instead of mourning, the garment of praise instead of a faint spirit; that they may be called oaks of righteousness, the planting of the Lord, that he may be glorified."* (Emphasis mine)

This Scripture reveals the nature of God's restoration and the fact that it is not just limited to physical deliverance but also covers emotional and spiritual healing as well. This truth alone encompasses the transformative power of God's love and extraordinary restorative design.

The prophet Jeremiah also spoke extensively about restoration. In Jeremiah 29:11 (NIV), God presents us a promise:

For I know the plans I have for you, declares the Lord, plans to prosper you and not to harm you, plans to give you hope and a future. — Jeremiah 29:11 (NIV)

This popular verse is frequently quoted and loved by many believers as the expression of God's purposed action in their lives. Many have come to associate this promise personally in their times of trial, and as a collective promise for the people of God. I know I have, and it is my hope that others do also.

Ultimately, the best example of God's promise of restoration is the Son of God Himself, Jesus Christ. Jesus often performed works of restoration, such as healing the sick, raising the dead, and even forgiving sins.

These miracles can only be explained by the "restoring" power of God that was at work in Jesus' ministry. In Luke 4:18-19 (NIV), Jesus said that he was anointed by the Holy Spirit to *proclaim good news to the poor, to set the oppressed free, and to recover the sight. —* Luke 4:18-19 (NIV)

... of people who were blind. In both Isaiah's original prophecy and Jesus' declaration, restoration was as clearly marked as the work that God does and is still doing in the world. Jesus being God's Son was indeed the promised restorer, sent to us out of God's love for fallen humanity.

The death and resurrection of Jesus Christ are so crucial to the beautifully laid out plan of restoration. On the cross, the Son of God bore the weight of all human sin and brokenness. Then, by rising from the dead, Jesus conquered sin and death, paving the way for new life. Romans 6:4 (NIV) says this glorious truth,

We were therefore buried with him through baptism into death in order that, just as Christ was raised from the dead through the glory of the Father, we too may live a new life. — Romans 6:4 (NIV)

This new life is the essence of restoration, transformation from death to life, and from brokenness to wholeness. Praise God!

In the most dramatic of ways, restoration got its greatest demonstration. This was the sum of God's plan. Christ's suffering and ultimate sacrifice brought healing and reconciliation to humanity, both then (for the original hearers and readers) and now (for all who repent and believe).

But he was pierced for our transgressions, he was crushed for our iniquities; the punishment that brought us peace was on him, and by his wounds we are healed. — Isaiah 53:5 (NIV)

Furthermore, the theme of restoration is not just a grand, overreaching concept, but also a personal reality for every believer.

Therefore, if anyone is in Christ, the new creation has come: The old has gone, the new is here! — 2 Corinthians 5:17 (NIV)

This verse describes the personal transformation that occurs when one becomes a follower of Christ.

Restoration is an ongoing process in the life of a believer. Philippians 1:6 (NIV) also assures us of this:

being confident of this, that he who began a good work in you will carry it on to completion until the day of Christ Jesus.
— Philippians 1:6 (NIV)

This passage proves that God is continually working in our lives, shaping us to become more like Christ. This process, known also as sanctification, is a journey of restoration where God heals our wounds, renews our minds, and transforms our hearts and our lives from glory to glory!

As believers, we often tend to live in the tension between the "already" and the "not yet." Humanity as a whole has anxiety over waiting in general. Right? We experience certain aspects of God's restoration now, but we also do tend to look expectantly forward to its complete fulfillment in the uncertain future. This hope shapes our lives and should also motivate us to participate in God's restorative work and plan.

Romans 8:18 (Amplified) is a snapshot of this tension and hope:

For I consider [from the standpoint of faith] that the sufferings of the present life are not worthy to be compared with the glory that is about to be revealed to us and in us! — Romans 8:18 (Amplified)

This verse reminds us that our current sufferings and the brokenness of the world are temporary, and that God's grace is sufficient. The glory that will be revealed far outweighs the present difficulties, and we, along with all creation, eagerly await the full realization of God's restorative work and plan for us.

We must understand that while we await the ultimate restoration, we are also called to be agents of restoration in the world. Jesus commissioned His followers/disciples to continue His work, empowered by the Holy Spirit.

In Matthew 28:18-20 (NIV), He commands...

All authority in heaven and on earth has been given to me.
Therefore, go and make disciples of all nations, baptizing them
in the name of the Father and of the Son and of the Holy Spirit,
and teaching them to obey everything I have commanded you.
And surely I am with you always, to the very end of the age. —
Matthew 28:18-20 (NIV)

This Great Commission is a call to each of us believers in Christ to participate in God's restorative mission. As we make disciples, we are helping to restore people to a right relationship with God. The body of Christ should be a community where restoration is lived out and extended to others in the same way Jesus did 2000 years ago.

THINGS TO PONDER...

In practical terms, participating in God's restorative work involves acts of compassion, justice, and most of all reconciliation.

1. In what ways might you begin to participate more in God's restoration in the earth and natural realm?

   _____

   _____

   _____

   _____

   _____

   _____

2. In what ways might you begin to participate more in God's restoration in the spirit realm?

   _____

   _____

   _____

   _____

   _____

   _____

3. I would like to encourage you to fast, pray, and make a list of Ten acts of Faith and works of Restoration that you can begin to participate in now, and in times ahead.

   _____

   _____

   _____

   _____

_____

_____

It is apparent that we are currently living in the end times of biblical prophecy, and therefore, there is no time like NOW to begin or continue to walk in restoration and the redemptive power of God, partnering with the Holy Spirit!

> *[Rather] is this not the fast which I choose, To undo the bonds of wickedness, To tear to pieces the ropes of the yoke, To let the oppressed go free And break apart every [enslaving] yoke?*
>
> *Is it not to divide your bread with the hungry and bring the homeless poor into the house; when you see the naked, that you cover him, and not to hide yourself from [the needs of] your own flesh and blood?*
>
> *Then your light will break out like the dawn, And your healing (restoration, new life) will quickly spring forth; Your righteousness will go before you [leading you to peace and prosperity], The glory of the Lord will be your rear guard."*
>
> *And the Lord will continually guide you, and satisfy your soul in scorched and dry places, And give strength to your bones; And you will be like a watered garden, And like a spring of water whose waters do not fail. And your people will rebuild the ancient ruins; You will raise up and restore the age-old foundations [of buildings that have been laid waste]; You will be called Repairer of the Breach, Restorer of Streets with Dwellings.*
> *— Isaiah 58:6-8;11-12 (AMP)*

This verse testifies to the importance of using our voice and acts concerning injustices, helping those in need, working toward unity and healing to restore many aspects of our own lives and others as well. It will become apparent that when we do this, we are showing God's desire for restoration as well as spreading his love and grace.

I pray that this devotional message has shown and made known God's commitment to renewing and changing our lives, and is also an offering of hope and comfort to those who seek healing and redemption through Him. For his Grace is sufficient, and hope is always a guiding light that leads us towards a fulfilling and restored life with Jesus.

Shalom.

Dear Heavenly Father,

As we conclude this devotional time with you, we pray with open hearts full of thanksgiving for this journey we have been on to fully understand Your restoration in our lives. We thank You for the hope, healing, and transformation You offer us Lord, and we ask for Your continued guidance and presence in our lives.

Please give us the strength to surrender to Your will, the courage to forgive as You have forgiven us, and the faith to trust in Your faithfulness to us in times of trials, because You are good no matter what.

I pray that we remain pure in heart and vessels for Your restoration in this world, as we encourage Your light and love to those around us. Lord, help us to walk in obedience and surrender to Your plans and purposes. We know that Your ways are higher than ours, and Your restoration may even be beyond our understanding at this moment. Yet, as we look forward to the promise of eternal restoration in Your presence, I ask that You fill us with grace, peace, and joy that comes every morning as we meditate on Your renewal, and may YOUR NAME be glorified in all that we do now and to come.

In Jesus's Name, Amen!

Arlana Holland Scola

Arlana is a Best-Selling Author, Soul Care coach, Corporate Wellness officer, and the founder and host of the *Renegade Women and Soul Care* podcast. She has been a featured expert panelist on various of the *Kingdom View* TV shows.

Arlana has a Master's Degree in Theology and has the special gift of encouraging others to care for their souls so that they can successfully achieve their own calling. Her specialty is equipping and empowering people to reach their goals. To this date she has equipped and empowered thousands!

For years she was a certified speaker for Stonecroft ministries where she impacted nearly ten thousand women. She is also the founder of the *Ruby Red Slippers Way* and the *Renegade Women and Soul Care Way*.

Arlana loves the outdoors, loves photography and loves horseback riding. She lives in San Diego with her husband, she has two sons and three grandchildren.

therubyredslippers.com

Day 24

Arlana Holland Scola

Authority in Christ

> *And he said to him, "I will give you all their authority and splendor; it has been given to me, and I can give it to anyone I want to. If you worship me, it will all be yours.*
> *— Luke 4:6-7 (NIV)*

In the book of Esther talks about *"a time such as this,"* well that time is now for us to realize and understand our authority in Christ! It is EASY to say and oftentimes hard to do!

As we consider this, let's think about the fact that God gave us His authority in the book of Genesis. First, He made everything perfect for us and then He blessed us with the authority to rule the earth. And thus, we began our lifelong struggle with accepting and standing within our God given authority.

What is authority in Christ? It is the belief in the fact that we possess spiritual power and influence because of the blood of Christ. We are given confidence and assurance in the words within the Bible because of this belief, and the authority that is bestowed upon us because of this belief.

Many years ago when I was in seminary, I attended a women's mini retreat. We were asked to take forty-five minutes to sit quietly with God and listen to what He had to tell each of us. I could not get comfortable in this room full of people. I changed my seat several times and finally left the room and was able to find some peace and quiet for myself. This is what the Lord shared with me:

Out of the Shadows

I (Arlana) have come out of the shadows, crept out of the cave of darkness and despair, following the light of God, crawling on my knees. Crying out for God's touch. Sure, that death was near, lurking in my heart, waiting for just the right time to destroy my soul. Mercy said no. Grace said no.

God said *"I will open your eyes to see me, I will mend your heart to love me, I will cherish your soul. I have work for you, you belong to Me and no one else. I have been the light on your path even when your eyes were closed. Because before I created you, I knew what you would do, and who you would become.*

You have hidden My Word in your heart. You are My gracious lovely daughter. You are strong, you are powerful, you are divine. I will continue to hold your hand as you share My love and My words with others. I will be there if you become afraid. The wind may come, the storms may blow, but I will carry you with My Words that you may carry others."

Within these words above, I realized that I was called into MY authority in Christ in that moment, and I have spent years refining what this means, and how to strengthen this authority in the midst of a fallen world. He has given to you and called you into this AUTHORITY as well!

There is the authority we are given in the Old Testament where God intercedes and takes care of us and provides for our needs and also there is the authority administered to us in the New Testament through the blood of Christ which lives and breathes within us during every moment of our lives here on earth.

We are going to look at how God calls us *"Out of the Shadows"* to stand in our authority. Sometimes, as women we think that we need permission to stand in authority. This is the lie! We were given authority, and we DO NOT need to ask for what is already ours. We have kingdom authority bestowed upon us, divine authority, and we are called to demonstrate this to others.

In the Old Testament, authority was from the outside in and in the New Testament our authority is from the inside out.

Now let's venture "out of the shadows" and into your God given authority!

The first Old Testament prophet was Isaiah and in chapter 61 he declares what still stands true for each of us today. A call to, and a declaration of, our authority. This is Isaiah prophesying to each and every one of us. Isaiah is considered to be the greatest of all of the prophets. It was the prophet's role to speak for God to His people in the Old Testament.

The Year of the LORD's Favor—Isaiah 61 (NIV)

"The Spirit of the Sovereign LORD is on me, because the LORD has anointed me to proclaim good news to the poor.

He has sent me to bind up the brokenhearted, to proclaim freedom for the captives and release from darkness for the prisoners, to proclaim the year of the LORD's favor and the day of vengeance of our God, to comfort all who mourn, and provide for those who grieve in Zion— to bestow on them a crown of beauty instead of ashes, the oil of joy instead of mourning, and a garment of praise instead of a spirit of despair.

They will be called oaks of righteousness, a planting of the LORD for the display of his splendor. They will rebuild the ancient ruins and restore the places long devastated;

they will renew the ruined cities that have been devastated for generations. Strangers will shepherd your flocks;

foreigners will work your fields and vineyards.

And you will be called priests of the Lord, you will be named ministers of our God.

You will feed on the wealth of nations, and in their riches you will boast. Instead of your shame you will receive double portion, and instead of disgrace you will rejoice in your inheritance. And so you will inherit a double portion in your land,

and everlasting joy will be yours

For I, the LORD, love justice; I hate robbery and wrongdoing. In my faithfulness I will reward my people and make an everlasting covenant with them. Their descendants will be known among the nations and their offspring among the peoples.

All who see them will acknowledge that they are a people the LORD has blessed.

I delight greatly in the LORD; my soul rejoices in my God.

For he has clothed me with garments of salvation and arrayed me in a robe of his righteousness, as a bridegroom adorns his head like a priest, and as a bride adorns herself with her jewels.

For as the soil makes the sprout come up and a garden causes seeds to grow, so the Sovereign LORD will make righteousness and praise spring up before all nations."
— Isaiah 61 (NIV)

We have been anointed and given authority to claim the good news. We have been anointed and given the authority to bind up the broken hearted. We have been given authority to set the captives free. We have been given authority to release prisoners from darkness.

We have been given authority to give them a crown instead of ashes. We have been given authority to give them the oil of joy instead of mourning. We have been given authority to give them the garment of praise instead of despair.

We have been given authority to stand as oaks of righteousness. We have been given authority to rebuild broken things. We have been given authority to restore things that are devastated.

We have been given authority over shame. We have been given authority to receive a double portion. We have been given authority to stand in the face of disgrace and to rejoice in our blessings.

We have been given authority to have everlasting joy. We have been given authority to reward people for their sorrows. We have been given authority to be a blessed people. We have been given authority to delight in the Lord.

We have been given authority to wear the garments of salvation and we have been given the authority to stand in his righteousness.

The authority that God has blessed us with is truly a constellation of strengths. The authority that we have been given is an eternal covenant which cannot be broken.

We have been given divine authority, kingdom authority, teaching authority, authority through humility, universal authority and all of that authority is multifaceted because of Christ's shed blood.

As we consider our personal God given authority, I want to mention some biblical women that have gone before us and stood strong in the authority bestowed upon them, and how they can continue to be an influence to us today. I will not go into each of their stories, I will leave that to you.

Mary, Jesus' mother, Ruth, Rebecca, Mary Magdalene, Susanna, Phoebe, Joanna, Rachel, Esther, Elizabeth, Mariam, Deborah, Hannah, Abigail, Hagar, Rahab, Mary and Martha, Lazarus' sisters, Lydia, Priscilla, Naomi, just to mention a few.

Each of these women have been in the shadows and found their way forward into their strength and their calling filled with God's authority. It looks different for every single woman that has ever lived and will ever live. What does standing in your specific authority look like for you, and what are you doing with your authority? God bestowed it upon us so that we could change the world in His name, one soul at a time.

There are times when we are afraid and don't really believe that we have what it takes to live out our authority in the world. God calls us out of the wilderness, out of the shadows, out of the darkness of brokenness and despair. We must trust, have faith, and believe in the calling.

Remember God's grace and mercy said that we could not be stopped. He has work for us to do, we belong to Him, and no one else! We are called to share His love and words with others. Each of our stories are for the people that God sends to us. We may never even know the effect our presence and authority has on a person until we get to Heaven.

There is glory in your story, in your challenge, and in your victory. Share it! Jesus came to earth with authority from God to teach humanity that they have authority. We have been talking about His story, His glory and His authority for over two thousand years. He died on the cross for us so that we could stand in His authority and tell our story of victory.

God is calling us higher with our story, and the authority He has given us. We have been given permission to unleash this authority into the world to change it. "For such a time as this" we are called. In the midst of a world that is full of discord and confusion, we are called. In a world where fear is a common word and common experience, we are called. In times like these we need to put on the armor of God and stand in our authority and fight for the love of Christ. Our authority gives us calm in the storm! And we are in the midst of a storm, a storm to keep us from God.

Stand in your glory and your authority and tell your story! The world needs what you have been through. The world needs to hear how God brought you through and restored your soul. Put the authority bestowed upon you into action. Be the change God created you to be!

THINGS TO PONDER...

1. Have you taken time to consider that we were given authority at the beginning of the book of Genesis? Think about that.

    _____

    _____

    _____

    _____

    _____

    _____

2. It's time to come out of the shadows. What steps will you take to come out of the shadows and into the light of your authority in Christ? Think about that.

    _____

    _____

    _____

    _____

    _____

    _____

3. Spend some time with Isaiah 61 and see how God speaks to you and demonstrates your authority and him to be shared with the world.

_____

_____

_____

_____

_____

_____

Dr. MB Busch

Dr. MB Busch is the President of *Heartbeat of Heaven Ministries* and a prophetic voice to the Body of Christ. She preaches that King Jesus can summon anyone out of darkness, and her passion is to set the captives free from any form of bondage, and to reveal the love of the Father.

Dr. Busch studied through the Bethel Supernatural School of Ministry. Redding, CA and The Patricia King Institute. She holds an Honorary Doctorate from Dayspring Theological University. She is married to Jeff, and both are certified inner-healing and deliverance counselors through Elijah House.

facebook.com/mb.busch.9

Day 25

Dr. MB Busch

His Wondrous Works

That I may publish with the voice of thanksgiving,
and tell of all Thy wondrous works.
— Psalm 26:7 (KJV)

God is still in the miracle business. How do I know? On January 31, 2008, upon receiving the baptism of the Holy Spirit, I was instantly and completely delivered from thirty years of alcoholism, drug addiction, and bulimia.

When the power of God hit me, I literally felt a demonic oppression leave, and with it, the desire to use alcohol or drugs ever again. I was a baby Christian, less than 90 days old, still sucking on a pacifier. I didn't have great faith. I didn't "walk out" my healing, nor would I have known how. All I knew was that the Creator of Heaven and Earth breathed on me, baptizing me with His Holy Spirit, and I was instantly set free.

I now understand that miracles are often received through people who have been given the gift of miracles from Holy Spirit (1 Corinthians 12:10). Joan Hunter is a personal friend of mine, and I have watched Holy Spirit move mightily through her to perform miracles and healings. Joan's ministry exists to equip believers to take the healing power of God outside the four walls of the church to the four corners of the Earth.

Who Held Back the Snow?

I met Michael in recovery eighteen years ago. Due to the anonymity of Alcoholics Anonymous, we will call him Michael. We didn't stay in contact, but years later I had an occasion to visit him at his business. During our visit, I learned that he had been "circling the drain" for two years. We refer to a person in this state as a dry drunk. He was actually planning a relapse for that coming Christmas, but God intervened.

Michael had been feeling nostalgic for Christmases gone by and, in his mind, there were certain conditions that needed to be met before he would follow through with his planned relapse. He had purchased the cognac, he had the location, and he had the Christmas music. But what he didn't have was the snow.

Jesus said, *"The thief comes to steal, kill, and destroy"* (John 10:10). The enemy of Michael's soul had a target on his back and thought it would only be a matter of time before his plan for Michael's life would come to fruition. The attack was so oppressive that it ultimately led him to end a fourteen-year relationship with the woman he was engaged to. The break up nearly destroyed him. He was traumatized, full of shame, tormented with grief, and riddled with anxiety.

As the months went on, Michael became overwhelmingly worse until he ended up in the emergency room. It was there that the doctors put him on five medications—four for depression and anxiety and one antipsychotic. He was circling the drain at a rapid pace, speeding toward the bottom.

It was December of 2023, and I knew that Michael needed a miracle. He was in traditional therapy, attending regular recovery meetings, and was heavily medicated. Yet none of this was setting his soul free from the trauma. I had prayed for God to intervene and set a plan in motion. Joan Hunter was in town teaching from her healing school curriculum. My thinking was, *If I could just get Michael there, God will work mightily though Joan, and he will get his miracle.* There was no question in my mind. It had already been settled in heaven and was about to manifest on earth.

Michael had hit bottom and was desperate to be free, so I didn't have to persuade him to see Joan. I had texted Joan in advance regarding his affliction. Of course, on the ride there, the enemy attacked Michael, and he began crying out, "God doesn't care about me. He's not hearing me because He's not answering my prayers!" I let him continue his rant because I knew that freedom was on his doorstep.

We arrived at Josiah Center and immediately went to a private room to await Joan's arrival. It was difficult to keep Michael calm while he was in such an agitated state but, somehow, I managed. It seemed like an eternity before Joan finally arrived. When she eventually got to us it was obvious to her that Michael needed a miracle and that this was no ordinary deliverance. In fact, when another group of people walked into our private area, Joan barked at them to leave immediately.

The stage was set for God to move mightily. Joan, myself, and two of her trained healing ministers gathered around Michael. He began to tell Joan how his downward spiral began a year earlier when he planned a relapse for Christmas. She asked him why he didn't follow through with it. He explained that the conditions had to be just right. The first one was that it had to be snowing, but it never snowed. "Michael," she said, "WHO do you think held back the snow?" Instantly, he was undone.

Joan went on to tell Michael that God DID in fact hear his prayers and that He wanted to set him free. She then proceeded to break off all trauma, shame, fear, grief, word curses, and depression, while the rest of us warred in the spirit. *"Now therefore, stand and see this GREAT thing which the LORD will do before your eyes!"* (1 Samuel 12:16 NKJV) (emphasis mine).

After a few minutes, all of us witnessed Michael's countenance completely reverse into one of peace and joy. All demonic oppression had been lifted. Who the Son set free—Michael—was FREE INDEED (John 8:36). Desperation had driven Michael to his knees and to a place of complete surrender. Today Michael has an intimate relationship with Jesus, he is off all medication, and he is doing service work for Alcoholics Anonymous.

This is a perfect example of David and Goliath. When David slew the giant, it wasn't the stone that killed him. The stone merely knocked him down. David then took Goliath's own sword—the weapon that was fashioned against him—and used it to cut off Goliath's head. Similarly, the enemy had used addiction, and the trauma associated with it, against Michael. But he turned that sword back on the enemy to help others who still suffer.

To grant us that we, being delivered from the hand of our enemies, might serve Him WITHOUT FEAR, in holiness and righteousness before Him all the days of our life.
— Luke 1:74–75 (NKJV) (emphasis mine).

These two examples of God's miracle-working power are very different. Mine was accomplished simply through God's power hitting me upon receiving the baptism of the Holy Spirit. And yet, I wasn't asking or believing for deliverance. I had already been sober for a year and *did not even know* that healing for addiction was available to me. I was taught that alcoholism was an incurable disease and that I would have it for the rest of my life. Wrong! Jesus shed His blood to heal us from all disease.

On the other hand, Michaels's miracle was accomplished through the laying on of hands, by the gift of miracles that Joan has been given by God. Holy Spirit used her as a vessel to heal Michael.

> *O Lord, my healing God, I cried out for a miracle and you healed*
> *me! You brought me back from the brink of death, from the depths*
> *below. Now here I am, alive and well, fully restored!*
> — *Psalm 30:2–3 (TPT)*

Who Held Back the River?

> *Then the priests who bore the ark of the covenant of the LORD*
> *STOOD FIRM on dry ground in the midst of the Jordan; and*
> *ALL of Israel crossed over on dry ground, until ALL the people*
> *had crossed COMPLETELY over the Jordan.*
> — *Joshua 3:17 (NKJV) (emphasis mine)*

Recently, through the entire night in a dream, I walked with Jesus as He discussed with me Joshua chapter three. He told me how God waited for the Jordan floodplain to flood before He parted the waters for Israel to cross into the Promised Land. Many Bible scholars say that it was a bigger miracle than the parting of the Red Sea because it was during the flood season of the Jordan. Let's unpack how this miracle applies to the modern-day believer:

> *"Then Joshua rose early in the morning; and they set out from*
> *Acacia Grove and came to the Jordan, he and all the children of Israel,*
> *and lodged there before they crossed over. So it was, after three days,*
> *that the officers went through the camp; and they commanded the people,*
> *saying, 'When you see the ark of the covenant of the Lord your God,*
> *and the priests, the Levites, bearing it, then you shall set out from*
> *your place and go after it. Yet there shall be a space between you*

and it, about two thousand cubits by measure. Do not come near it,
that you may know the way by which you must go, for you have not
passed this way before.' And Joshua said to the people,
'Sanctify yourselves, for tomorrow the Lord will do wonders among you.'
— Joshua 3:1–5 (NKJV)

A personal revival of intimacy with the Lord paves the way for one to receive their inheritance and subsequent harvest. The ark of the covenant was representative of the LORD'S presence, and carried by the Levities, the ark advanced toward the Jordan's banks. The people were admonished to maintain a space of 2000 cubits—just a Sabbath's day journey—between themselves and the ark.

This space reminds the Christian that an attitude of Sabbath rest must lead, rather than drive, the believer into the revival of intimacy and eventual possession of spiritual and natural inheritance. This path is seldom taken and the Hebrew children had not traveled this route before. Revival of inheritance does not travel the well-trodden roads of tradition. Revival follows God's advancing presence into uncharted territories of promise. Let's look at the miracle that God performed for His children then and what He will do for the believer today:

"So Joshua said to the children of Israel, 'Come here, and hear
the words of the Lord your God.' And Joshua said, 'By this you shall
know that the living God is among you, and that He will without
fail drive out from before you the Canaanites and the Hittites and
the Hivites and the Perizzites and the Girgashites and the Amorites
and the Jebusites: Behold, the ark of the covenant of the Lord of all the
earth is crossing over before you into the Jordan. Now therefore, take for
yourselves twelve men from the tribes of Israel, one man from every tribe.
And it shall come to pass, as soon as the soles of the feet of the priests who
bear the ark of the Lord, the Lord of all the earth, shall rest in the waters
of the Jordan, that the waters of the Jordan shall be cut off, the waters

that come down from upstream, and they shall stand as a heap.'
So it was, when the people set out from their camp to cross over the
Jordan, with the priests bearing the ark of the covenant before the people,
and as those who bore the ark came to the Jordan, and the feet of the
priests who bore the ark dipped in the edge of the water (for the Jordan
overflows all its banks during the whole time of harvest), that the waters
which came down from upstream stood still, and rose in a heap very far
away at Adam, the city that is beside Zaretan. So the waters that went
down into the Sea of the Arabah, the Salt Sea, failed, and were cut off;
and the people crossed over opposite Jericho. Then the priests who bore the
ark of the covenant of the Lord stood firm on dry ground in the midst of
the Jordan; and all Israel crossed over on dry ground, until all the people
had crossed completely over the Jordan."
—Joshua 3:9–17 (NKJV)

Inconvenient and uncomfortable situations characterize revival and harvest. The flooded Jordan presented the tribes with a serious problem. Yet God had commanded His people to cross this rampaging waterway in the most perilous of times—at flood stage.

The ark of the covenant, borne by the anointed Levites, set out before the people. Trusting and trembling, the ark-bearers set their feet into the troubled waters and watched a miracle take place. Christians should consider that when life's situations flood the banks of their human experience, revival and harvest are potentially on the horizon.

The River Jordan was symbolically flooded during the season of barley harvest. Barley is representative of a type of spiritual harvest from the preaching of the Word during difficult times. So, those who desire to harvest the fruits of God's Word must be willing to follow God's presence into tumultuous territory, trusting Him to lead them on dry ground to a harvest on the other side. Just as the Lord did for the children of Israel, He will do for the believer today.

And Joshua said, "By this you shall know that the living God is among you, and that He will without fail drive out from before you the Canaanites and the Hittites and the Hivites and the Perizzites and the Girgashites and the Amorites and the Jebusites: Behold, the ark of the covenant of the Lord of all the earth is crossing over before you into the Jordan."
— Joshua 3:10–11 (NKJV)

Jesus goes before us and clears the path of stumbling blocks—all the hurdles that the enemy has set before us. Notice that the Scripture says, "Without fail." Recently He spoke this word to me:

The baptism of fire My church is about to go through is not for the faint of heart. This purging is necessary for My TRUE bride to rise up from the ashes triumphant, without spot or wrinkle (on her wedding gown). Beware and "be aware" of the hurdles that the devil puts in front of you, as they are designed to cause you to stumble and fall. But fear not, My overcomer! For I will be there to guide you over and around each one. So take My hand, and watch Me go to war on your behalf. We have just begun a great journey, and I am there to equip you for this end time battle. And you shall overcome every fiery dart the enemy sends your way.

About two years ago, a woman working in the café at my gym approached me. She said she had a dream where she saw me on a road holding Jesus by the hand. He was leading me around every pothole in the road so I wouldn't stumble and fall. Wow! Amazing God!

Beloved, what you are going through is no surprise to God. We all have times of tests and trial, and sufferings. We may be wandering in a spiritual wilderness for a season but rest is coming. In the meantime, He will provide for you as He did for the children of Israel. They had fresh manna every day! True rest is when we place our trust in Jesus Christ and Him alone.

God wants to bring a mighty invasion of power into your life. Perhaps there are a few things that the Lord has to correct before He does. When a river flows, it must have banks. Otherwise a flood can destroy a large amount of land. We're all hungry for the river but we must have some banks or boundaries. Benny Hinn said, *"We have to be able to say: This is not of God. It's over here, not over there. So much work today is pure flesh, yet people have labeled it as of the Spirit. It is not the Spirit because it is not centered on Christ."*

Beloved, are you ready to walk on dry ground into your promised land? God is ready, willing, and able to move heaven and Earth for you. Press into Him more than ever, and watch Him go to war on your behalf. I will leave you with the words of King David as he was placing the ark of the covenant in the Tabernacle of David and instituting praise and worship day and night:

Oh, give thanks to the LORD! Call upon His name; make known His deeds among the peoples! Sing to Him, sing psalms to Him; talk of all His wondrous works! — 1 Chronicles 16:8-9 (NKJV)

THINGS TO PONDER...

1. Do you believe God is still in the miracle business?

    _____

    _____

_____

_____

_____

_____

2. Can you remember a time when you needed a miracle and God provided it for you?

_____

_____

_____

_____

_____

3. How did that affect you and those around you?

_____

_____

_____

_____

_____

Mandy Leigh

Mandy Leigh is the Survivor On Fire Transformation Coach. She is a conference/retreat speaker and facilitator and a Best Selling Author. Her story includes overcoming abuse, sex trafficking, addiction, divorce and mental health disorders. She now Coaches trauma survivors to rise up out of the ashes of their past so they can burn bright in a dark world. She takes them on the journey from the pit to the platform, coaching them to break the silence, cultivate their authentic voice, and share their story with the world. Her mission is to shift the culture for Christ through 100,000 survivor stories by 2030.

facebook.com/mandy.leigh555
www.survivoronfire.com
instagram.com/coachmandyleigh

Day 26

Mandy Leigh

The Truth About Restoration

Come, let us return to the Lord; for he has torn us, that he may heal us; he has struck us down, and he will bind us up.
— *Hosea 6:1 (ESV)*

Restoration is messy, let's face it. The word restoration always sounds so inviting... so welcoming, and something we all desire... until it comes time to go through the process. If you have ever worked on restoring an old house or an old car, then you know what I mean. It is a massive undertaking! Many times, you will have no idea how big of an undertaking it is until you are well into the project.

There are tearing down of walls, and ripping up of carpets, and floorboards. Many times, you may find mold or other infestations causing you to have to tear down more than anticipated. Often the old wiring needs to be ripped out and new wiring installed, not to mention, the plumbing!!

The project often seems endless! Many times, it is much easier to abandon the project, half done, than to persevere forward—and many often do. Continuing that push through and continue through to completion are almost always the ones that have a vision they just cannot let go of. They see the beauty in the old house, and they know the reward of restoration far outweighs the cost of the labor.

The same is true in our lives. Restoration does not always look like what we think it's going to look like. In fact, often it looks the exact opposite of what we think it should look like, and it doesn't feel any better either.

I know my restoration story began with me falling and severely injuring my neck! I was in a downward spiral in my life and going fast down a dead-end road. One night I was out at a night club, partying with a friend of mine and I thought it would be fun to attempt to reenact the scene from the movie *Dirty Dancing*. You know—the one where Patrick Swayze lifts Jennnifer Grey up above his head for "the lift"? (Come on, it's ok to admit you have watched the movie). Well, the truth is that neither one of us was trained for this type of move, and we were both highly intoxicated. I am sure you can imagine what happened next! The planned attempt failed miserably, and I ended up faceplanting headfirst onto the hard ground. Yes, it was a painful fall, but honestly, I was so intoxicated that I didn't even really feel anything until the next morning.

When I woke up, I could not move my head or my neck, because I was in so much pain. I went to the closest urgent care, and they immediately sent me to the trauma unit, at the hospital. Through a number of scans and MRI's they discovered an injury to my C3 and C5 vertebrae, and would not let me go home, and admitted me for overnight observation.

It was in that hospital room that God got ahold of me. He spoke to me with a voice so clear and calm and said *"You are a beautiful daughter of The Most High King. You are highly favored and deeply loved."* No one had ever spoken such beautiful words to me before in all my life. I knew these words were straight from the heart of God. I knew these were the words of my Heavenly Father.

Then He gave me a vision. In this vision, I saw a figure of the most beautiful woman I had ever seen in my life. She had long, dark flowing hair and she was wearing a beautiful white flowing gown. She was so peaceful, so serene... even ethereal. As I gazed at this woman, I realized that I knew her and it suddenly dawned on me that this was a vision of me, as my highest self, in my glorified being, and how God sees me. It was the most beautiful vision and the one that I clung to for the next few years as God continued the restoration process in my life.

It hasn't been easy, or pretty. It's been really hard and very, very messy. In fact, I've abandoned the project multiple times. But God! He always leads me back to His Vision for this old house. That vision has kept me going when I wanted to give up. It has given me so much hope, and inspiration, to know that there is a version of me that is so perfectly whole, and beautiful, and that all this hard work is going to be worth it one day. Just like someone that is working to restore an old house, or an old car does not give up because they have a vision of the end result.

The vision God gave me of myself in my perfectly restored being has kept me going and given me the fuel I needed when all I wanted to do was give up. You see, He has a plan for my life, and He won't stop working until who I am matches the way He created me, as long as I allow Him to do the work in me. He has a plan for your life too. In fact, He has a plan for the entire world. His plan is to restore the entire world and all created things unto Himself and establish an order of peace in place of chaos.

In Acts 3:20-21 (TPT) we read this: *"And he will send you Jesus, the Messiah, the appointed one. For he must remain in heaven until the restoration of all things has taken place, fulfilling everything that God said long ago through his holy prophets."*

The Greek word the author of this passage, Luke, uses here for restoration is the only time this word is used in the entire New Testament, and it is the word *apokatastasis* in the original Greek language. This word packs a powerful punch, and it literally means the restoration of ALL creation to the original state of perfection. That is God's plan for this world, and I believe for ALL created things. One day, ALL THINGS will be restored, according to everything God has said, including lands and cities, governments, and the relationship God has with human beings. God will establish an order of peace in place of chaos.

One of the Hebrew words for peace is Shalom. However, Shalom does not always come in the way we believe it should. It comes on the heels of conflict, and war, and violence, and is only obtained by tearing down, and ripping apart of old ordinances, customs, and societal structures.

If you break apart this Hebrew word, letter by letter, it literally means *"to destroy the authority that establishes chaos"* and that does not look or feel peaceful, at first. The breaking apart of an old pattern and the birthing of something new typically causes much pain and loss. The truth is that the restorative plan that God has for this earth will include much of the same. Everything as we know it will be challenged and confronted and we must be willing to tear down the old to establish the new. It will not look at all like peace at first, but God's plan of restoration will prevail, as He promised, to match His vision for His creation.

Just like in my life, and in your life, God has a vision of who you are in His eyes, according to how He created you. His plan is for who you are on earth to be just as you are in Heaven. He desires to restore you to the perfect version of yourself, just as He originally designed you to be. He desires to restore communion with you and be in deep intimacy with you. This is not just for some day when you get to Heaven! This process is happening right now, if you are willing, and if you will choose to embrace true SHALOM!

Will you welcome Shalom into your life and home, even if it is a painful process? Even if it means giving up who you are? Releasing the right to be "right"?

Letting God tear down your idols and altars that you've erected to yourself, your children, your spouse, your ministry, your business, your own comfort? Your religion? This will not be pretty. For a lot of us, this process is messy and scary and super painful, but oh, so necessary to place King Jesus in His rightful place in our lives and destroy the authority that establishes chaos and restores peace.

You are going to have to let go of everything you have ever known, and be willing to embrace the new, no matter what it looks like, and no matter what it feels like. It is going to challenge your cultural, societal, and religious norms, and it is going to cause a great deal of conflict. It is going to mean tearing down of things, and ripping out of things, in order that the new may be built up.

And they shall build up the ancient ruins; they shall raise up the former devastations; they shall repair the ruined cities, the devastations of many generations. —Isaiah 61:4 (ESV)

The truth is restoration is messy, but the reward of restoration is ALWAYS worth it.

And the Lord restored the fortunes of Job, when he had prayed for his friends. And the Lord gave Job twice as much as he had before. —Job 42:10 (ESV)

I will restore to you the years that the swarming locust has eaten, the hopper, the destroyer, and the cutter, my great army, which I sent among you. —Joel 2:25 (ESV)

Come, let us return to the Lord; for he has torn us, that he may heal us; he has struck us down, and he will bind us up. —Hosea 6:1 (ESV)

THINGS TO PONDER...

1. What areas of your life need to be torn down so that God may build you back up?

_____

_____

_____

_____

_____

_____

2. What does the restoration of all things mean to you? Do you believe all means all?

_____

_____

_____

_____

_____

_____

3. Ask God to give you a vision of you through His eyes, of how He created you. What does this vision look like? What do you think this will do for you?

_____

_____

_____

_____

_____

_____

_____

4. Are you willing to tear down anything God asks you to tear down in order to allow the new to be built?

_____

_____

_____

_____

_____

_____

_____

Libby George

Libby George is an International Award-winning Broadcaster, communicator, teacher, and prophetic inner healing practitioner. She is an anointed mentor specializing in restoring brokenness, and equips, and trains in prophetic soul healing.

Libby is an igniter and has a revelatory gift as a prophetic Seer to release revelatory strategies, raise leaders, and equip and activates holistic inner healing, prophetic intercession, deliverance, and purpose.

Libby trains individuals and groups offering a range of equipping programs from creating greater intimacy with God, prophetic foundations, to inner healing and powerful spiritual warfare strategies.

edenclinic.co.nz/

Day 27

Libby George

Reformation of the Heart

*They conquered him completely through the blood of the lamb
and the powerful word of his testimony. They triumphed because
they did not love and cling to their own lives,
even when faced with death.*
— Revelation 12:11 (TPT)

Positioning our heart for overflow and the profound transformation that comes from a surrendered life to God is the threshold of a refiner's fire. When we align our will with His, and truly surrender, we are at the mercy of the Master Craftsman. He will complete the good work in you He has begun. This is a partnership of surrender.

The Journey of Inner Healing

A life fully surrendered to God is the highest calling. It is this commitment that purifies our conscience so we can hold the mysteries of heaven in our hearts.

Over the years, my personal journey from darkness to light has revealed that the greatest treasures on earth are in the heart. Regardless of external circumstances, a heart aligned with God can experience true freedom and prosperity of soul and spirit, even amidst challenging trials.

Inner healing is an essential aspect of this journey. It involves unlocking spiritual senses and preparing the soul for stillness, so we can hear the voice of His faithful nature with greater clarity and insight.

Keys to Position Our Heart to Hear His Voice

Key 1: Posture Your Heart

Begin by finding a quiet place free from distractions. In this solitude, bring everything before the Throne of Grace: your burdens, passions, talents, health, finances, family, and circumstances. Surrender all before your King. This act of surrender is the first step in positioning your heart for overflow.

Imagine bringing all that weighs you down and all that brings you joy and laying it at the feet of Jesus. This symbolic act of placing everything before Him demonstrates your trust and dependence on His sovereignty. It is in this place of surrender that you begin to open your heart to the possibility of overflow.

Key 2: Reflection

Reflect on where the Holy Spirit is in your life right now. Allow Him to move like a gentle breeze, ministering to your heart. Be sensitive to His tangible presence and remember the mercies of God's grace in your life. Reflect on times when you experienced His faithfulness and were carried through storms. This reflection aligns your heart with His nature.

Think back to moments when you felt the undeniable presence of God guiding you, comforting you, and providing for you. Allow these memories to flood your heart with gratitude and awe. As you dwell on His goodness, your heart becomes fertile ground for His presence to overflow.

Key 3: Ask

Ask God to reveal His perspective to you. Seek His wisdom and guidance, asking Him to show you how He sees you and what His plans are for you. This act of asking open questions is a door to divine revelation and insight.

In your prayers, be specific about your requests. Ask God to illuminate areas of your life that need transformation. Seek His counsel on decisions you are facing and ask for His vision for your future. This posture of seeking and asking positions your heart to receive His direction and overflow with His wisdom.

Key 4: Trust

Trust in the revelations and insights you receive. Trust your sanctified imagination, your thoughts, your feelings, and impressions. What is God revealing to you right now? Trust that He is speaking to you and guiding you according to His will.

Trust requires a deep sense of surrender and a willingness to let go of control. It involves believing that God's plans are better than your own plans, and that His timing is perfect. As you cultivate trust, your heart opens wider to receive the overflow of His promises and purposes for your life.

Key 5: Revelation

Revelation asks for more revelation. Then, wait until you perceive and receive more. Reflect on what you have just experienced and journal your insights. This continual dialogue with the Holy Spirit deepens your understanding and trust in His guidance.

Revelation often comes in layers. As you spend time in God's presence, He reveals Himself and His plans for you. Keep a journal to document these moments of revelation. Reflect on them regularly and allow them to shape your heart and mind. This ongoing process of revelation positions you to live in a constant state of overflow.

Reformation of the Heart

Becoming more like Christ, and living a life that honors Him, is a continuous journey of growth, learning, and deepening our relationship with God. It involves a willingness to self-examine and surrender. It requires confronting areas in our lives that are not always easy to acknowledge or face; yet, essential for experiencing the fullness of abiding in and aligning with His will.

Jesus said,

Whoever finds their life will lose it, and whoever loses their life for my sake will find it. — Matthew 10:39 (NIV)

This paradoxical statement underscores the importance of surrendering our lives to gain true life in Him. The suffering we experience is the process of dying to oneself, allowing the old man to be put to death so that Christ may live in us.

Lessons from Peter and Judas

The stories of Peter and Judas offer profound lessons in managing the heart. Peter, despite his passion, was overcome by fear and denied Jesus three times. Yet, the Holy Spirit transformed him from a self-centered coward into a great leader and founding Apostle. Judas, on the other hand, was consumed by offense and betrayal, leading to his destruction. Both loved Jesus, but their responses to their failures differed significantly. Peter's repentance and transformation through the Holy Spirit exemplify the potential for renewal and surrender.

Peter's story reminds us that failure is not the end. When we repent and allow the Holy Spirit to work in our lives, we can be restored and used mightily for God's Kingdom. Judas' story, however, serves as a warning of the dangers of harboring offense and not seeking reconciliation with God.

These contrasting outcomes highlight the importance of managing our hearts well and continually surrendering our introspective perceptions to God's will.

A Call to Obedience

Jesus' journey to the cross is the ultimate example of obedience and surrender. In the Garden of Gethsemane, Jesus expressed His anguish and desire to avoid suffering, yet He surrendered to God's will, saying,

Not my will, but yours be done. — Luke 22:42 (NIV)

This act of obedience paved the way for our redemption and reconciliation with God.

Abraham's faith journey also illustrates this call to obedience. His trust in God was greater than his trust in his own emotions and logic. To walk in this kind of relationship with God, we must lose our lives according to His purposes, aligning our will with His.

Obedience often requires stepping out in faith, even when the path is unclear, or the cost is high. It involves trusting that God's ways are higher than our ways and that His plans are for our good, and not to harm us. As we walk in obedience, we position our hearts to experience the overflow of His blessings and the fulfillment of His promises. Trust and faith are our constant companions and the enduring fortresses that thrust us forward, yet protect the advance.

Reformation is a Practical Process

Reformation is a practical process of transformation. Practical steps for reforming our hearts involve a logical process. It always begins with an ability to be honest with oneself and allows us to pull down the objections and the walls that we use to protect ourselves.

Developing the skill to self-examine oneself with grace and acceptance while partnering with conviction produces a pure heart. When we can examine ourselves without judgment and shame, then we can receive grace to heal.

Truth realigns our identity with God's will and purposes. When we resist aligning with Him, we continue to stay stuck in the mindsets of pain and trauma. We struggle to heal.

When you reflect on God's faithfulness by recalling moments of His intervention and the grace in your life, allow these memories to take you into a greater depth and capacity of gratitude. It is here that you will find your strength and trust in Him.

Relationships Reflect the Measure of a Person's Heart

Are you quick to forgive, or are you easily offended and keep a record of those who wronged you?

The whole earth was cursed by the fall of Adam and Eve and eagerly awaited the day for the revealing of God's lineage to take back their rightful place over the earth.

All atonement and supplication for our transgressions have been certified, verified, and stamped "endorsed." Yet how many of us toy with the thoughts of revenge and unforgiveness of heart when we are wronged?

Jesus told us to turn the other cheek, forgive 70 x 7 times, and prefer and consider others greater than ourselves. This is God's ultimate plan.

In the book of Genesis, we see two significant moments where Joseph, who was sold as a slave by his brothers, many years later confronts his brothers with a spirit of forgiveness, highlighting his understanding of God's overarching plan and his willingness to forgive their transgressions against him.

God's Warning to Cain

Then the Lord said to Cain, 'Why are you angry? Why is your face downcast? If you do what is right, will you not be accepted? But if you do not do what is right, sin is crouching at your door; it desires to have you, but you must rule over it.
— Genesis 4:6-7 (NIV)

When God warns Cain about the danger of harboring anger and resentment. This is a timeless lesson on the importance of self-awareness, self-control, and moral responsibility. It teaches that while negative desires and emotions confront us, we have the power and responsibility to master them, choosing actions and outcomes that align with the divine will of God.

The discretion of a man makes him slow to anger, and his glory is to overlook a transgression. — Proverbs 19:11 (NKJV)

The manifestation of God's transformation has a tangible impact on the relationship we have with others. If you are not seeing this, then ask God why? Ask Him if there is something you are missing. A blind spot, or an oversight? For it is in relationships where love shows up, or it shows us we simply do not have it. You cannot avoid the process of love, genuine growth, submission, forgiveness, and unity. This is a vital part of the purging process when it comes to true reformation of the heart.

The Power of Inner Healing

Inner healing is a vital part of positioning our hearts for overflow. It involves addressing past wounds, traumas, and lies that hinder our relationship with God and others.

One effective approach to inner healing is the practice of "clean language" in prayer. This means praying open-ended questions with the Holy Spirit and having an expectation of faith to receive the unexpected reply.

I call this clean language. A term used in counseling circles, where we ask open-ended questions without judgment or a preconceived assumption. In other words, if you come to God with an agenda, a set list of requests, and God has something He wants to convey or reveal to you, you could easily miss what God is wanting to impart to you. He often wants to give us much more than we can imagine.

When you come to pray and engage in God's presence, you are coming before the Throne of Grace. You are entering the Holy of Holies with the Divine Creator and Sovereign Majesty, Lord, and Creator our God.

Living in the Overflow

You were created to shift atmospheres with the presence of God living inside and through you. You are a vessel that carries all the promises of heaven inside you. Once you realize it is not about you, but more about your humility, reliance, and surrender, then the overflow of heaven will flow with greater power and impact through you.

Peter's shadow healed the sick. Yet this was not about how great Peter was. It was about the grace of God that flowed through Him and the calling on his life to lead and birth the church. In his human frailty, he still struggled with his instinct for Hebrew culture and religious conditioning.

Yet his calling graced him with the supernatural outpouring of the Holy Spirit. His surrendered humility allowed God to move powerfully through him.

Allowing God to reform your heart and purify your heart. Draws you into the overflow of God's fullness of presence and power. It involves continually seeking His guidance, trusting His plans, and obeying His commands. It means being a vessel of His love and grace, ready to be poured out and to pour out the river of God that flows from His throne to others.

Conclusion

May this chapter inspire you to position your heart for overflow, allowing God's presence to permeate every aspect of your life, reforming and transforming you into a vessel of His love and grace. So be it, Amen.

Activation Exercise: Heart Restoration

When you wake in the mornings and before you fall asleep, a great practice is to ask the Holy Spirit if there is anything in your heart that needs attention? Ask the Holy Spirit, would you scan my heart and reveal anything that would deter me from my path or from hearing and aligning with your ways and your will?

Next, ask God to reveal His perspective to you. Seek His wisdom and guidance, asking Him to show you how He sees you and what His plans are for you. This act of asking open questions is a door to divine revelation and insight.

In your prayers, be specific about your requests. Ask God to illuminate areas of your life that need transformation. Seek His counsel on decisions you are facing and ask for His vision for your future. This posture of seeking and asking positions your heart to receive His direction and overflow with His wisdom.

THINGS TO PONDER...

1. Find a Quiet Place: Create a peaceful environment where you can focus on God without distractions.

   _____

   _____

   _____

   _____

   _____

2. Invite the Holy Spirit: Ask the Holy Spirit to be present and to guide you through the reconciliation and healing process.

   _____

   _____

   _____

   _____

   _____

3. Surrender to God: Lay the things revealed before God and ask Him to realign your heart and mind with His truth.

   _____

_____

_____

_____

_____

_____

4. Release Forgiveness: Repent from partnering with the things God has revealed to you. Turn away from what is not from God in your heart and release forgiveness to others and yourself.

_____

_____

_____

_____

_____

5. Receive Healing: Allow God to minister to your heart and receive His love and grace.

_____

_____

_____

_____

_____

_____

6. Journal Your Experience and Ask for More: Write down the revelations and insights you receive. But never assume God has finished with you. He is always wanting to engage more with you. So even when you receive insight, ask Him if there is more He wants to reveal to you. And wait... often, He just wants to blow you away!

_____

_____

_____

_____

_____

_____

7. Thanksgiving and Praise: Reflect on God's grace and His goodness towards you. Enter His gates with thanksgiving and his inner courts with praise.

_____

_____

_____

_____

_____

Dr. MB Busch

Dr. MB Busch is the President of *Heartbeat of Heaven Ministries* and a prophetic voice to the Body of Christ. She preaches that King Jesus can summon anyone out of darkness, and her passion is to set the captives free from any form of bondage, and to reveal the love of the Father.

Dr. Busch studied through the Bethel Supernatural School of Ministry. Redding, CA and The Patricia King Institute. She holds an Honorary Doctorate from Dayspring Theological University. She is married to Jeff, and both are certified inner-healing and deliverance counselors through Elijah House.

facebook.com/mb.busch.9

Day 28

Dr. MB Busch

Picking Up Your Mantle

For many are called, but few are chosen.
— Matthew 22:14 (NKJV)

"*For many are called, but few are chosen.*" These are the words of Jesus.

In today's fast-paced society, I find that so many people want the anointing and the high-calling but are not willing to walk through the fires of repentance and purification to obtain it.

The following commentary in *The Revival Study Bible* is from A.W. Tozar, American pastor, author, and spiritual mentor:

> *The cross we want is that which will come to us from being*
> *in the will of God. It's not a cross on a hill or a cross on a church.*
> *It's not a cross that can be worn around the neck. Willingness to suffer*
> *for Jesus' sake—this is what we've lost from the Christian church.*
> *We want our Easter to come without the necessity of a Good Friday.*
> (Reference made to Romans 8:17)

I went through a period of time where each morning when I woke, Holy Spirit would ask, "Daughter, what's in your wallet?" This went on for several weeks. I thought He was preparing me to sow a financial seed somewhere. Then one morning, I was reading the story of Jesus in the Garden of Gethsemane in *The Passion Translation*.

> *Then Jesus led his disciples to an orchard called "The Oil Press."*
> *He told them, "Sit here while I pray awhile." He took Peter, Jacob,*

and John with Him. An intense feeling of great horror plunged His soul into deep sorrow. And He said to them, "My heart is overwhelmed with anguish and crushed with grief. It feels as though I'm dying. Stay here and keep watch with Me."

He walked a short distance away, and being overcome with grief, He threw himself facedown on the ground. He prayed that if it were possible, He would not have to experience this hour of suffering. He prayed, "Abba, My Father, all things are possible for You. Please—remove this cup of suffering! Yet what I want is not important, for I only desire to fulfill Your plan for me."
—*Mark 14:32–36 (TPT)*

Notice Jesus said, *"Yet what I want is not important, for I only desire to fulfill Your plan for Me."* Beloved, are you willing to pray that prayer? Are you willing to pay the price that is required to pick up your mantle—your assignment—and take your position in the body of Christ? Holy Spirit is asking you now, "What's in your wallet?" He specifically told me what needs to be there, "There are four things I require from My leaders: gratitude, rectitude, fortitude, and servitude." Notice He said *requires,* not desires. Let's unpack each of these.

Gratitude—Rejoicing in Your Portion

Do you rejoice in your portion? Do you wake up grateful every day for all He has given you and all He has called you to do? King David knew:

Yahweh, You alone are my inheritance. You are my prize, my pleasure, and my portion. You hold my destiny and its timing in Your hands. Your pleasant path leads me to pleasant places. I'm overwhelmed by the privileges that come with following You!
— *Psalm 16:5–7 (TPT)*

An important aspect in discovering your calling is to allocate a set time each day to fellowship with Holy Spirit. It is in the secret place that He reveals His plan to us. Often, He doesn't show us the cover of the puzzle box, but rather, He gives us the pieces one by one. We cannot receive these pieces of revelation without intimacy with Him. Fellowshipping with God is unplugging from the world and spending time with Him. It could be your devotional time in the morning, or at night before bed, or simply talking to Him throughout your day while rejoicing in His goodness.

One morning I hit the snooze alarm because I stayed up later than usual catching up on back episodes of *This is Us*. After several attempts, I finally got out of bed thirty minutes later than my normal time. I poured coffee and sat in my chair to enjoy it before going into my prayer closet. That's when I heard, "Punctuality is important to Me."

Wow, that pierced my heart! Since becoming a believer, I've been getting up during the fourth watch at 4:00 a.m. for a date with Jesus and to fellowship with Him. About a year ago, I contemplated going back to bed after I woke, but the Lord spoke and repeated to me what He said to His disciples in the Garden of Gethsemane, "Will thou not stay awake with Me for one hour?" Ouch, that broke my heart.

Friend of God, let NOTHING hold you back from your divine purpose. You were created to be an intimate friend of God. Without great intimacy with Holy Spirit, there can be no mantle to pick up.

Rectitude—Morally Correct Behavior or Thinking

One day the Lord said to me, "Anoint yourself for burial." I was like, *What do you mean?* He was saying that dying to self is not a one and done. It is a process we must go through every day as we pick up our cross and follow Him. He was preparing me for my "dark night of the soul." He then said, "Shema," which according to Yisrael Wikipedia means obedience in Hebrew. Aka: to submit to. It literally means: to listen, heed, hear, or do, and I was about to find out in real time why He was speaking this to me.

In August of 2011, I was sent to prison for something that happened eight years earlier when I was addicted to drugs and alcohol. Although I had been serving in ministry for four years, God allowed me to go to prison, and heaven became silent for eight weeks. When the silence finally broke, one of the first things He said to me was, "Daughter, I had to get you out of the world to get the world out of you."

This time in prison was a separation, a consecration, and a purification of the highest kind. It was my training as a prophetess of God. It was ten hours a day in the Word and on my face in prayer. I experienced encounters with Jesus and had angelic visitations, all the while being about my Father's business. There was no cell phone or television, just Jesus.

It was the best of times, and it was the worst of times. I was taken away from everything I knew—my marriage, my ministry, my church, my friends, and my family—all to prepare for the high calling on my life. During times of great sorrow, I pressed in and chose to obey and believe the Word of God over my circumstances. I ended up finding unspeakable joy in prison because He rewards those who diligently seek Him (Hebrews 11:6). Living within the boundaries of the Word of God will develop rectitude in your life.

Here is a love declaration from the Father's heart toward you regarding rectitude:

"My beloved, I beseech your beauty. When you and I are alone together, magnificent things transpire in the glory realm. Feel My loving arms pull you into the shelter of My wings. You are My treasure. You are My joy! Your King greatly desires your beauty, your purity, and your holiness. You are set aside for royal purposes. Relish in My care and bask in My love." — Jehovah Kabod, King of Glory

Fortitude—Courage under Adversity

One night I had an amazing dream. I was looking at a table, and Jesus came up and pulled out a chair and invited me to sit. I asked Him what table this was, and He said, "It is the table of suffering."

He then said, "The one who sits here, is willing to endure all things."

So I am willing to endure anything if it will bring salvation and eternal glory in Christ Jesus to those God has chosen.
— 2 Timothy 2:10 (NLT)

Blessed are you when they revile and persecute you, and say all kinds of evil against you falsely for My sake.
— Matthew 5:11 (NKJV)

Then Jesus said to His disciples, "If anyone wishes to follow Me [as My disciple], he must deny himself [set aside selfish interests], and take up his cross [expressing a willingness to endure whatever may come] and follow Me [believing in Me, conforming to My example in living and, if need be, suffering or perhaps dying because of faith in Me]. — Matthew 16:24 (AMP)

What an honor it is to be persecuted for the sake of the Gospel. Are you willing to suffer for Jesus and His Gospel? The Bible says in Philippians 3:10 that we are to partake in the fellowship of His sufferings. This is not always something we like to mediate on, but it's true. And though He allows us to suffer at times for the sake of the Gospel, we know that we are more than a conqueror through Him (Romans 8:37).

Several years ago, the Lord woke me up in the middle of the night, and said, "I will smite those that smite thee." According to vocabulary.com, smite means to strike with a heavy blow using a weapon. Whoa! The hair on the back of my neck rose up when I heard Him say this. Our Warrior King goes with us into battle and smites the enemy with a heavy blow. Just knowing this gives me fortitude to press on.

This is what the Lord says to you about fortitude:

When you come into that place in your heart that you know that you know that NOTHING is impossible to those who believe, then I will shower you with delicacies from heaven. Receive from Me an increased sanctity of mind and a reservoir of hope.

Breathe in the fragrance of Me, as pleurisy has no place in My kingdom. Anxiety, doubt, and unbelief are shattered when you come to the perfect knowledge of who I AM for you.

Calibrate your thinking. For you will count it all joy when trials come against you.

Seek a permanent place of refuge, child. It's in My heart.

Servitude—A Bondslave for Jesus

Elijah was traveling to Gilgal, Bethel, and Jericho before the Lord took him up to heaven in a whirlwind. He told Elisha three times not to follow him, but Elisha did anyway. He knew that the Lord God of Israel had appointed him as Elijah's successor, but he was still tested three times. In this instance, Elijah repeatedly urged Elisha to remain behind to test his determination and to be formally recognized as his successor. Persistence is a key trait of a faithful prophet.

Then Elisha said, *"Please, let me inherit two shares of your spirit."* Elijah replied, "You have asked for something difficult" (2 Kings 2:9–10 HCSB). Why did Elijah say, *"You have asked for something difficult?"* Notice what was coming.

There were fifty sons of the prophets that stood as witnesses. They saw the Jordan River part and Elisha walk through on dry ground. Yet, they still insisted that they send out men to search for Elijah, suggesting that the Spirit of the Lord had carried him away to another place.

Elisha said not to send them, but they pressed him to the point of embarrassment until in verse seventeen, Elisha succumbed to the pressure and agreed that they could search for Elijah. Of course, they didn't find him, and their unsuccessful search for his body confirmed that a miraculous work of God had occurred.

What's the lesson here? Mantles don't come easy, and they're not automatic. If Elisha was tested three times, you can expect to be tested. Not everyone will recognize that you have inherited a mantle and will want proof. Later, in 2 Kings 2:21, Elisha threw salt into a spring of water that was bad, and the water was healed. Then they believed.

If you want the heavy anointing and the oil, expect to be crushed. The anointing isn't cheap. God doesn't wave a magic wand. There will be testing and trials before you can serve the Lord with your mantle. The following Scripture speaks to me so well about how we feel when we get to the other side of the trial:

To grant us that we, being delivered from the hand of our enemies, might serve Him without fear, in holiness and righteousness before Him all the days of our life. — Luke 1:74–75 (NKJV)

This is what the Lord says to you about servitude:

My faithful servant, do not entertain the wind and the waves. Come dance upon the sea with Me, and you shall see the mantle I have bequeathed unto you.

More will be revealed in the coming days. For I will pour out My goodness upon you.

Do not faint. Do not give up hope. For your Royal King who sits on the throne, takes delight in your every move.

Rest assured, the enemy of your soul will pay exceedingly for every sorrow and for every trauma he has brought your way. Your Bridegroom King cometh to avenge you.

His Grace Covers You

In closing, let me reassure you that God does not require perfection from us. We will make mistakes along the way, but that's okay. In His vast mercy, He will lovingly correct us and set us on course again. In fact, as I am typing this, the Lord says, "Tell them that there is recompense in failure." Recompense means compensation for loss or harm suffered.

Beloved, your mistakes have not hindered God and His plan for your life. He is not disappointed in you. Don't give up, and don't give in. The enemy would love for you to lose hope, but the King of kings says to you right now:

"Your destiny is calling you, beloved. For surging within you is the River of Life.

More will be revealed in the coming days. In the meantime, dive into the deep things that await you in My Holy Word. Being catapulted to your divine destiny is as sure as the light of day! My grace covers you."

One Sunday in church, I heard preaching on the following passage in Isaiah:

> *I am God, and there is none like Me! I declare from the beginning*
> *how it will end and foretell from the start what has not even*
> *happened. I decree that my purpose will stand, and I WILL*
> *fulfill My every plan.* — *Isaiah 46:9–10 (TPT)*

During the message, the presence of the Lord came in with great fire and poured oil on my head. Then several days later, upon opening my eyes in the morning, the Lord spoke something similar to me, "I am the Lord thy God and like Me, there is no other!"

I love the following Scripture:

> *When you pass through the waters, I will be with you; and through*
> *the rivers, they shall not overflow you. When you walk through*
> *the fire, you shall not be burned, nor shall the flame*
> *scorch you.* — *Isaiah 43:2 (NKJV)*

He says, "I *will* be with you." He doesn't say, I might be with you. Wow... what a Savior! Even if we look at the wind and waves and sink like Peter did, He will pull us out. He will never leave us nor forsake us... EVER.

I love the expression, "If you want to walk on water, you have to get out of the boat." Once you get a full revelation of this, you will become fearless. You will be willing to step out in faith and be a witness for Jesus. You might even take a risk and challenge something that goes against His Word. Beloved, what is He asking you to do? *If God be for us, then who can be against us?* (Romans 8:31). I love this verse and quote it often. Let's flip it around though. Are you unconditionally for God? No matter what the consequences?

The teaching notes in The Revival Study Bible include a quote that I absolutely love from the great evangelist and revivalist Dwight L. Moody:

> *God can take care of us when we pass through deep waters. God can take care of us when we pass through the fires. God is able to take care of us if we will stand up for Him. Honor God, and your God will honor you!*

> *What you have to do is to take your stand upon God's side. And if you have to go against the whole world, take that stand, dare to do right, dare to be true, dare to be honest. Let the consequences be what they may.*

Finally, beloved, align yourself with the Lover of your soul through intimacy, obedience, and sacrifice. Remember that gratitude, rectitude, fortitude, and servitude don't come easy. God does not hand out mantles like candy. Many are called, but few are chosen. I will leave you with the following word He gave me to encourage you in the process of becoming fearless:

> *Drink deeply of Me and receive an impartation of holiness and purity. My Spirit reigns mightily in your life, and I will keep thee in perfect peace. Do not fear man nor life's challenges. For they are put there to arm you with strength and sharpen your skills for battle. Soak in My mercy.*

THINGS TO PONDER...

1. Many are called, few choose to answer the call. Are you willing to pay the price of answering the call?

    _____

    _____

    _____

    _____

    _____

    _____

2. Are you aligning yourself with the Lover of your soul?

    _____

    _____

    _____

    _____

    _____

3. Are you living in fortitude—courage under extreme adversity?

    _____

    _____

    _____

_____

_____

_____

4. Are you living in rectitude—a morally upright walk?

_____

_____

_____

_____

_____

5. Are you practicing servitude—do you have a heart to serve, putting Jesus' desires above your own and obeying His call?

_____

_____

_____

_____

_____

_____

6. Are you living in gratitude—being grateful even in challenging situations?

_____

_____

_____

_____

_____

_____

Lu Ann Topovski, M. Div., MBA

Lu Ann Topovski obtained her Master's in Divinity degree through Ashland Theological Seminary in 2007, and then her MBA in 2010. She is host of *The Kingdom View*, has owned two counseling centers, published five books, and was a contributing author in three Best Selling books. She is president and founder of *Integrity Developers, The Kingdom View,* and *Kingdom Global Influencers.*

Lu Ann believes as we heal from emotional wounds, we see clearer and no longer operate from an oppressive or offensive spirit, but rather we desire to do what God has directed us to do. We rise above our old patterns as we build our relationship with God by reading the Bible and prayer. This includes speaking in tongues of angels as stated in 1 Corinthians 12-14.

thekingdomview.com

youtube.com/@integritydevelopersfoundation

facebook.com/TheKingdomView2022

facebook.com/p/Rising-Above-100070471415885

linkedin.com/in/lu-ann-topovski-m-div-mba-19556632

Day 29

Lu Ann Topovski, M. Div., MBA

Our Kingdom Family

So then you are no longer strangers and aliens [outsiders without rights of citizenship], but you are fellow citizens with the saints (God's people), and are [members] of God's household.
— *Ephesians 2:19 (AMP)*

As members of God's household, we are a family. We don't always act like a family, but we are. Our gifts complement each other and when we work together, we are stronger as a family unit. It is important for us to see the good gifts each one has and honor their position within the Kingdom.

We also have a mutual enemy who wants to divide us. He wants to break and tear down each of our individual families, so we feel pain and weak emotionally. In some cases, we must work harder for the things God is leading us to do for Him because we are busy picking up broken pieces within our own family. This is often exhausting, and this is where our enemy wants us—distracted and exhausted.

However, when we work together, we are unstoppable. Our unity in Christ is the glue which holds us together.

Because of the work accomplished by Jesus Christ on the cross, and because He rose again to life on the third day, we have the opportunity to be Sons and Daughters of God Almighty. This is not just a privilege. God has plans for each one of us and His strategy for our success coincides with us working together. The choice to follow King Jesus is ultimately ours—and it is an adventurous journey.

When we are open to what God has designed us to do with and for Him in this spiritual war, then we are ready to prepare for war. Once we know our identity in Christ, we must then ask, "What is our position?" We then ask for revelation and wisdom to carry it out.

Our Strength and Power

As 'born again' children of God we now have Christ in us, the promise Jesus gave us. The question is, do we operate in the Christ within us, or know how to?

When Jesus died for us, He said, *it is finished*. This means our enemy no longer has a right to our life or soul. It also means we have the power, through Christ within us, and our spoken words, to fight back, and shut the mouth of the dragon—and stop the arrows he flings toward us.

Yet, this was not all our gracious Heavenly Father had in store for us. He wanted His fractured, broken family back! He still wants us back! He wants us whole again. He wants what the enemy stole, and He wants us to be keenly aware of our enemy's tactics so we can fight the good fight of faith and win, be happy, fruitful, and multiply.

> *Beloved, I pray that you may prosper in all things*
> *and be in health, **just as your soul prospers.***
> *— 3 John 1-2 (NKJV) (emphasis mine)*

This is the heart of the Father for us. He wants us to be healthy, wealthy, and wise—and it starts with the health of our soul.

Our Heavenly Father loves us so much that He wanted us seated with Jesus at His right hand—right now. He wants us to know these things so we can grasp this fact and behave like the children of God that we are. He has plans for us, and they are good! It is up to us, our own free will, and choice, to stand at the door and knock, asking Him for our next assignment.

And God raised us up with Christ and seated us with Him in the heavenly realms in Christ Jesus, in order that in the coming ages he might show the incomparable riches of his grace, expressed in his kindness to us in Christ Jesus. For it is by grace you have been saved, though faith and this is not from yourselves, it is the gift of God. — Ephesians 2:6-8 (NKJV)

This is an honor and privilege. When we understand this concept, that we are royalty with Jesus, and of the household of God, then and only then do we start to realize our identity in Christ. This is what the enemy is after. If he can hide our identity in Christ from us, he knows we will believe we are powerless. However, when we come to realize our heavenly position, our desire to have a genuine relationship with the loving Godhead is magnified. With this personal relationship our faith and courage grow because our soul identifies with Christ

By knowing our identity in Christ, we see our purpose, and understand there is NO competition in the Kingdom of God. We are fitly joined together and when we are all doing what we were created to do, then we have joy working together with God and for His Kingdom.

The Enemy

The enemy would like us to believe otherwise. He wants to steal, kill, and destroy us and our families. His main goal is to separate marriages, and then the family. This in turn weakens the family unit, and often the individuals.

His goal to dismember the family has not changed. We can see clearly that these tactics have been the downfall of the family, the body of Christ, our true identity, and humanity.

This is why we need to protect our family, including our Kingdom family. When fragmented, we must do our part to make it right. We also must rely on the Godhead and pray asking God for restoration. This is the opposite of gossiping, holding grudges, and not forgiving. We must mature in this area to grow into the family of God that He designed us to be.

All of us are created to be a part of God's family and within God's plan is our earthly family. We therefore need to work together to destroy the works of the enemy and do our part to keep the peace.

So, we need to understand who the enemy really is and how he can cause so much chaos. As we know, he aims to destroy us and our understanding of our identity. Why?

Basically, it's because he didn't win his attempt to overtake the Godhead. He is therefore mad at God for kicking him out of the third Heaven. He had influence over one third of the angels, he was the most beautiful angel, and created beautiful music. He was the assistant to the Word (Jesus) and he lost his attempted coup.

So, why did he want to overthrow the Godhead?

Some theologians believe this arch angel was jealous of what God was about to do next. He was going to create another being (man) in His own image, thus, making him a little lower than Elohim, one of the Hebrew names for God (Psalm 8:5 ASV).

As we know, angels are spiritual beings who were created by God to be His servants, and God has given them different hierarchical authority and power to do His will. When God was about to make mankind, He was placing him/them in between God and the angels in terms of authority and position within the Kingdom of God.

When Adam and Eve were created, that was their position—until satan deceived them and legally took their position away from them. However, Jesus came and rescued us from this cursed position (Old Testament law). We are now redeemed by His blood and, by knowing this fact, we now know our rightful place and authority which overpowers the *"darts of the enemy."* (Ephesians 6:10-18)

Lucifer was his name and his failed attempt to take over got him thrown out of heaven and stripped from his duties (Isaiah 14:12-17) along with one third of the angels who are now demonic entities.

This was how deceived with pride he was, he actually thought he could overthrow God—until God threw him down to the earth like lightning (Luke 10:18).

He has not changed. His tactics are the same. However, our God loves us so much, that He has shown us how to fight against the devil and his demons—and win.

The Whole Armor of God

In Ephesians chapter six we read of our spiritual weaponry and armor.

Finally, my brethren, be strong in the Lord and in the power of His might. — Ephesians 6:10 (NKJV)

First, let me point out that we are to be strong in the Lord, not in our own power. When we fight the enemy, it is not within our own power that we win. We kill and destroy our enemy's tactics with our words of faith and by the power of Christ living inside us.

This is the Holy Spirit, our "Counselor, Helper, and Comforter" that Jesus said He would send to help us in the very moment of our situation. When we ask Him for assistance in any situation, He will give us the answer, and that is what we must do.

> *Put on the whole armor of God, that you may be **able** to stand against the wiles of the devil.*
> *— Ephesians 6:11 (NKJV) (emphasis mine)*

What are the "wiles" of the devil? They are the tricks and deceptions used by our enemy to deceive, harm, and trouble people, especially Christians. This means we must be wise to his ways, as well as ways to overcome him. This takes Bible reading and discernment which is one of the gifts of the Holy Spirit (1 Corinthians 12:10).

When we read further, we see in Ephesians 6:12 (NKJV),

> *For we do not wrestle against flesh and blood, but against principalities, against powers, against the rulers of the darkness of this age, against spiritual hosts of wickedness in the heavenly places.*

Some might ask, how do we 'wrestle' or overtake principalities and rulers of the darkness? How can we 'wrestle' with spiritual hosts of wickedness in the heavens? This seems like a job for superman or superwoman.

Well, saints, that is exactly who we are in Christ. We are the ones our Heavenly Father has chosen, and we are called upon to help overtake the one who sets out to destroy God's family and what He has created.

What we must realize at the core of our being is this, we are workers together with God in Christ as 2 Corinthians 6:1-2 tells us. So, as workers together with Him, we must trust what He tells us, and His ways.

His ways might not be what we are used to, but as we step out into what we believe God is telling us to do, we see the results. Then, it becomes easier to hear Him, and therefore, move forward with Him the next time He calls upon us, or when we ask for help.

Why don't some Christians know this? Good question! It is because some of God's chosen leaders, who started out wanting to serve Him, have either not been taught, or they turned to traditions and religious rhetoric ways over the guidance of the Spirit of God.

How do I know? Because I used to be one of them—until I was so oppressed by the spirit of religion and narcissism, I could not think for myself. So, I began to do what the Spirit of God was guiding me to do. I spoke in tongues, (1 Corinthians 12:10) in my heavenly language, and received revelation. When I did what I was guided to do, I was released from oppression. It was not easy, but I trusted His guidance and eventually, I was free to follow Christ, and not religion or tradition.

I learned that as I stood on the revelatory Word of God received by Holy Spirit, I was able to overcome every situation the enemy threw at me. It took massive courage, and at one point, I knew it was the only way to live, and in my case, stay alive. God has not failed me—ever.

Therefore take up the whole armor of God, that you may be able to withstand in the evil day, and having done all, to stand.
— Ephesians 6:13 (NKJV)

Sometimes, it is in standing, and patiently waiting, that we lean into Scriptures or speak in tongues to strengthen ourselves. This is what I did until I received my breakthrough. As I spoke in tongues, I received revelation and wisdom from God on my next step. That is what literally saved my life on many occasions.

As we read further along in Ephesians 6:14-15 (NKJV) it states, *"Stand therefore, having girded your waist with truth, having put on the breastplate of righteousness and having shod your feet with the preparation of the gospel of peace."*

We see here that it is the truth, righteousness, and being prepared with the Gospel (giving us knowledge and therefore peace) so we can stand with confidence before the enemy. When we speak words of truth we know from scripture, or what God downloads into our mind, that is the truth that sets us free.

Above all, taking the shield of faith with which you will be able to quench all the fiery darts of the wicked one. And take the helmet of salvation, and the sword of the Spirit, which is the word of God. —
Ephesians 6:16-17 (NKJV)

Beloved, we need to understand that we gain faith, the most paramount piece of armor, when we read our Bible.

Faith comes by hearing, and hearing by the Word of God.
— Romans 10:17 (KJV)

This is one of the ways the enemy will try to persuade and deceive us because he knows there is power, and knowledge filled within the Bible. This is exactly why he doesn't want us to read it.

Verse 17 states the Word of God is literally the sword of the Spirit. This is how we kill the enemies lies and fight our battles. It is by the words in the Bible and the words of our testimony that we stop the fiery darts of the enemy. Our words and decrees are powerful in the spiritual realm. We must always remember this fact. This is how we quench every fiery dart and arrow from the enemy. Discernment from Holy Spirit is our partner here. (1 Corinthians 12:10).

*Praying always with **all** prayer and supplication **in the Spirit**,*
being watchful to this end with all perseverance and supplication
for all the saints. — Ephesians 6:18 (NKJV) (emphasis mine.)

When the Apostle Paul wrote this letter to Timothy who was overseeing the church at Ephesus, Paul encouraged Timothy and the church to pray in the Spirit, or in tongues. This means we must do the same as it strengthens our spirit. It is a powerful piece of our weaponry, and part of the whole armor of God.

This heavenly language is undetectable by our enemy and his entourage. The Bible tells us it is a language of angels (1 Corinthians 13:1). It strengthens our personal spirit, and we often receive revelation and wisdom.

Paul writes in 1 Corinthians 14:18 that he thanks God that he speaks in tongues more than anyone. Perhaps that is why he wrote more books in the New Testament than any of the other Apostles.

Closure

To reiterate, we are part of God's family, and it is important that we are unified. This takes maturity in knowing our identity in Christ, our position within the body of Christ, and knowing how to fight this mutual enemy. We need to fight the way Ephesians 6 tells us to fight, and we must cling to our identity in Christ. Remember, we have a purpose and as we walk, run, ride, drive, or fly we must do it with His wisdom.

We must also remember that our fight is not against flesh and blood, meaning with our brother or sister, but it is against the darkness of this world, and that is what influences people. When we fight spiritually, we stop being offended by someone who doesn't believe like us. Instead, we see commonality and work together in truth.

To be clear, the enemy does not want us to know our identity in Christ, or know the authority we have, because if we do, he knows he is dead in the water. When we make decrees with our words and do what God directs us to do, we win—EVERY time.

The truth is the enemy has no power over us unless we give it to him or if we are ignorant of our rights and authority. All he knows to do is deceive like he did with one third of the angels in heaven, with Eve in the garden, and with all of us at one time or another.

We as children and heirs of God need to realize we are no longer living in the Old Testament administration. We are living in the New Testament administration and Jesus died to give us our authority back.

We sit with Jesus, right now, in the heavenlies. It's time to take back our power individually, within our families, and within the Kingdom of God. When we understand this concept in our soul (mind, will, and emotions), we can take our position to the fullest degree possible and win with the boldness of Christ that gives us strength!

THINGS TO PONDER...

1. Are you clear on your identity in Christ? If not, search the Scriptures and read for yourself. Then, take a quiet moment, and ask God to explain your identity to you more clearly.

　　　　　　　　　　　　　　　　　　　　

　　　　　　　　　　　　　　　　　　　　

　　　　　　　　　　　　　　　　　　　　

　　　　　　　　　　　　　　　　　　　　

　　　　　　　　　　　　　　　　　　　　

2. Take a moment, position yourself in a quiet space with soft or prophetic music, and ask God where He has positioned you in the body of Christ.

3. While you are still in that moment with Him, ask Him for revelation on what He wants you to do within that position.

    _____

    _____

    _____

    _____

    _____

4. Next, ask God for wisdom on how to walk it out.

    _____

    _____

    _____

    _____

    _____

5. Write this down and go back to it from time to time asking God for new revelation and wisdom.

    _____

    _____

    _____

    _____

    _____

Day 30

Lu Ann Topovski, M. Div., MBA

The Great Commission

*Then Jesus came to them and said, 'All authority in heaven
and on earth has been given to me. Therefore go and make disciples
of all nations, baptizing them in the name of the Father
and of the Son and of the Holy Spirit, and teaching them to obey
everything I have commanded you. And surely I am with
you always, to the very end of the age.*
— Matthew 28:18-20 (NIV)

As most of us know, this Scripture passage is known as the *"Great Commission."* A commission is a command or assignment given by someone in authority. At this point in history, Jesus had died and rose again. Judas Iscariot was gone and Jesus needed to give an update on the spiritual development within the Kingdom of God. He was now telling the eleven remaining apostles that all authority in heaven and on earth had been given to Him and with that authority He was commissioning them to make disciples of people from all nations. He was giving them the power and authority to do so.

He wasn't saying to baptize in water for the remission of sins, although that was important by John the Baptist as he was the forerunner before Jesus. So, in retrospect, we too must repent of our sins. However, what Jesus said was to baptize in the name of the Father, Son, and Holy Spirit.

When people are water baptized these days, we typically hear the one baptizing the person say, *"I baptize you in the name of the Father, Son, and*

Holy Spirit" right before submerging the person into water. This is very powerful as when one rises out of the water they sense and feel the power of the Holy Spirit within. This new power sensation is Christ in us, the hope of glory.

Jesus continued to instruct His apostles by telling them to teach people to obey everything He, Jesus, commanded and assured them that He was always with them, even until the end of the age. The end of the "age" has not come. We are still in that age as Jesus has not come back for His church yet. However, He gave us the Holy Spirit, (Christ in us), as our Counselor, Shepherd, and Comforter until we leave this earth by our last breath, or when Jesus returns.

We, in the meantime, need to recognize the times and seasons. Currently, we are in the beginning stages of the third great awakening. We have moved from the Church era to the Kingdom era where people are waking up spiritually and sensing the movement of the Holy Spirit within them and all around the globe.

So, it is imperative that we listen to the Christ in us. It is also important for us to pay attention to the prophets as the Bible tells us:

Surely the Sovereign LORD does nothing without revealing his plan to his servants the prophets. — Amos 3:7 (NIV)

The late prophet Bob Jones prophesied in 1975 that one billion souls would be saved. Recently, however, prophets like Emma Stark, Chuck Pierce, Robin Bullock, and others have prophesied over a billion souls would be saved and one prophet says four billion. Now that is a huge number. We all can feel the shaking—and it's about to get stronger.

This has begun. Many of us feel this in our spirit and see it all around us in the natural world. This spiritual awakening is enhancing the commission to those called to go into all the earth and make disciples of the nations. This includes baptizing all nationalities. This time has arrived.

The nations are all around us, not only through the internet, but also those with whom we work. We are surrounded by all nationalities throughout the world in our communities, in our workplaces, and even in our homes. Meetings and conferences can be attended by the click of a link and can include people from around the globe.

The moment is now for those of us who are aware of these times, and open to the Spirit's promptings. We are being led by the Spirit of God to speak life, truth, and Scripture into the atmosphere where we stand, and into those who stand before us. We are planting seeds and making disciples by our obedience and knowledge of how to baptize in the name of the Father, Son, and Holy Spirit. This is being done in tandem with our knowledge of Scripture, and by the promptings of the Holy Spirit.

This is the time for the church, the ecclesia, to awaken from their spiritual slumber of selfishness programmed by society. The time has come to rise in spiritual awareness, love for Christ, and for mankind. It is time to forgive, repent, and rise into our positions within the Kingdom of God. There is no time to waste, as this opportunity for everyone is now.

Those of us who feel this move of the Spirit of God, very strongly desire to be exactly who we have been created to be, and where we are called to be in this very moment in time. We feel the pull and desire for restoration to God, ourselves, and mankind. We are falling in love with the Godhead because we are experiencing His presence and therefore desire to move as directed. This is an adventure of a lifetime, and a ride we will always remember!

As mentioned in the previous chapter, our warfare is spiritual in nature. It is not about spears, swords, guns, tanks, or physical ammunition.

Although we need to know how to fight with and against these ways as well. However, our spiritual warfare is with our faith infused words, commands from Holy Spirit, and personal decrees. We fight by the revelation given to us, and as we ask for wisdom and strategies to walk each assignment out, He gives it to us. Our assignment could be on our own, or it could be with a group of Christ-filled glory carriers.

These very acts of obedience bring restoration within the governmental body of Christ, the ecclesia. This in turn helps to bring forth the positioning of the nations within the church body. This takes maturity in our understanding as we reign in the Kingdom of God here on earth—in the natural.

Commissioning Angels

We are told in Scripture that angels are assigned to us.

*See that you do not despise one of these little ones. For I tell you that in heaven **their** angels always see the face of my Father who is in heaven. — Matthew 18:10 (NIV) (emphasis mine)*

The way I read this; the word angels is plural which means more than one angel is assigned to each of us.

There is a war going on in the heavens and it will not stop until Jesus comes back for His church and our enemy is thrown into the lake of fire. This war in the heavens and spiritual realm include God's angel armies who were not persuaded by Lucifer.

We can literally call on these angelic hosts to help us in our personal and spiritual warfare. I have done this, and it is a power of love for His children that I have witnessed more than once in my lifetime.

For he will command his angels concerning you to guard you in all your ways; they will lift you up in their hands, so that you will not strike your foot against a stone. — Psalm 91:11-12 (NIV)

This is a powerful promise, and I have experienced God's love for me in this way, and in the lives of my loved ones. We all have probably encountered angels at one time or another, possibly without realizing they were angels assisting us. Or maybe we have wondered, "Was that an angel?"

It has been a huge blessing for me as I have been on the receiving end of being assisted by these angelic hosts. For instance, I was in a five-car pileup on the freeway (which I caused). It was so bad that the engine dropped in my SUV. I was told later that if it had not dropped, my legs from my knees down would have been severed.

When I got out of my car, dazed and confused, a man walked up to me on my left. He asked me if I was okay. I stated I was okay, but my shins were a little sore. I asked him which car he was driving. He stated he was not in the accident but was a doctor and stopped by to see if I was okay. I shared with him my shins were sore, but I was fine. He asked me again, and again, and I assured him I was fine.

I then looked to my right to see the other cars in the accident. When I looked back to my left to speak to the doctor, he was gone. I did not see him anywhere. I did not see an "extra car" that was not in the accident. I believe he was an angel and was sent to protect me and my legs.

Another time when I was driving, I was coming up to a railroad track. My newborn baby girl Taylor, (my first miracle baby) was in the car with me and I began to slow down as I was approaching railroad tracks. It was late at night, and even though there were no lights at the railroad tracks, no bells ringing, no arm coming down to stop on-coming traffic from the tracks, I felt a very strong urge from either an angel or Holy Spirit to STOP!

This message in my mind and in my spirit kept getting stronger and stronger as I drove closer to the railroad tracks. So, I thought, I had better stop, just in case. I stopped right in front of the tracks, and as soon as I did, a train went flying by. If I had tried to cross the tracks, both my baby and I would have been hit by the train and probably killed. This is why it is vital to listen to what the Holy Spirit is telling us in every moment.

About 20 years later, I received a call from my daughter Taylor, and she told me my son, Spencer, (my 2nd miracle child) was in a bad motorcycle accident. I felt in my spirit it was not good. I prayed immediately and asked God to send His host of angels around my son, and to specifically send Archangel Michael to protect him.

It turns out, my son was hit by a semi-truck while riding his motorcycle, and it was nothing short of a miracle that he survived. I found out later, a woman from "Mt. Carmel" stopped by the accident and told the emergency squad, who thought my son was 'dead on arrival', that she felt a pulse.

This caused the EMT medics to intubate him immediately which kept him alive. I believe this woman was an angel who later visited my son in the hospital to see how he was doing.

The reason I share my personal stories is to simply point out that we have angels assigned to us and we can ask God to commission angel armies on our behalf.

We can ask God to send His angels to assist us, and we must listen to the promptings of the Holy Spirit, or the angels sent to warn us. Our

Heavenly Father has provided for us a heavenly host to assist us in our lifetime here on earth. We have been given provisions to be protected, to be restored, and to take our positions to fight the war of the century we are situated in. We just need to know what is available to us.

We find what we need in the Bible, and we rely on the gift of Christ in us to relay messages to us as needed. This builds our relationship with the Godhead and prepares us for our great commission.

There is more, a lot more, to understand and to discover in our own personal relationship with the Lord. It is a personal journey precious and undeniable. When we are allowing ourselves to be led by the revelation of the LORD, then we cannot go wrong. This is our faith journey, and it is not always easy, but it becomes easier as we learn to keep in step with the revelation(s) given to us by the LORD. Then, as always, ask Him for wisdom on how to walk it out.

Unless the LORD builds the house, the builders labor in vain.
Unless the LORD watches over the city, the guards stand
watch in vain. — Psalm 127:1 (NIV)

This precious and loving gift of Christ in us is given to all mankind who accept Jesus as Lord and Savior. It is like the powerful explosion of dynamite within us (*dunamis* power in Greek) which helps us every moment of the day. It is time for us to discover on our own where this journey with Christ will take us, and where we fit within the Kingdom of God. This is part of our great commission.

Together with Christ and God's angel armies we fight the enemy who will try to steal, kill, or destroy us. This is when we need to remember our arsenal and comrades. We have angels on our side to assist us, we have fellow

Christians, and Christ in us is constantly giving us revelation, direction, and even warnings. It is up to us to take heed of the warnings and speak words from our mouth to call forth the angels and ask for revelation.

This journey is an adventure. We are privileged to be called sons and daughters, and when we are knowledgeable of our artillery and authority in Christ, we are all up for the challenge. Remember, we were literally created for our assignments and for such a time as this. It is up to us to say, "yes" and continue our journey in this Kingdom movement.

THINGS TO PONDER...

1. Have you had a time in your life where you were visited by an angel? If so, when was it and how were you guided?

2. Have you been prompted by the Holy Spirit in areas of trouble in your life? Have you listened to Him? What happened?

_____

_____

_____

_____

3. Have you called on angels to assist you in times of trouble? If so, when and what occurred?

_____

_____

_____

_____

_____

_____

4. Ask the Holy Spirit to reveal to you the angels that He has assigned to you to co-partner with the angelic in this season of transition.

_____

_____

_____

_____

_____

_____

5. What is your understanding of YOUR Great Commission?

    _____

    _____

    _____

    _____

    _____

6. Are you ready to baptize others in the name of the Father, Son, and Holy Spirit?

    _____

    _____

    _____

    _____

    _____

Day 31

Lu Ann Topovski, M. Div., MBA

New Wineskins

Neither do people pour new wine into old wineskins.
If they do, the skins will burst; the wine will run out and
the wineskins will be ruined. No, they pour new wine into
new wineskins, and both are preserved.
— Matthew 9:17 (NIV)

As Christians in this new reformation era, it is important to understand the third person of the Godhead, Holy Spirit. When we understand His position, we understand the tools given to us to fight the good fight of faith. This new Kingdom era thinking requires that we become mature Christians in our understanding of the Scriptures, our authority in Christ, and the tools given to assist us on assignments by Holy Spirit.

Many of us have been taught Scriptures, and yet, some denominations do not teach about the position of the Holy Spirit or His gifts. Some religions are often like the Pharisees and Sadducees of 2000 years ago. Their ritualist ways did not answer prayers, heal the sick, mend marriages, heal relationships, or heal inner wounds. We see the same in some religions and denominations of today. There is no power of God within their rituals.

The power of God given to Christians is in Christ alone. It is through the revelation given to us that changes our world-view, transforms our lives, and assists us in helping others. We receive revelation within Scriptures and from Christ within us. This might sound foreign to some Christians but not to those of us who truly have a relationship with Jesus, and worship Him with our spirit and in truth daily.

Because we have Christ in us, we are in Him and He is in us. We walk with Him daily, just as Adam, Eve, Enoch, Noah, Moses, Elijah, Deborah, Esther, David, Daniel, the Apostles, Pricilla, Aquilla, and many other saints. It is up to us to keep asking, knocking, reading, and then trust His leading.

Jesus came to fulfill the Scriptures as well as teach the Scriptures. He taught often in parables, including about our talents, oil in our lampstand, sowing seeds, mustard seed believing, wine skins, and others. He did this to get our attention and to help us think differently.

Jesus also came to heal the sick, bring sight to the blind, help the poor, die for our sins, and free us from the control of the enemy. Now, we are to rule and reign with Jesus from our spiritual position, at the right hand of the Father. This takes faith in the Scriptures and trust in our relationship as we literally communicate daily.

Jesus is the ruler of everything, and yet He wants a relationship with us. To do that, we must understand His ways and be open to His promptings. As Christians, we must ask ourselves these questions:

1) Do we truly realize who Jesus is and the impact He has made—and is still making?

2) Or do we know about Jesus like a person in a textbook?

Many of us were taught about Jesus, but not taught how to have a real relationship with Him. Many of us were not taught about the gifts of the Holy Spirit including speaking in tongues, yet these gifts are for us to help us fulfill our calling. This is the meat of the Word.

For everyone who partakes only of milk is unskilled in the word of righteousness, for he is a babe. — Hebrews 5:13 (NKJV)

I was brought up in Brethren and Baptist denominations, which have solid foundational teachings of Scripture. When I was 16 years old however, a friend of mine shared 1 Corinthians 12-14. These scripture passages are about the gifts of the Holy Spirit including speaking in tongues. I was never taught these scriptures before, and I was amazed when my friend spoke in tongues. I was fascinated!

I began to meet with a full gospel ministry who believed in these gifts. At age 18, I bought a Young's Concordance, did Word studies on my own, took Bible classes, and excitedly returned to one of my childhood church families sharing my findings.

However, I was told they did not believe or teach about those gifts. I was baffled! Then I was accused of being in a cult because the full gospel church I attended believed in the gifts of the Holy Spirit. It was especially however, because I believed in and spoke in tongues that I was ostracized.

I felt like the Lord was telling me to love them and let Him lead me. So, I did.

Fast forward 20 years, I attended Ashland Theological Seminary, which has a Brethren foundation. They were being moved by the Holy Spirit and received a prophecy that "The broken are coming." They allowed other denominations and women to attend the seminary and were not as strict as other seminaries in terms of having to be of the "Brethren" denomination to attend.

When I attended Ashland Theological Seminary (ATS), there were over 50 different Christian denominations, including the three mentioned above from my teenage years.

Ashland Seminary is a gift to the body of Christ as these 50 different Christian denominations represented the student body and clearly, we did not all believe the same way. Yet, we learned from each other, and clarity was seen in the Scriptures.

Sure enough, even if someone was not taught the gifts of the Holy Spirit, or about women in ministry, or the 5-fold ministry, they could not refute that these very important subject matters still existed in the church. Iron sharpens iron, and I was grateful for the years I attended. I often stated that what was taught at ATS should be taught at all pulpits. That, however, was the choice of the student(s) attending, and the denominations they served.

As part of the student body, we were expanding our thinking and allowing Christ to teach us in our spirit, as well as being taught Scriptures by the professors. We were washing our understanding with the Scriptures and allowing Christ to stretch our thinking by oiling our wineskins of understanding.

As we continue to expand our spiritual understanding, outside of religious walls we become more diverse in our thinking. It is advantageous for us to believe the Bible, attend a Bible believing church, speak in tongues, and grow in Christ. This is washing and oiling our spirit and soul (wineskin).

The Bible is very clear and if it states, *"I wish that you all spoke in tongues,"* (1 Corinthians 14:5) we should believe it is possible or at least do our due diligence to understand by personal study. Let's allow the Spirit of God to teach us, as He builds our understanding and deepens His relationship with us.

We are in a new, faster paced era now. If we stay in religious mindsets, we will crack under the pressure of not understanding what God is doing. A spirit of religion will try to hinder a Holy Spirit revelation into a mind with religious unbelief. It doesn't work. This is why we must study to show ourselves approved, gaining knowledge to break the stronghold of a religious spirit trying to influence us (2 Timothy 2:15).

This can bring contention among Christians, but it mustn't be. We must continue to love, pray, and allow the Holy Spirit to work in the person's heart. Sometimes, we just plant the seed.

Paul was having a similar situation with the church in Corinth telling them,

> *I fed you with milk and not with solid food; for until now you were not able to receive it, and even now you are still not able.*
> — *1 Corinthians 3:2 (NKJV)*

Many Christians are in this same boat, but God is calling them out of the infant stages and into the maturity of adulthood.

This is why we must be open to Scriptures and to the revelation we receive from Christ who speaks to us daily. This is the new wineskin. We expand our thinking by this communion with Holy Spirit.

When we sit quietly with our Lord and ask Him to speak to us, as we wait, He will speak. He speaks to us in various ways: in dreams, visions, during praise and worship, during a sermon, and at various times of the day. This might be a new concept of receiving revelation for some Christians, but it will not stop. In fact, it's happening more rapidly.

These are the times to keep in step with the Spirit of God because He is on the move, and He is not stopping until His battle is won. We just happen to be a part of His army. He wants our participation. We have been perfectly positioned for His purposes and when we are in position, we feel exhilaration and love it! It feels right, because it is. He does know best, even if we don't understand at times.

As mentioned, multiple times within this devotional, we are seated in the heavens with Jesus, and we have authority in Christ to carry out our specific assignments. We must know at the deepest level that when God speaks to us, we have the authority to decree it. This is our job. This is where it all begins. As we speak what He tells us we watch it eventually come into existence.

We don't have to be a prophet to receive revelation from God. In fact, we can all prophesy one by one as 1 Corinthians 14 tells us. So, when we are given a revelation, know this, God is entrusting us (you and me) to speak it for Him, or keep it to yourself until He tells you when to release the Word. Ask for discernment, and He will give it to you. He will do the rest. We are workers together with God and our mantra should be:

Where You go, I go.
What You say, I say.
What You pray, I pray.

Angel Armies

The other thing we must understand is that we have angel armies at our beck and call. When the Lord gives us a word of revelation, we not only speak it and decree the revelation at the right moment, we also can ask the Lord to release His angel armies to make straight our way, move the enemy out of the way, and carry us through until the end. We can ask God to send His angel armies to what we need for our families, ministry needs, and health. They are here for us, and Father God wants us to ask for their help.

This is us giving our "Yes!" to God's assignments. It is us going "all in" and requesting God to release His angels to assist us. This verbal action is our "yes" response in the spiritual realm. This gives Kingdom precedence at a higher supernatural level, releasing the plans of God, and activating angel armies to help us to prevail and win stunning victories. We will see incredible interventions from the angels when we give the order to do so.

This is a mature mindset in the body of Christ and within the ecclesia—which is the Greek word for church in the New Testament. This is the word Jesus used over 100 times in the New Testament. So, it must be important to understand who we are as His church. We are part of God's governmental rule, and we all have positions of authority.

This church (ecclesia) is a governmental ruling body in the spirit realm. This is what Jesus meant when He said He would build His church on—the revelation of Christ in us. The Christ in us gives us the revelation in a certain matter, just like Father God gave Peter the revelation that Jesus was the Christ. This is how Jesus builds His church to maturity. This is why we must have a relationship with Him if we want to participate.

He has mighty plans for each of us, and it is vital that we understand that our wineskin needs washing and re-oiling from time-to-time to make us pliable for what He is about to do in our lives. He has plans for all of us and moves in ways that outsmart the enemy, thereby positioning us for each of our new assignments.

Some of God's moves we might not understand. Some of God's moves might catch us by surprise. It could be a divorce, financial difficulty, a death, job loss, or a move out of state. We might not understand, but God is positioning us for His purposes and glory. We must lean into Him during these times of uncertainty. It will give us His Shalom peace.

Sometimes it may appear as if we are losing a battle, or what we want in our life. However, this King's Gambit move which out-strategizes our opponent, sets us up in a "checkmate" position as we follow along with what the Spirit is showing and speaking to us. Our job is to simply trust and keep in step with the Holy Spirit.

There have been many tragedies and disappointments in my life, and I often wondered, "Why God?" There was a failed marriage, my son was hit by a semi, financial problems, family disappointments, ministry set-backs, more accidents, and deaths. Yet, God was with me every step of the way. I walked through each of these *shadow* of death experiences, and had no fear, but rather I had strength beyond belief. I spoke in tongues often, and received revelations, visions, dreams, and comfort from sources I didn't know existed.

These past few years it has been non-stop tragedy after tragedy. I felt like a Samurai in constant battle. In January 2024, within one months' time, I had several family members hospitalized multiple times, a deer hit my daughter's car, and the car was totaled, she was distraught. My 93-year-old Dad fell and was hospitalized, and within a week he passed away—and I wasn't at the hospital when he passed. At this point, it was all I could do to hold it together. The very next day, someone hit my daughter and totaled the car she just bought!

This is when I heard the Lord say, *"Go to praise and worship tonight. I have something for you."* I said, *"Okay Lord, but YOU are going to have to get me there."*

Just like our Lord, He got me to the church on time. After leaving the hospital with my daughter, I was able to drop her off at her house, and then drove to the church.

I remember walking into the church and finding my place.

Typically, I would stand with my hands held out, ready to sing and receive. However, at this point I could not physically stand. I was so weak in my body and soul. I sat in my chair, put my hands over my face, and wept. I didn't even know what to pray. So, I began to speak in tongues.

I immediately had a full-blown vivid vision. I was literally, *"caught up in the Spirit."* I believe I was in the 3rd Heaven. In this vision, my earthly Dad (who passed away the day before) walked up to me and held his hand out for me to take. I put my hand in his hand, and he began to dance with me. Mind you, in the natural realm, tears are falling down my cheeks. I remember my Dad was younger in appearance and not the 93 year old I saw the day before.

He turned me around and around as in a ball room style dance. I saw my aunts, uncles, and grandparents who passed before my Dad. They were off to the right side of us watching us dance and were cheering us on.

This vision went on for a very long time and while having this vision, suddenly, I heard a song playing from our worship team in the natural realm. As I listened to the words, I stood up from where I was sitting and began to sing along. It was directly related to the vision I was having in that very moment.

I closed my eyes again while still standing, and went back into the vision, and saw my relatives singing along with us. It was as if heaven and earth came together as one. It was at that time the Lord revealed to me that I was attending my earthly Dad's homegoing. Tears flowed... and yet, this gave me peace, hope, and happiness—knowing where my Dad was, and that he was okay.

I share this with you, my friends, to tell you, that with your relationship with the Lord, He gives YOU exactly what you need, at the time you need it most. Although I miss my Dad, his love, support, and wisdom, I know He is okay, I feel his presence in my heart, and I will see him again. Our loving Heavenly Father gave me exactly what I needed in that very moment. It gave me the strength and peace I needed to walk on—and deal with what was in front of me.

It showed me how much our Heavenly Father, our Lord Jesus Christ, and Holy Spirit loves me—and my Dad, as this was a gift to my Dad and relatives as well. It also showed me that I will see my Dad and relatives again, when I leave this earth and walk into my homegoing one day. It showed me how real heaven is and how our loved ones are waiting for us to come to our eternal home.

God also loves you, my friend. He is here for you, and wants you to take His hand, and follow Him. It is a ride that you will cherish for the rest of your life here on earth, and in heaven above. Enjoy every moment!

THINGS TO PONDER...

Take some time to journal and reflect on the following:

1. Have you had an encounter with God?

_____

_____

_____

_____

_____

_____

2. If so, what was it?

_____

_____

_____

_____

_____

_____

3. Ask Holy Spirit to reveal more to you about that.

_____

_____

_____

_____

_____

4. What have you experienced about the gifts of the Holy Spirit in 1 Corinthians 12-14?

_____

_____

_____

_____

_____

5. Would you like to learn more about them?

   _____

   _____

   _____

   _____

   _____

6. If so, ask the Holy Spirit to reveal more to you and activate the gifts within you with greater revelation, understanding, and power.

   _____

   _____

   _____

   _____

   _____

7. Ask the Holy Spirit to reveal to you where He would like you to go in Scripture.

   _____

   _____

   _____

   _____

_____

_____

8. Ask the Holy Spirit what else He wants to show you about Himself.

_____

_____

_____

_____

_____

_____

9. Ask the Holy Spirit to reveal to you by revelation what He wants you to know.

_____

_____

_____

_____

_____

_____

10. Write down your experiences. Take time to journal and reflect each day on your experiences and insights.

_____

_____

_____

_____

_____

_____

11. Ask Him to lead you into greater truth and understanding.

_____

_____

_____

_____

_____

_____

Libby George

Peggy A. Grimes

Lu Ann Topovski, M. Div., MBA

This next section is a gift to you, the reader.
The Lord so graciously gave three of us specific prophetic
words for you.

Please pray before you read each one and
feel the love of the Father,
Son, and Holy Spirit as you read.

Love and Blessings,

Lu Ann

— Prophetic Declaration —

Libby George

The Rise of the Remnant:
A New Decree for a New Era

20 August 2024

In mid-August 2024, I attended a conference in New Zealand, where Jane Hamon released a powerful revelation about the body of Christ and insight into the times we are stepping into. Jane spoke of her new book, *Confronting the Thief*, emphasizing the need to take back what the enemy has stolen and declare "Divine Recovery." She compared our current time to that of Esther 8:8 when the King gave Esther and Mordecai the authority to make a new decree over the Children of Israel.

It is time to decree your promises, walk in victory, and break the curses that have robbed your calling, identity, and victories. We are called to rise up as an army, cancel the assignments of hopelessness, and overcome spiritual poverty. The days of the church reigning over believers with disbelief and fear are over! We will no longer allow the truth of our identity to be stolen. We are rising beyond the constraints of four walls, advancing in true kingdom power, authority, and identity.

We are stepping into the legacy of a holy priesthood and the inheritance of the Kingdom of God. The earth has been groaning for this day when the sons of God would be revealed. We are transcending into the mysteries and revelation of our heavenly identity as children of God, transformed by the blood of Yeshua and adopted into His promises and legacy. We are manifesting the limitless nature and fullness of the blueprint of His DNA through the blood of Christ.

No longer will we be robbed of the truth, silenced, into powerless lives void of miracles, signs, wonders, and intimacy with our Heavenly Father. It is time to step beyond the grasp of an anti-Christ spirit hiding behind the legitimacy of religiosity and logic. Hopelessness, fear, and the constraints of controlling strongholds have lost their grip on the remnant.

Through Christ's sacrifice, we receive His revelation of true righteousness and an abundant life, overflowing with the riches, provision, authority, dominion, and glory of God. Nothing we have done or can do will change our destiny as co-heirs through His grace, love, and faithfulness of His promises, when we are one in Him.

Jane Hamon compares this time to Esther 8, where King Xerxes gave Esther and Mordecai the authority to make a new decree. This new authority to write a new decree in the king's name, using his signet ring to seal it, was irrevocable. This new decree allowed the Jews to defend themselves against their enemies on the day appointed for their destruction.

This moment mirrors the current state of the Church. If we liken the remnant to Queen Esther replacing the established beautiful Queen Vashti, who refused to expose her nakedness.

In this season, the remnant is rising, just as Esther rose to take her place. The remnant is mirroring the events of Esther and stepping into a new era of divine authority, reclaiming everything that was stolen, and stepping into bold, new authority, granted to her through favor and intimacy. While we witness Queen Vashiti, banished.

We are in a season where generational curses will be broken and everything the enemy stole from us will be repaid in full with interest. We have been given the King's authority to command victory over the ten sons of Haman, symbolizing complete victory over the enemy's plans. Future generations will walk in fullness of power, authority, and victory.

"In the earth, God is releasing a new frequency that will transform and shift all creation." The earth has been groaning, for the sons of God to take their place. Creation yearns to align with the fullness of her glory as the son's step into their true destiny and authority.

I woke up several days before writing this and heard the father say, "You can create eternity now." Some might find this unscriptural or even sacrilegious, but it reflects the limitless nature of sonship and the reality of our royal lineage. The privilege of adoption through Christ's blood and the surrender of self allows us to co-labor with God in creating the new world and New Jerusalem as foretold in the Book of Revelation.

Romans 8:15-17 (NLT), *"So you have not received a spirit that makes you fearful slaves. Instead, you received God's Spirit when he adopted you as his own children. Now we call him, 'Abba, Father. For His Spirit joins with our spirit to affirm that we are God's children,"* and the reality of Gods deepest desires anchored in the father's heart. The privilege of sonship and the oneness of abiding in Him.

I see in the spirit, a new Jerusalem arising on the horizon. I am not speaking of this world but of what has been foretold in the book of Revelation. And there is an invitation to the sons of God as co heirs to participate and co-labor in this new creation.

Just as Adam co-labored creation with God on earth. Genesis 2:19-20 God involved Adam in the act of caring for and naming the animals, giving identity to the creatures God created.

The concept of a "New World" and "New Jerusalem" in the Bible, particularly in the Book of Revelation, represents the culmination of God's plan for humanity and the renewal of creation.

Revelation 21:1-2 (NIV):

Then I saw a new heaven and a new earth, for the first heaven and the first earth had passed away, and there was no longer any sea. I saw the Holy City, the new Jerusalem, coming down out of heaven from God, prepared as a bride beautifully dressed for her husband.

The concept of believers coexisting in two realms—earthly and heavenly—speaks to a dual existence found in Ephesians 2:6, where we are spiritually positioned in heaven, sharing in Christ's authority and victory. John Calvin emphasized the "mystical union" with Christ, where our life is hidden with Him in God (Colossians 3:1-3). N.T. Wright speaks of "inaugurated eschatology," where the Kingdom of God is both a present reality and a future hope. *"Our citizenship is in heaven, and we eagerly await the transformation of our lowly bodies into His glorious body"* (Philippians 3:20-21).

The power of decree in the Bible refers to the authority given to believers to speak God's will into existence. When we align with God's word and decree with faith, our words can bring about change in the spiritual and natural realms. Jesus demonstrated this power, speaking healing, deliverance, and even life into existence.

In the book of Esther, Queen Esther and Mordecai made a new decree that destroyed Haman's ten sons and saved the Children of Israel. You have been given full authority and endorsement by the King of Kings to make decrees in faith and alignment with God's will, transforming atmospheres and realities, and aligning now with heavens mandate.

As I finalize this word, I awoke again early, this time at 4am... hearing the father say drink from the fountain of life. As I meditated on His words... I had a sudden urge to read all the words Jesus had spoken in all four gospels. So I encourage you to do the same. Soak in the words Yeshua spoke, and drink from the fountain of life.

ACTIVATION:

1. Ask the Holy Spirit what He wants you to decree over your life, family, community, and nation.

   _____

   _____

   _____

   _____

   _____

   _____

2. Step out as a mighty warrior in faith, believing you have been given the authority to shift atmospheres, recover what has been lost, and restore what has been stolen.

   _____

   _____

   _____

   _____

_____

_____

3. Decree and declare with boldness, co-laboring with Yahweh to bring about His promises, power, and purposes.

_____

_____

_____

_____

_____

_____

— Prophetic Word —

Peggy A. Grimes

❝ *Seek first My Kingdom! The days are darkening and will require much more strength and dependence on Me to navigate through your days. This is a time to strengthen your faith, drawing closer to Me. I am preparing My people for battle --not a physical battle, but a deep spiritual battle! All you see happening right now are the 'birth pains' of your deliverance. As a woman pushes through to bring birth, you too must push through to draw nearer to Me.*

I am raising up an army of those who will fight My final battle against evil; to take their position in My body of 'sold out,' committed, and battle-ready believers who will eagerly enter onto the spiritual battleground to stand ready to fight evil on every side. As they stand on the heights prepared for battle, they will watch as My Son, through His blood sacrifice, will defeat every enemy; just as I instructed Jehosaphat, King of Judah, to stand and watch as God destroyed His enemies at En-Gedi (2 Chronicles 20:15-24). He was told to prepare for war, but the victory was Mine. It will be that way again. Like Jehosaphat, prepare yourself for War! TAKE YOUR POSITION. Then watch and see what I will do!"

— Prophetic Word —

Lu Ann Topovski, M. Div, MBA

I have given you more than you can fathom. You are my chosen remnant, and I have not forgotten you. You are precious in My heart. You are sent here for a purpose well known to Me, and you must trust each move and assignment I give to you.

We together will win this war and battle. The enemy, the forever loser, will not win even though he thinks he has outsmarted Me. It is laughable. His moves are not as strong as My power within you, so you must take your position and trust there is nothing new under My sun.

Speak boldly as I place in your heart what to speak. Be bold as I have equipped you with armor that is unbreakable. Do your part and I will do My part. Know this, I love you with a deep and burning love. You have not been brought up to know My ways, but I will teach you, and you will learn strategies from Me and My Bible.

Bless you, My child. We will all be together soon, and you will see the purpose of My calling for you more clearly in the coming days. Until then, make a way for those who come after you. I have a purpose for them, and they too will carry My torch just as you have and will continue to do.

Shalom.

More from Kingdom Global Influencers!

"For the word of God is alive and active. Sharper than any double-edged sword, it penetrates even to dividing soul and spirit, joints and marrow; it judges the thoughts and attitudes of the heart" (Hebrews 4:12 NIV).

The contributing authors in this 30-day devotional have been guided by the Holy Spirit to share a Word with the Kingdom—NOW. The God-inspired chapters are filled with hope, healing, joy, strength,forgiveness, and love and illustrate the power of God's Word.

God is calling you to a deeper relationship with Jesus and spiritual growth. May you be transformed by a Kingdom Word—NOW.

To give back, 25% of the proceeds from this book will be used to support human trafficking survivors.

www.ingramcontent.com/pod-product-compliance
Lightning Source LLC
Chambersburg PA
CBHW060854120626
46553CB00001B/81